Praise for
Armin A. Brott

"Brott writes honestly and earnestly.
His wry sense of humor will be
a relief to hassled parents."
—*Time* magazine

The Military Father

"As an Army brat I know firsthand that it's not only our military men and women who serve the country—their spouses and children serve proudly as well. Armin Brott has contributed his own brand of service with this wonderful book—a great resource with useful checklists and advice that covers every stage of childhood. It will help ease what are difficult journeys."

—Linda Powell, daughter of General Colin Powell, U.S. Army Ret.,
former Chairman of the Joint Chiefs of Staff

"Too often, those who do the most for us are supported the least. Military fathers would certainly fall into this category. Brott's wonderfully informative book, *The Military Father,* is not only a much needed salute to the importance of these unique dads but it is also a 'field manual' for their most important front of all—the home front."

—Roland C. Warren, President, the National Fatherhood Initiative

"Armin Brott talks dad to dad in *The Military Father,* giving service men practical ways to stay connected with their wives and children during deployment."

—Karen Pavlicin, author of *Surviving Deployment* and
Life After Deployment

The Expectant Father

"Quite simply the best guidebook to date for both the prospective father and his partner in their journey through the nine months of pregnancy.... A must for fathers-to-be."
   —John Munder Ross, Ph.D.,
      author of *What Men Want* and editor of *Father and Child*

"Don't get pregnant without it! A first-rate guide for all dads-to-be."
   —Vicki Lansky, author of *Feed Me, I'm Yours* and contributing editor to *Family Circle* and *Sesame Street Parents*

"This book is the *What to Expect When You're Expecting* for men.... If you know an expectant father, first baby or not, make sure he has this book."
   —*Full-Time Dads*

The New Father

"Read a book? Who has time? But you'd be wise to find some so you can take advantage of a fabulous resource...*The New Father*."
   —*Sesame Street Parents*

"...addresses the many needs and concerns of dads with sensitivity, wisdom, and good humor...a helpful road map through the often bewildering country of fatherhood."
   —Brad Sachs, Ph.D., Director, The Father Center

"This book would make a great gift for any new dad."
   —Lawrence Kutner, Ph.D., columnist, *Parents* magazine

Fathering Your Toddler

"In this third book of his perfectly targeted book series for the modern dad, Brott demystifies child development...and make[s] fathers...enjoy the vital role they play in their kids' lives even more. A great addition to any parenthood library."

—*Child* magazine

Fathering Your School-Age Child

"Brott...drolly delivers readable, practical guidance on fathering. Covering each year from three to nine, the chapters focus on the developmental states of child, father, and mother/partner as well as their relationships to one another. Considerable knowledge from parenting experts is woven into the text, and special issues (e.g., children with special needs, divorced dads) are also explored."

—*Library Journal*

"This, thankfully, is not another one of those goofy, dumbed-down books (think sports metaphors and caveman references) that make such amusing—but unhelpful—gifts for dads. In fact, this is as informative as any traditional parenting book out there (including those aimed at the moms), and in some ways even better. Busy dads will be grateful for Brott's accessible tone and quick-and-painless format—bullet points get the basics covered on what's going on with your child, yourself and your relationship with your partner at each developmental stage."

—*Newsday*

The New Father series
by Armin A. Brott

The Expectant Father
Facts, Tips, and Advice for Dads-to-Be

The New Father
A Dad's Guide to the First Year

Fathering Your Toddler
A Dad's Guide to the Second and Third Years

Fathering Your School-Age Child
A Dad's Guide to the Wonder Years, 3 to 9

The Single Father
A Dad's Guide to Parenting Without a Partner

Father for Life
A Journey of Joy, Challenge, and Change

Also available in audio

The Expectant Father

The New Father

THE MILITARY FATHER

By Corporal Victor Castro, 3rd Battalion, 6th Field Artillery, U.S. Army

The Military
FATHER

A Hands-on Guide for
DEPLOYED
DADS

Armin A. Brott
FORMER U.S. MARINE

Abbeville Press Publishers
New York • London

Editor: Susan Costello
Copyeditor: Miranda Ottewell
Cartoons Editors: Meg Parsont, Cynthia Vance
Production Editor: Erin Dress
Production Manager: Louise Kurtz
Typesetter: Angela Taormina
Designer: Misha Beletsky

First edition
10 9 8 7 6 5 4 3 2 1

For cartoon credits, see page 325

Paperback: ISBN-13: 978-0-7892-1031-9
Hardcover: ISBN-13: 978-0-7892-1030-2

Library of Congress Cataloging-in-Publication Data

Brott, Armin A.
 The military father : a hands-on guide for deployed dads / Armin A. Brott.
 p. cm.
 Includes bibliographical references and index.
 ISBN 978-0-7892-1031-9 (pbk. : alk. paper) — ISBN 978-0-7892-1030-2 (hardcover : alk. paper)
 1. Father and child—United States. 2. Soldiers—Family relationships—United States. 3. Children of military personnel—United States. 4. Families of military personnel—United States. I. Title.

 HQ756.B767 2009
 355.1'2—dc22
 2009000362

For bulk and premium sales and for text adoption procedures, write to Customer Service Manager, Abbeville Press, 137 Varick Street, New York, N.Y. 10013, or call 1-800-ARTBOOK.

Visit Abbeville Press online at www.abbeville.com

Contents

Part I: Predeployment
You're in the Army...or Navy...or Marines...or Air Force...
or Coast Guard Now

Part II: Deployment
During Deployment: Boots on the Ground,
Hitting the Deck Running, or Haze Gray and Underway

Part III: Post-deployment
Okay, So Now What Do We Do?

Appendices

To all those who have served our country with honor.
My heartfelt appreciation as a father,
a Marine, and an American.

Acknowledgments

This is the seventh volume in what has become known as the *New Father* series. Over the course of writing those books (plus twelve more on other topics), I've come to realize that the process of coming up with ideas and putting words together is just the beginning. Turning those ideas and words into an actual book is a pretty big job—one that is best done with a hardworking, committed group of talented, creative, passionate, and incredibly helpful people. And that's exactly what I was fortunate enough to have throughout this project. So let me take a moment to introduce a few dozen of them and express my gratitude and thanks, in no particular order, to a bunch of people, without whose support—in a variety of ways—this book would still be gathering digital dust on a flash drive instead of resting comfortably in your hand.

Publisher Bob Abrams and Cynthia Vance Abrams, who believed in and supported this project—and everything else I've done—from the beginning. My editor Susan Costello, who, as she has many times before, gently, patiently, but firmly guided the manuscript through every step and kept me on track. The rest of the Abbeville team: Louise Kurtz, who supervised the production and Misha Beletsky, who designed the book. Erin Dress, Briana Green, and Michaelann Millrood helped with promotion and marketing, Miranda Ottewell, who copyedited it all; Meg Parsont who juggled her roles as cartoonist wrangler, publicist, and pal with remarkable skill; and Nadine Winns, who does a little bit of everything—all of it very well—and somehow keeps smiling throughout.

Mark Baker, Victor Castro, Steve Dickenson and Todd Clark, Julie Negron, Charles F. Wolf, and Basil Zaviski, who contributed many of the cartoons you'll be chuckling at as you go through this book. They're not only talented artists but they have an insider's view from previous or present affiliations with the military (see pages 326–27). Major Scott Howell, who supplied a ton of research, offered his guidance, and shared a huge amount of insider knowledge about all things military. Laurie Knight, who was also a researcher, and provided an invaluable perspective as an Army spouse. Alison Banholzer, Gracie Blackburn, Veronica Brown, Andrew Langer, Leah McDermott, Brannan Vines, and many others, who shared their personal stories and wisdom, as did Laura, Carrie, April, and the other women of the civiliansinraq Yahoo! group (yes, that's the right spelling). Kerry Tucker and Bill Reese of Military OneSource, who read early drafts, made some great suggestions, and have really championed the cause. Bill and Vicki Crouch, who also offered some helpful comments on the manuscript. David Walbridge, who added his sense of humor. And finally, the many men and women I interviewed who asked to remain anonymous. Some are or were in the military, some were spouses, and some were under cover in all sorts of fascinating places, but all were great sources of information and ideas.

Many people opened their Rolodexes and made introductions. Jimmy Boyd (who I'm convinced is running the entire Western hemisphere) and Scott Williams at the Men's Health Network, who have opened so many doors it's impossible to count. Bob and Elly Gordman, who never seem to run out of rabbits to pull out of their hat. (Typical comment from Bob: "Oh, I may be able to help with that. How 'bout a [fill in the blank with exactly what I was looking for]?") Jim Levine, who saw something in me nearly 20 years ago and has been making connections ever since. Mike Mombrea, who put through some key calls and who's an integral part of the future of Mr. Dad. And Bob Stien, who besides helping me is making the world a better place for dads and daughters (and sons too).

Ron Goldberg, a friend who's had my back since we were four, and who's always kept the computers—and the plumbing—running. My dear friend Darren Kessler, with whom I've logged thousands of miles over the years, and who, many times has dragged me kicking and screaming out of my cave to have a beer. Stephen Leist, who jump started my head and has been a softball coach, chairman of the board, biking buddy, and all-around great friend. And Jon Shuster, who's last on this list only alphabetically, and who must have cauliflower ears from letting me bend them so many times.

Finally, Mom and Dad, for more than I can possibly say here.

By MSG Mark Baker (RET), U.S. Army

Introduction

Over the years I've received more than a thousand letters and e-mails from fathers (and mothers) asking for advice on every conceivable parenting topic—from "What are some workouts I can do with my pregnant wife?" and "Help! I'm about to be a new dad but I've never touched a baby before" to "Should we pay our kids to do chores?" and "My teenage daughter came home with liquor on her breath! What did I do wrong?" Although each question is a little different, what the writers really want to know is how to build strong relationships with their children and be the best possible parents.

But starting in late 2001, I also began getting very different questions, things like, "I'm in the Marines. My unit is shipping out to Afghanistan next month, and I'm going to miss the birth of my baby. What can I do to remain close to my wife?" and "My husband is deployed in Iraq. How can I help him be part of our children's life when he's 8,000 miles away?" and "I've been gone for so long. Will my wife and kids still need me when I come home?"

As a former Marine myself (I know, I know, once a Marine, always a Marine), these questions hit me especially hard. And I was reminded of the day, back when I was in boot camp, that my chief drill instructor barked to a fellow recruit who'd made the mistake of revealing that he had just gotten married, "If the Marine Corps wanted you to have a family, you moron, they'd issue you one!" Fortunately, things have changed quite a bit since then. (Although there's still an awful lot of camouflage floating around.)

Until about 1973, the United States used an involuntary draft to bring in the soldiers, sailors, airmen, and Marines needed to staff the military services. Almost all of them were unmarried men without children. But today, well over half of active duty, reserve, and National Guard personnel are married, and nearly 40 percent have kids. Given that the vast majority of these service members will be deployed at some point, there are literally *hundreds of thousands* of dads (and quite a few moms too) who will be separated from their family. Looking at that from another angle, nearly two million children—three-quarters of whom are under twelve—will be separated from a parent (and that doesn't include the children of civilian contractors or of the nonmilitary government employees, who are stationed overseas and away from their families).

Like their civilian counterparts, deployed military fathers want to be involved, play an important role in their children's lives, and feel needed and valued by their family. But they face some additional challenges: Is it possible to stay connected across time and distance? How can you build or maintain relationships with people you can't even touch? If you're divorced and your children are with your ex-wife, you may feel at an extra distance from your kids. How can you stay involved with them?

I wrote *The Military Father* to answer those, and many other questions. Perhaps more importantly, I also wanted to reassure every one of those deployed fathers (and mothers too) that he plays a vital role in his children's lives—one that goes well beyond changing diapers, driving the carpool, and being a living, breathing ATM machine. And finally, I wanted to give deployed dads the tools they need to keep those relationships strong.

Of course, being thousands of miles and a dozen time zones away from each other complicates things. Teaching your child to ride a bike or throw a curve ball is going to be tough, and good-night kisses are out for a while. But with today's technology, you may be able to read bedtime stories to your children, help them with their homework, tell them silly jokes, show them how much sand you dump out of your boots every night, teach them about geography, see their science fair projects and school plays, and remind them of how much you love them and how proud they make you.

Bottom line: you are irreplaceable. Being deployed is going to be an adventure. An exhausting, difficult, dangerous and sometimes rewarding adventure. Sure, there will be all sorts of challenges, mistakes, and emotional ups and downs. But it can be done—and this book will help. It *is* possible to stay connected to everyone in your family, and it *is* possible to remain a major influence in their lives. I'll get back to that in a minute.

Who's This Book For?

The Military Father is written primarily for dads serving on active duty, in the Reserve, or in the National Guard in any of the five branches of the U.S. military: Air Force, Army, Marines, Navy, and Coast Guard. However, there are three other very important groups:

♦ Deployed civilian contractors. At any given moment, there are well over 100,000 civilians working in a variety of capacities alongside the U.S. military. The majority of these civilians are men, and quite a few are dads.

♦ Many of the 90,000 civilians who work overseas for government agencies—State Department, Departments of Defense, Commerce, Agriculture, and others.

♦ Dads who stay home while their wives are deployed—something that's happening more and more often.

What's in This Book?

Like the other volumes in the New Father series, *The Military Father* is organized chronologically, but rather than using the child's age as a way to measure the time, I've structured the book around the three broad phases of deployment. **Part I** is devoted to predeployment. We'll talk about how to prepare yourself, your kids, and your wife for your absence and how to put systems in place that will help keep those relationships strong while you're away. In **Part II**, we'll focus on what happens during the actual deployment, how to implement those predeployment plans, and specific ways to stay connected and involved with your wife and children. In **Part III**, we'll look at what happens when you get home. Yes, the deployment is officially over, but sometimes it's harder to reintegrate back into your family than it is to be gone. Each of these three parts includes several chapters.

What's Going On

Each of these chapters is divided into three main parts:

♦ **What's going on with you**, where we'll look at what you may be feeling and thinking, and how those feelings and thoughts may play out in your behavior.

♦ **What's going on with your wife**, we'll focus on your wife's emotional journey.

♦ **What's going on with your children**, where we'll explore what your children are going through.

Although this book is written primarily (but not exclusively) for deployed fathers, one can't possibly understand them without a firm grasp of what's happening on the home front. There are many good resources out there that cover that topic, and you'll find similar information in the best of them. Books by Karen Pavlicin (*Surviving Deployment* and *Life After Deployment*) and Eliane Dumler (*I'm Already Home* and *I'm Already Home Again*) were especially helpful.

The more you know about what's happening emotionally and psychologically on all fronts, the easier it'll be to help them and yourself cope with the deployment. (Oh, you'll still go through the ups and downs, but this way at least you'll be expecting them.) It will also allow you to keep your expectations reasonable and prepare you for how they—and you—will have changed over the course of the deployment.

Oh, and in case you were worried, being deployed isn't all bad news—not by a long shot. The tax benefits and salary bonuses can relieve some financial pressures, and deployments tend to be good for career advancement. Deployments may make you and your wife feel more competent and confident. After all, if you can make it through this period, you can make it through anything.

Staying Involved

This is where we get into the concrete steps you can take to stay involved with your wife and your children. As with the **What's Going On** chapters, each of these is divided into three sections:

- ♦ **Looking out for number one.** Knowing you're making a difference in the lives of your wife and children will make you feel more like an integral part of your family. In addition, knowing they're doing well will keep you focused on the job at hand. You'll cope with the stresses of deployment much better if you're confident that your family is okay. Plus, if your worries about what's happening at home distract you too much, you could jeopardize your life, your buddies' lives, and the success of your mission. Not a good thing at all. In these sections we'll focus on things you can do for yourself—getting in a little "me time" now and then is very important. But don't count on having the time for a bubble bath...

- ♦ **Staying involved with your wife.** Your children aren't the only ones who are affected by your deployment. In fact, almost 60 percent of service members say that the number and length of deployments has hurt the stability of their marriage and put a strain on their family. Yes, you'll be apart, and no, it's not going to be much fun. But deployment is definitely *not* a death sentence for your marriage. In fact, supporting each other and knowing that you're both working toward the common goal of keeping the family strong often brings deployed couples closer. The more support she gets from you and the more you reassure her that you love her, the happier and more confident she'll be (it's actually mathematically impossible for her to hear "I love you" too many times). That's good for her, good for the kids, and will be good for you when you get back. Your wife is also the link between you and your children. If she feels that you're making an effort to keep your relationship with *her* strong, she'll be much more supportive and encouraging of your relationship with the kids.

♦ **Staying involved with your child(ren).** When you're a part of their lives—even at a distance—your children will cope better with the stress of your deployment, have fewer behavioral problems, do better in school, think more creatively, get along better with peers, be less likely to abuse drugs or alcohol, and be less likely to get pregnant or get someone else pregnant. Since the majority of children with deployed parents are under seven, I'm focusing mostly on that age group. However, there's plenty of valuable information on staying involved with kids from seven through the teen years.

But Wait, There's More

Throughout the book I've included a number of special sections, including:

♦ What deployment is, who gets deployed, for how long, and where.

♦ Unique issues that affect civilian contractors and nonmilitary government employees.

♦ Challenges facing Reservists and National Guardsmen when they leave— and then return to—their civilian life.

♦ Knowing your legal rights. A number of laws offer special financial and legal protections to reserve and active duty military. These are very useful to know about. Oh man, are they useful.

♦ What to do if your wife is going to have your baby while you're deployed— besides worry.

♦ How to stay involved as a single parent.

♦ Dual service couples, where dad *and* mom are both in the military (and may be deployed at the same time).

♦ Dealing with combat stress or physical injury.

♦ What happens when Mom is deployed and Dad is the trophy husband. (Congratulations on that, by the way!)

♦ Easy-to-use predeployment checklists.

♦ A detailed overview of child development, from pregnancy through eighteen years old.

♦ A whole chapter written just for moms, on how to support your husband during the deployment.

A Note on Terminology

Airman, Marine, deck ape, flyboy, FNG, GI, ground pounder, grunt, gyrene, jarhead, JSR, leatherneck, puddle jumper, REMF, sailor, salt, soldier, squid, swabby, warrior, zoomie...

Early on the writing process I realized I had to come up with a single word to describe the people serving in the military without alienating anyone. (Call a Marine "sailor" or someone in the Air Force "soldier" and you'll start a riot.) So after a lot of discussion, I settled on "service member."

Wife

In the other books in this series I usually refer to the mother of your child as your "partner." My goal has always been to make sure you have the tools and resources you need to be the kind of dad you want to be, and I don't think it's my place to make judgments about whether you're married, about to be married, "seriously involved," or "it's complicated." The military, however, isn't as open-minded. If you're not married, the nonmilitary partner essentially doesn't exist—whether you have children or not (although biological or adopted children of the military partner do). She won't be covered by your insurance or have any medical/dental benefits at all, isn't eligible for survivor benefits if you're injured or killed, can't shop on base, won't get job hiring preference, won't be able to live with you in on-base housing. Oh, and "wrongful cohabitation" (which just means living together while not married) is a violation of article 134 of the UCMJ and could get you dishonorably discharged. For that reason, in this book I'm assuming that the mother of your child is your wife.

Male, Female, He, She...

Because the majority of military service members are men, I generally refer to them as "he," except in specific cases where I'm talking about female service members. On the other hand, military *kids* are just as likely to be male as female. I can't stand the painfully neutral expressions "his or her" or "he or she," and find "s/he" ridiculous (plus, how are you supposed to pronounce it if you're reading it out loud?). The solution? I tried to alternate between "he" and "she" by chapters. In almost all cases, the words are interchangeable.

The All-Important Disclaimer

I'm not a pediatrician, financial planner, accountant, lawyer, military commander, or congressman, nor do I play one on TV (although I am a veteran and do have a radio show). This means that even though all the medical, financial, legal, and military advice in this book has been reviewed by experts and proven to work by real people who have been through what you and your family are experiencing, you should still check with an appropriate professional and/or your CO or boss before trying it out on yourself and your family.

PART I

Predeployment

You're in the Army...or Navy... or Marines...or Air Force... or Coast Guard Now

1.

What *Is* Deployment, Anyway?

Understanding the Basics

The official definition of *deployment* is the "movement of an individual Sailor, Soldier, Airman, Marine, or an entire military unit, from the home base to any other area in order to accomplish a mission." Your definition, however, or your family's, will probably be a little different. For example, *you* might define deployment in terms of distance or time spent away from your family and friends, or in terms of missed birthdays, sports events, and piano recitals, or even the birth of your child. Your children might think about bedtime stories, bike rides, or good-night kisses missed. And your wife might use all those terms plus, as I've heard several military spouses put it:

- Days spent worrying about you.
- Nights spent crying herself to sleep.
- Times she has to answer the question, "When will Daddy be home?"
- Months of not being quite whole.
- The number of toilets she has to plunge by herself.

Who Gets Deployed?

Today, around 1.4 million service members are on active duty in one of the five branches of the U.S. Armed Forces: the Air Force, the Army, the Navy, the Marines, and the Coast Guard (which is technically part of the Department of Homeland Security). That's down over 30 percent from just over 2 million in 1990. With that kind of decrease, it makes sense that the military would start relying more and more on Reserve forces and the National Guard to pick up the slack. Unfortunately, at about 800,000 strong, the total Reserve force is nearly 30 percent smaller than it was in 1990 (when there were 1.1 million members).

Given the perfect storm of more and more operations and a shrinking number of service members, the question is no longer *whether* you'll be deployed, but *when.* And the longer you stay in the military, the more deployments you'll probably see. According to a recent report by the RAND Corporation, in their first term, about half of Army and Air Force enlisted personnel, two-thirds of the Marines, and three-quarters of Navy personnel were deployed at least once. In their second hitch, about one-third of Navy personnel, one-half of Air Force personnel, nearly two-thirds of Army personnel, and nearly three-quarters of Marine Corps personnel had at least one deployment.

Again, the story is pretty much the same for Reservists. According to the Department of Defense, about two-thirds of Reservists have been mobilized, and over 70 percent of them (about half of the total) have been deployed. You didn't really think you were going to serve all your time in Duluth, did you?

What about Mobilization?

The terms *mobilization* and *deployment* are sometimes used interchangeably, but they're really quite different. Mobilization is what happens when Reserve or National Guard units are called up to active duty to prepare for combat or in the case of national or international emergency. Once a unit has been mobilized, it may or may not be deployed (actually, about 70–80 percent of the time it goes beyond "may" and into "will definitely.")

Put a little differently, mobilization is the "get ready" phase; deployment is the "here we go" phase; being there is the "OMG" phase.

How Much Notice Do You Get, and How Long Does Deployment Last?

Well, it depends. If your unit gets called up to deal with the aftermath of a hurricane or some other natural disaster, you might have to drop what you're doing and report for duty within a few hours. Or you could simply be put on alert (meaning you won't be able to leave town until you get orders to deploy or are told to stand down. If you do get deployed, you'll probably be gone only a couple of days or a week).

Regular training missions typically last from a few days to a few months, and you'll usually know all the details several months in advance. In wartime, deployments are often on a schedule, and you can find out where and when you're going as much as a year in advance. Or not. Given the nature of our world today, there's a definite possibility of completely unannounced deployment. As jarring as this kind of situation will be for you, it's going to come as a far bigger shock and surprise to the family you'll be leaving behind. ("Mom, is Dad driving me to hockey today, or is he going to Iraq?")

How long you're gone will depend on the mission and the branch of service you're in. For the Air Force, deployments are usually about four months; for the Navy and Marine Corps, six to seven months; and for the Army and National Guard, a full year. Of course, those numbers are subject to last-minute changes, so do your planning with a grain of salt. Or sand.

Many deployments—particularly those that will take more than a few months—are preceded by training periods that last an average of about ninety days. In most cases, active duty service members—who typically do some training on an ongoing basis—have a shorter training period than Reservists, who may require a little extra time to dust off those skills.

Because civilian contractors are not in the military, they have a lot of choice about where they get deployed and for how long—they can always quit if they don't like the deal they're getting. But because they're working for the U.S. government, most contractors have to go through a hiring process that includes security clearances and health screenings—a process that sometimes takes months. Once the paperwork is complete, though, they may be expected to leave within two or three weeks. Some contractors will be deployed for as long as a year, others just three or four months. Some may serve their entire stint "in country" (without coming home); others may do three to four months in country, get four to six weeks' vacation at home, then do another three to four months abroad. Just think of all those frequent-flyer miles....

Let's Not Forget about the Civilians

With the recent privatization of war in Iraq, Afghanistan, and other places, there are nearly as many civilian contractors and subcontractors working there as military personnel. These contractors, who work for companies like DynCorp International, Blackwater USA, and KBR, do everything from providing private security and training local law enforcement to serving food in mess halls and delivering mail in government compounds. Because, like their military counterparts, these deployed civilian contractors are usually separated from their family, they'll experience many of the same emotional upheavals. And although they're not technically in the military, they'll still get deployed, often wear a uniform, and occasionally eat food with sand and dust in it.

Another group that's often overlooked is civilian government employees. About 45,000 people work outside the country for the U.S. Department of Defense. Another 20,000 work abroad for the State Department (that's two thirds of their entire workforce). But contrary to the stereotype of diplomats gallivanting around the world wearing tuxedos and drinking cocktails, seventy percent of those employees are in "hardship" posts, meaning that they may be subject to terrorist threats, violent crime, harsh climate, social isolation, or other factors.

What Kinds of Deployments Are There?

According to the U.S. Department of Defense, the American military is deployed in over 150 countries. The foreign service is even more far-flung with a presence in 180 countries and over 40 international organizations. The number of service members varies greatly, ranging from only a handful in places like Malta, Estonia, and Mongolia to about 30,000 in Japan, 57,000 in Germany, 25,000 in South Korea, and tens of thousands more in Iraq and Afghanistan.

The range of missions is almost as varied as the number of countries. Of course, most of the deployments we hear about have to do with deposing dictators, the global war on terrorism, and the various conflicts and outright wars we're involved in. But there are plenty of others. Remember the slogan, "Join the Army, see the world"? You may get sent places to protect, to build infrastructure, or even just to stand around and look fierce.

Regular training exercises, for example, which rarely make the news, are an integral part of life in the military. As military commanders (like everyone else) become increasingly reliant on technology, service members constantly need to be trained on the latest weapons, equipment, and tactics. Training exercises also serve a public relations function, a way for the military to tell the rest of the world that it would be a mistake to mess with us or our allies.

Here are just a few of the hundreds of missions American service members have been deployed to achieve:

- Peacekeeping in Sierra Leone, Sudan, India, Haiti, East Timor, the Balkans, and the Middle East.
- Anti-drug operations in Central and South America and the United States.
- Delivering emergency relief supplies to Bolivia, Ethiopia, Paraguay, and Georgia.
- Fighting fires in California, Oregon, and Tennessee.
- Providing security for the Winter Olympics in Utah.
- Improving water supplies, digging wells, building schools and housing, transporting hospital equipment, and providing humanitarian aid for millions of victims of tsunamis, earthquakes, hurricanes, tornadoes, and other natural disasters in the United States and dozens of countries around the world.

As you can see, in each of these situations the needs of the operation go far

When You're In, You're In. When You're Out, You Could Still Be In

Now here's something that will come as a shock to some readers. Did you know that every enlistment contract is actually for eight years? It's true. Say you signed up for and served four years of active duty, or you signed up for and served six years in the Reserve. At the end of that time you'll get an honorable discharge. But instead of being able to kiss the service good-bye forever, you'll spend the difference between what you served and eight years in what's called the Individual Ready Reserve (IRR). The IRR is technically an inactive kind of service. You don't have to report for duty, you don't have to attend weekend drills, and you can grow your hair as long as you want to. But you're subject to recall if Congress or the president says they need you. Anytime, any place.

There's also what's called "stop loss," where even though you've retired or been discharged, you can be recalled if you've got training or expertise in something the military needs. If that isn't a lesson on the need to read the fine print, I'm not sure what is.

beyond infantrymen, tank drivers, and fighter pilots. Just think of all the support they require: transportation, communications, food preparation, sleeping arrangements, construction of entire buildings (which often have to be built from scratch), medical support, intelligence gathering, security, and interpreting. Depending on the situation, some or all of these functions may be performed by civilian contractors. But whether they wear a U.S. government uniform or not, all of these people are essential to the success of every mission.

Making a List and Checking It Over and Over and Over

As we talked about earlier, when it comes to deployment, it's a question of when, not if. And because that "when" could happen with little or no advance notice, your personal affairs should be in order at all times. Like right now. I strongly suggest that you also put a system in place—long before you deploy—to ensure that your family will have access to whatever information, support, and resources they might need while you're away. Besides giving your wife some much-needed peace of mind, this is good for you too. Imagine you're on a raid somewhere, and all of a sudden you start worrying about whether you told your wife the passwords for your online banking, or whether she knows that the car registration is about to expire. This isn't like those times when you can turn your car around and go back home to make sure you turned off the oven. In combat, your distraction and lack of focus could put your life and that of your buddies in even more danger than they're already in.

In the appendices, on pages 249–57, you'll find a comprehensive worksheet that you can use to keep track of all your predeployment to-do lists. If you're on active duty, you may have already taken care of some of these items. If you're a Reservist, though, it's a lot harder to keep deployment preparation issues on top of your mind—you've got plenty to keep you busy in your civilian life. Unfortunately, that means you've got some extra work to do—and you'd better start soon, before the rumors of deployment get too loud. But for right now, whether you're on active duty or in the Reserve, I want to highlight several absolute essentials.

1. No DEERS, no bucks. Immediately after you find out that you're being deployed, item number one on your to-do list should be to make sure that all of the information in the Defense Enrollment Eligibility Reporting System (DEERS) is accurate. DEERS is what the military uses to determine eligibility for a whole host of benefits, including health care. Even the slightest error or omission could result in your family not being able to get the care or the benefits they're entitled to.

If you're on active duty, you're already enrolled in DEERS. But double-check your info anyway, especially if you've had any major life event, such as changing branch of service, moving from enlisted to officer, getting married or divorced, or having a baby or adopting one. If you're in the Reserve or National Guard, you'll have a chance to update your DEERS info during the mobilization process.

To get properly enrolled in DEERS, you'll need to bring copies of:

♦ Birth or adoption certificates or guardianship papers for all your dependents who are twenty-one and younger.
♦ Social security numbers for yourself and everyone else in your family.
♦ Marriage certificate from your current marriage.
♦ Child support orders, if any.
♦ Your mobilization and/or deployment orders.

2. Get ID cards. After you've finished updating DEERS, and while the whole family is together, make sure everyone ten and older has an ID card—they'll need to flash it to get on base, shop in the PX, use recreational facilities, and get medical care. If you and all your dependents have ID cards, great. But check the expiration dates. If a card is set to expire while you're gone, take care of the renewal now. If you're a Reservist, you'll need to get ID cards for your family. And you may need a new one for yourself, too, since the ones for active duty personnel are a different color.

3. Take care of the legal stuff. There are several documents that you do not want to be scrambling around trying to put together the day before you leave, and because they're so important, you may need a little help. That help is available for free, whether you're active or Reserve, through your legal assistance officer or judge advocate general (JAG). These documents are:

♦ **A will or trust.** If the worst happens and you don't come home, and you don't have a will or trust in place, a court—not you—will ultimately decide how your assets and property will be divided. This could include everything from bank accounts to your lucky Pez dispenser collection to your car. Having a will or trust is especially important if you're in a blended family, where you and/or your wife are stepparents. When preparing a will or trust, pay special attention to who will be the executor (the person who makes sure your wishes are carried out), and who will be the guardian of your children in case you and your wife die. During predeployment training you'll most likely prepare a standard will. If you have complicated assets or confusing child-care plans, though, you might want to start the process before training gets underway.

♦ **Powers of attorney.** These are legal documents that authorize anyone you select (as long as that person is twenty-one or older) to act on your behalf. In most cases that person will be your wife. But it could be a parent, relative, or trusted friend. Powers of attorney come in three flavors. If you aren't absolutely sure which type you need, ask your legal assistance officer for some guidance.

◊ **A general durable POA** appoints one person to be your representative in *everything*. This person will have access to all of your private information and finances, and can sign your name to any legal document. You can revoke this POA at any time.

◊ **A health-care POA** appoints one person to make medical decisions for you if you happen to be incapacitated and aren't able or competent to make medical decisions for yourself.

◊ **A special (or limited) POA** appoints someone to be your representative on one or more specific matters. You can have as many limited POAs as you want. For example, you might want one person to handle your family's finances, another to sell your fishing boat, and another to get your kids enrolled in private school.

Some people are a little wary of drawing up a POA—and it's hard to blame them. I've heard numerous stories from service members and civilian contractors who've lost everything while they were deployed. Granting a POA is a lot like giving someone all your credit cards. And your checkbook. And your PIN number. And the keys to your mint-condition 1964 Corvette. And then dropping them off in Las Vegas for the weekend. It's a trust thing. In most cases, you'll be giving your wife the POA. If you don't think you can trust her with it, you've got a real problem in your marriage.

4. Make a calendar. A really big one. And put everything into it: paydays for you (and your wife, if she works); due dates for monthly bills as well as not-so-monthly things like when you need to change the oil in the car and rotate the tires, clean furnace and air-conditioning filters, and pay your property taxes, homeowners' insurance, and nonmilitary life insurance. Go ahead and include personal dates as well: birthdays, anniversaries, school events, sports games, recitals, and so on. Then make two copies. One stays home with your wife, the other goes with you. If you're pretty sure you'll have Internet access while you're deployed, you might want to use an online calendar such as Google (calendar.google.com), which you, your wife, or your kids can update whenever you need to. It can also e-mail or text you reminders of big events so you can send cards or flowers. Remembering a special anniversary or birthday will earn you big romance points—redeemable when you get home.

5. Take a walking tour of your house. The idea here is to show your wife all the chores you normally take care of but that she'll have dumped in her lap pretty soon. This is no time for memory games or mind reading, so bring along a pad of paper and write it all down for her. Must-see sights on the tour:

♦ The breaker panel, and how to tell when a circuit has tripped. If you have a fuse box, show her how to tell if a fuse is blown and where the spares are kept.

♦ Water, gas, and electrical meters.

♦ Emergency shutoff valves for the water and gas.

♦ The automatic sprinkler system and how to use it.

♦ The thermostat and how to program it.

♦ Where you keep the hammer, screwdrivers, ladders, and other tools.

♦ Where you keep the extra keys to the house.

♦ How to fix the garage door opener if it comes off the track.

♦ How to change a tire or recharge a dead car battery with an electric charger.

♦ How to use the power lawn mower.

♦ How *not* to use the power lawn mower.

♦ What kind of oil to mix with how much gas for the weed whacker.

♦ Things you've been meaning to take care of for months but never quite got around to, like the sliding glass door that always sticks, the cable TV box you have to bang to get to work, or the toilet that won't stop running after you flush it.

♦ Anything else that's normally your territory. Basically this is the time to show her all the guy knowledge you've accumulated over the course of your life—how to fix, find, and finagle everything else we men hold sacred. Luckily, you probably won't have to teach her how to field-dress a moose.

6. Start gathering documents. The checklists in the Appendices go into this in more detail, but here are some of the highlights:

- ◆ **Service-related records.** At the very least, your wife will need a copy of your deployment orders.
- ◆ **Personal records.** Social security cards; birth, marriage, adoption, guardianship, and other certificates.
- ◆ **Medical.** This includes immunization records, policy numbers, medication, allergies, and your family care plan (see page 33). It should also include any medical records for your pet. Seriously. You don't want a late-night call from back home asking when Fluffy needs to be wormed.
- ◆ **Financial.** Pay stubs, statements, and account numbers for all savings, checking, brokerage, trading, credit union, and retirement accounts, as well as for mortgage, electricity, garbage, water, phone, cable, property taxes, and other bills. If you're the one who pays the bills and you don't already use online or automatic bill paying, now is a great time to set it up. You'll save her a huge amount of time and hassle.
- ◆ **Owner's manuals, pink slips, receipts, and warranty information.** For your car, the dishwasher, microwave, refrigerator, washing machine, dryer, cell phones, and anything else you can think of.

7. Emergency contacts. This list will include the person or people your wife can contact if one of your allotments doesn't get deposited when it should (which happens more often than you'd think), your home warranty company, claims lines for auto and home insurance, credit cards (in case one is lost or stolen), tradespeople (plumber, electrician, handyman), babysitters, and helpful neighbors. You might include your favorite pizza delivery place, for those nights when she's too bushed to cook. You can thank me later.

By Gunnery Sgt Charles Wolf, U.S. Marine Corps

Special Circumstances for Active Duty Service Members

Married to the Military

There are about 84,000 couples serving on active duty where husband and wife are both in the service. Of those couples, 36,000 have children. These dual-service couples are subject to the same relocations and deployments as service members who are married to civilians, and there are no assurances that they'll even be assigned to the same base. Although one might think it would be a terrible thing to take Mom and Dad from their family at the same time, it does happen. So if you're in a dual-service marriage, there are two very important things you should do. The first is optional, although you'd be silly not to do it. The second is mandatory.

1. Apply for a Joint Spouse assignment. Each branch of the service has a Joint Spouse program, and in order for you and your wife to have even a glimmer of hope of being assigned anywhere near each other, you'll *both* need to apply for it. Under the program, your branch of service will *try* (there are absolutely no guarantees) to accommodate your request, which, on average, they do about 80 percent of the time. But wait. Their definition of *accommodate* could be very different from yours. What they mean is that you'll be assigned within a hundred miles of each other. If you're both in the same branch of service, there's a pretty good chance you could be assigned to the same base. But if you're in different branches, good luck. It's unlikely that you'll find bases for two branches very close together. And it's even less likely that one of you will find a job on the other's base (it's rare, for example, to find a Marine Corps contingent on an Army post). Again, you'll *both* need to apply for Joint Spouse. If you're engaged to another service member, consider getting married sooner rather than later. The earlier you put in for Joint Spouse, the better your chances of getting it.

2. Complete a family care plan. A family care plan (FCP) is a document that lays out how you'd like your child(ren) and any other family members who aren't able to care for themselves to be looked after in the event that you and your wife are deployed at the same time. If you're a dual-service couple or a single parent (more on that below), an FCP is mandatory. FCPs differ slightly from branch to branch, but at the very least, they all contain provisions for:

+ **A short-term care provider.** Someone living nearby who has agreed to accept care of your children twenty-four/seven, if you get deployed with no notice.
+ **A long-term care provider.** Someone—not necessarily living nearby— who will care for your children if you're deployed for a long period of time.

You and your wife should have an FCP in place at all times. And you should review it at least once a year to make sure the information in it is up-to-date. In addition to filing the FCP with your respective units, you and your wife should keep a copy in a safety deposit box and give copies to anyone who's designated in the plan as a caretaker. Because FCPs are individually tailored to your family's unique needs, we won't go into any more detail here. Your commanding officer is responsible for ensuring that you understand the requirements of and properly complete the FCP, and he or she should be able to direct you to a judge advocate general (JAG), chaplain, personnel officer, or other military support agencies, depending on your questions or particular needs.

"Next to my two years in the Marines, you're the best thing I've ever done."

What if You're a Single Dad?

None of the branches of service allow single parents to enlist. But if you became a custodial single parent because of a divorce or the death of your wife, or you share custody with your ex, the service won't boot you out. They won't give you any special treatment either. (Don't feel bad. The military prides itself on not giving *anyone* special treatment. They're like that.) Unlike in civilian life, where parents are encouraged (or forced, depending on your perspective) to put their children first, in the military, the unit and the mission come first every time. You won't get any extra leave, nicer quarters, shorter workdays, or any exemptions from deployment or training. You'll be just like any other service member—except that you'll have to complete a family care plan (see page 33 for more details). If you don't, you could end up with an "involuntary separation"—in other words, be thrown out.

A special note if you owe child support. If you're on active duty, your child support order was probably set using your base pay and other allotments, and not much will change while you're deployed. But if you're in the Reserve, you've got deployment orders, and you anticipate that your earnings will drop during your activation, you could have a real problem. So put this book down, grab your military orders and copies of your divorce decree, custody agreement, and child support orders, and double-time it down to the family division of your local county courthouse. If you have a lawyer, contact him and have him meet you there. Like getting married, adjusting child support is much easier to do in person—and almost impossible to do after you've shipped out.

What you want to do is request a downward modification of your child support order. Theoretically, that should be easy. Child support is usually calculated as a percentage of your salary. So if you're not going to be making as much as you are now, your payments should be lowered accordingly. The problem is that many family law courts disregard the facts and keep the order the same, implying that you're trying to cheat the system by keeping your income artificially low.

Even under the best of circumstances, though, modifying a child support order—especially downward—can take as long as a couple of months to work its way through the system. But if you get deployed on a day or two's notice, you won't have time to get the modification approved before you leave.

Either way—whether you get a Neanderthal judge who refuses to lower your obligation, or you don't have enough time to actually get the order in hand—you could find yourself in real trouble. I've heard from more than a few Reservists who fell behind on their child support and were arrested, heavily fined, or punished in some other ridiculous way when they came home. The fact that they'd been putting their life on the line to defend our country didn't seem to count for much.

Dads-to-Be: Is There Any Chance of Coming Home for the Birth?

The official answer is most likely no. However, unit commanders have a lot of leeway, and there are definite advantages to being an officer or a seasoned veteran with several combat tours under your belt. If you're lucky enough to talk your way into taking a stateside trip to be there for the birth of your baby, don't count on being able to stay longer than a few days.

That said, if your service offers a mid-tour leave program, you may have as much as two weeks to return home. Then, it's just a matter of scheduling your mid-tour leave to coincide with the birth. The problem is that only 5 percent of babies are born on their actual, "official" due date. About 25 percent are born earlier, and 70 percent arrive later. Overall, though, about 80 percent are born within seven to ten days of the due date. Still, since you're not going to get a written guarantee from your baby (and how would you enforce it anyway?), planning your leave around a specific date isn't terribly wise. Ideally, your baby will be born full term and your wife will go into labor on her own. However, she wants you to be there for the birth as much as you do. So if her doctor feels that it's medically safe (the health of your wife and baby are *always* the top priority), you and your wife may want to discuss induction or other less natural ways of jump-starting labor. But don't push too hard on this. Finding the right words so you don't come across as self-centered and insensitive is not going to be easy.

So maybe you should consider other factors. For example, when would your wife want you there the most? Before the birth, when it becomes difficult for her to move around? During the birth itself? Or after the birth, when she is still recovering and really needs the extra support? Of course, the answer to this question is different for everyone, and knowing how much support your wife has close by (in the form of family or friends) will influence your decision. Just to be safe, it's definitely worth having a discussion with your wife.

If you're a civilian contractor, you may want to get this issue resolved before you start your hitch. Some companies are on very strict timetables, and if your taking a week off in the middle of a major project could blow the entire project, they won't let you leave. There's also the issue of who pays for the transportation. Most companies will cover your airfare to the job at the beginning of your term and back home at the end. Any non-company traveling you do in between could be on your own nickel.

Are There Hardship Cases That Could Keep Service Members from Deploying?

Theoretically, yes, but don't count on it. If you have reason to think that your deployment will cause you or your family a significant hardship, start by discussing the matter with your CO. If there's a true emergency that you can't possibly resolve before you ship out, you *may* be able to delay your deployment until the crisis has passed. Each branch of service has review boards that consider hardship cases, but approvals are rare. If your particular hardship has to do with money, keep in mind that there are laws in place to protect you while you're deployed. See pages 38–39 for more information.

How Much Deployment Is Too Much?

Operational tempo (or OPTEMPO)— the number and frequency of deployments—has always been a part of every service member's life. But as the number of our military engagements rises and the size of the military shrinks, OPTEMPO has increased. A number of research teams are investigating how service members and their families are affected by deployments that are closer together and last longer. But to date, there's no magic number. Of course, your unit's OPTEMPO will depend on its mission. Some support units may see twenty or thirty short-term deployments every year. Other units may go two years between deployments. Commanders of many combat units try to follow a schedule of twelve to fifteen months of deployment followed by a year at home, hoping to allow their units to recover from the stress and spend some time with their family. But they aren't always successful. It's not at all uncommon for service members to see four or more deployments over the course of six or seven years. The numbers keep on changing. And not in your favor.

When it comes to the Reserve forces and National Guard, there are actual laws in place that mandate a certain amount of time between deployments (one such law allows for twelve months of deployment out of every six years in the Reserve). However, in times of war or national emergency, those laws are often mothballed. In addition, some units offer "voluntary" deployments before the required "at-home" period is up. Consequently, a lot of Reservists feel compelled to "volunteer" because everyone else is doing it, or because they think it might advance their career.

Those non-military government employees have some pretty serious OPTEMPO issues as well. According to the American Foreign Service Association, well over half of the Foreign Service has been assigned to a hardship post within the past five years. Over the same time period, over thirty percent have served in an unaccompanied position. And a full 20 percent of the Service has spent time in a war zone in Iraq or Afghanistan.

Civilian contractors, of course, have the most flexibility and are free to turn down assignments or quit their job entirely if they want to avoid the stress of multiple deployments. But good luck trying to find a stateside job that can match the high pay and tax benefits of overseas assignments.

Special Circumstance for Reservists and Guardsmen

Federal Protections

As a responsible adult, part of your job is to keep your financial affairs as close to being in order as possible. Unfortunately, being deployed can really mess with your budget and bank accounts. The good news, though, is that there are several laws designed to help you out. These are the Servicemembers Civil Relief Act (SCRA) and the Uniformed Services Employment and Reemployment Rights Act (USERRA). Let's take a closer look at each one.

SCRA

The SCRA is set up to get creditors off your back—or at least not quite so close to your jugular. Under this law, you have to demonstrate that your income has been so drastically reduced by military service that it's difficult or impossible for you to make payments. Under the SCRA you could qualify for:

♦ A cap on high-interest rate mortgages and credit cards.

♦ Protection from eviction (in some cases).

♦ A break on your state and federal taxes.

♦ A delay on all civil court actions, such as bankruptcy, foreclosure, or divorce proceedings.

♦ The right to break an apartment or car lease, as long as you entered into it before being mobilized. You may also be able to avoid eviction.

Several important restrictions on the SCRA:

♦ Interest rate reductions only apply on debts you ran up *before* your stint on active duty began.

♦ You're still ultimately responsible for the debt.

♦ You must let your creditors (banks, insurance companies, lenders, etc.) know well in advance that you've been called to active duty. And be prepared to offer proof that you won't be able to make the payments.

♦ You're protected under the SCRA only during the time you're on active duty. Once you're back home, you're on your own.

For more on the SCRA, visit MilitaryOneSource.com, which keeps up-to-date information on the SCRA, especially its relationship with mortgage difficulties, or contact your unit or installation legal assistance office.

USERRA

A lot of Reservists and guardsmen worry about what will happen to their job if their unit is deployed, and USERRA is designed to give you some peace of mind. Under USERRA—which applies to just about any employer, public or private, large or small—if you have to leave your civilian job because of "service in the uniformed services," you're entitled to return to that job, at the same level and salary you would have reached had you not been deployed, as long as *all* of the following are true:

1. You had a civilian job.
2. You gave your employer advance written notice that you had been deployed.
3. Your military service is for five years or fewer.
4. You are released from service under "honorable conditions."
5. After returning from deployment, you report back to your civilian employer or submit an application for reemployment in a timely manner.

Knowing your rights under USERRA and any other laws is a good first step. But if your boss and coworkers don't understand or support your military obligations, they can make your life and your job miserable—no matter how many laws you can cite. According to Employer Support of the Guard and Reserve (esgr.org), an organization within the Department of Defense, most employment conflicts can be avoided by being candid with your employer about your obligations as a member of one of the Reserve components. Here are some of ESGR's tips for keeping the people you work with and for on your side:

- ♦ Don't take your employer's support for granted. Keep your boss informed about what you do in the military and when you do it.
- ♦ Let your boss know the vital mission that is supported by your participation in the National Guard or Reserve.
- ♦ Let your boss know how your military experience and training will make you a more capable civilian employee.
- ♦ Take time to recognize the sacrifice your boss and coworkers make when they support you.
- ♦ And I'd add, start thinking about taking the gang out for a drink when you get back. A round or two of beer can go a long way toward building mutual support and feelings of goodwill and understanding.

By Basil Zaviski Co. F 425 Airborne Infantry, U.S. Army

Do You Own Your Own Business?

Under the best of circumstances, deployments can be tough on Reservists and their families. But if you own a small business, the costs could be even higher. The first big decision you have to make is what's going to happen to the business while you're gone. Will you be able to turn the reins over to someone else and keep things running smoothly? Will you have to temporarily close the doors? Will you close up shop permanently or declare bankruptcy? If you're not sure which of these options is the best one for you and your family, you may want to get some advice. The Office of Veterans Business Development of the Small Business Administration (sba.gov) and the Small Business Development Center (sbdcnet.org/sbdc.php) are great sources of information.

If it turns out that you'll have to close your business, whether temporarily or permanently, you'll need to let all of your customers and creditors know and legally appoint someone to handle all the details in your stead. Closing a business can sometimes be a drawn-out process, and you probably won't be able to see the whole thing through before you leave.

Hopefully, though, you'll be able to keep the business going. If so, you've got a lot to do.

♦ **Take care of the legal end.** You'll need to have a power of attorney (see page 29 for more) that appoints one or more people to run the

business while you're gone. Carefully outline their responsibilities and the amount of control you're giving them.

- **Have a business plan.** If you haven't already got one, now's a good time to put one together that details the goals of the business and how you'd like to accomplish them.
- **Start letting people know.** Talk with your banker, creditors, lawyer, accountant, insurance agent, and of course your employees.
- **Train, train, train.** It's essential that you have people in place who can fill your shoes while you're gone. If you're not completely confident that you can just hand the keys to someone and leave, you may want to give that person a trial run during one of your annual two-week drills. Or, if that doesn't work out, take a short vacation and let him or her handle everything. Don't forget the sunscreen.
- **Get help if you need it.** The SBA's Military Reservist Economic Injury Disaster Loan program provides loans to small businesses that need to cover expenses when a key employee is deployed. These loans, which can range from a few hundred dollars to over $2 million, are designed to help you meet ordinary operating expenses and pay your bills. You won't be able to use the loans to replace actual income or profits or to expand the business. You can apply for these loans online, at disasterloan.sba.gov.

Now for the Good News

There are some definite benefits to being deployed as a Reservist.

- ◆ **Taxes.**
  - ◇ If you're enlisted or a warrant officer, the money you earn while deployed in a combat zone (CZ) is not subject to federal income tax (each state has slightly different regulations on this, so check with yours. If you're an officer, your CZ income is untaxed up to a certain level).
  - ◇ Because your income from your civilian job will be lower, the amount of taxes paid and the overall tax rate will drop.
  - ◇ You can get an automatic extension of the federal tax filing deadline. The deadline is 180 days plus the number of CZ days served.
  - ◇ If you're activated for at least six months, you may be able to withdraw money from your 401(k) or other similar plan without paying the 10 percent penalty for early distributions.
- ◆ **Education benefits.** The time you spend on active duty will qualify you for certain benefits under the GI Bill. In addition, many colleges and universities have reduced tuition programs for veterans.
- ◆ **Low-interest veterans' loans for vehicles, business, and home purchase.** The requirements are sometimes a little quirky, but the rates are usually below market.
- ◆ **Vocational, mental health, and disability benefits.** Hopefully, you won't need any of these, but if you do, it's nice to know you're covered.
- ◆ **TRICARE (the military's health-care plan).** While you're on active duty, a small premium will be taken out of your check, and your family will have complete medical and dental coverage with zero copays and zero forms to fill out (this may be the only time in your military or civilian life when you won't have any paperwork as long as you see a military provider, so enjoy it while you can). There are some requirements (such as having to see a primary care physician before getting a referral to a specialist), but this coverage is excellent.
- ◆ **Your salary.** Although conventional wisdom says that Reservists' income falls when they're activated, economist David S. Loughran and his colleagues at the RAND Corporation found that only 17 percent of Reservists experienced a loss, while 83 percent said their income actually increased. Whether you're in the 83 percent or the 17 percent group, be sure to stop by your employer's HR department. A growing number of companies are picking up the difference between deployed Reservists' active duty pay and their regular salary. Hey! Free money! Well, almost.

Special Circumstances for Civilians

An Advantage (👍) and Several Disadvantages (👎)

👍 FINANCES

Your income can more than double while you're overseas. Your room, board, movies, gym membership, and just about everything except cigarettes and candy bars is covered by the company. Plus, your tax liability is smaller, since a big chunk of money earned outside the country is exempt from taxes. If you manage all this extra income properly, you can come home with a windfall that can slingshot you into a far better life. I've heard from civilian contractors who've taken contract jobs to pay off debts, and one man was actually able to save enough to pay cash for a home. Be aware, though, that you'll be working hard for every penny. Most contractors work about twelve hours per day, seven days a week, for the duration of their contract. This isn't usually as bad as it sounds, since most of the places you're likely to go won't have much in the way of entertainment anyway.

👎 PERSONAL AND FAMILY LIFE

If you and your wife are going through some tough times, or you're dealing with a child who has drug or alcohol problems or is in trouble with the law, taking an overseas contract job is *not* going to magically make things better. In fact, I can pretty much guarantee that it'll make them worse. Taking a contract job and then spending your time worrying about an alcoholic wife, a pregnant teen daughter, or a son in jail will trash your productivity and could result in your getting written up and fired. I strongly recommend that you get your personal and family life in order before shipping out.

👎 FREEDOM

If your job takes you to a country where we're engaged in a war, there's a very good chance that you'll be spending twenty-four hours a day on a military base or a camp that looks and feels like one. It may simply be too dangerous for you to go "outside the wire" (leave the compound). Back in the United States, even full-time, active duty military can leave their base, eat out in restaurants, go camping, or visit family. But you won't be able to. Hey, that's why you get the big bucks.

🔋 JOB

Here's the rule: When you're hired for a contract job, there is no guarantee that you'll be able to keep working for the company when you get back stateside. Overall, fewer than 10 percent of contractors are able to transition to full-time employment. In a lot of cases, that's because many of the overseas jobs being filled—like food service, laundry, and washing trucks—don't exist anywhere except outside the country. In addition, you may have been recruited from a city where the company doesn't have facilities, so even if they do have jobs available, you'd have to uproot your family and move to Houston or wherever.

Unlike activated Reservists, there's no guarantee that the civilian job you're leaving to take the contract job will take you back. If you're leaving a job you can easily get back into when you get home, you're okay. But if the contract job will bump you off a nice stateside career path, be very sure the rewards more than offset the risks. This generally means cash. Lots and lots of cash.

Coping with Emergencies

Generally speaking, civilian contractors try to be flexible. If there's a true emergency, the company will do what it can to accommodate you, but if you just want a few days off because you're tired, or you want to go to your high-school reunion or help your wife pick out drapes, good luck.

The hitch is that many companies will require you to make an application through the Red Cross, which will investigate the emergency and, if they verify it, make a request on your behalf that you be allowed to go home. If the Red Cross turns you down, there's nothing to stop you from quitting your job. There's also nothing to stop your employer from refusing to hire you back again.

The Cycle of Deployment

As we've talked about earlier, because of the number of countries and conflicts the U.S. military is engaged in, deployments are more frequent, longer, and less predictable than they were a few decades ago. But as unpredictable as the deployments themselves are, there is a very predictable, consistent pattern to the way service members and their family react to deployment—regardless of when or how it comes about. These reactions, which can be physical, behavioral, emotional, and psychological, form what many researchers and the military call the "cycle of deployment."

On the most basic level, the cycle has three major phases: predeployment,

deployment, and post-deployment. Each phases is further divided into several stages. Although there are lots of ways of slicing up the cycle, I like the one used by Karen Pavlicin, author of *Surviving Deployment*. On pages 46–48 you'll find a brief overview of the cycle based on the author's basic breakdown and augmented with information I've gathered from interviews with service members and their families.

Understanding the cycle and the psychological, emotional, and behavioral upheaval that can come with each phase and stage will help everyone in your family better cope with and adapt to your deployment, and can go a long way toward keeping your relationships with each other—especially your kids—strong while you're away. At the very least, it can be very reassuring to know that the crazy thoughts and feelings you're having or the bizarre behaviors you're seeing from your wife and children are completely normal (except if you've got teenagers. Their behavior is *always* going to be a little crazy).

In broad strokes, here's what the cycle looks like. We'll go into a lot more detail in the chapters that follow.

"I'd feel safer if you were an ex-marine with a gun collection."

Phase 1: Predeployment

This phase, which can last from a day to a year or more, officially starts when the service member receives his deployment orders, and ends just after the last good-bye. The predeployment phase is all about preparing you and your family for what's ahead.

- **Stage 1: Shock, denial, anger, and more.** Whether you're on active duty or in the Reserve, there's always a certain amount of shock at receiving orders to leave your family and your routines. After the shock, it's natural for anger to kick in—at anything and everything—as well as a complete refusal to believe the deployment is actually going to happen. From there on, the emotions that you and your wife experience will be all over the place.

- **Stage 2: Acceptance.** Once the emotional upheaval has settled, reality sets in, and you and your family will start coming to terms with the idea that you're actually going to be gone. For some families, this is a period of great closeness, when everyone wants to spend as much time with each other as possible, building up a reserve to last them through all those months when you'll be separated. But for many families, it's a pretty tense time, as each person finds a different way to begin adjusting to the coming new reality.

- **Stage 3: Emotional detachment and withdrawal.** You're going to be spending more and more time with the other guys in your unit, forming closer bonds, learning to work together as a team, and preparing yourselves for your mission. But the more time you spend with your buddies, the less you'll have for your family. At the same time, your wife has been preparing herself for your departure, and she may withdraw from you emotionally and physically. As for your kids, they may also be withdrawn and angry, "punishing" you in advance for leaving them.

Phase II: Deployment

This is the actual separation, which, like the predeployment phase, can last anywhere from a few days to a year or more.

- **Stage 4: Emotional disorganization.** You're off—and now those mixed emotions from stage 1 come roaring back. On one hand, you and your wife might actually feel some relief that the goodbyes and predeployment tension are behind you and that you can both now focus on the task at hand—you on your mission, she on helping the family resume some semblance of normality. On the other hand, you're all starting to miss each other, and you're worried about how you'll adjust to the uncertainty of your deployment.

♦ **Stage 5: Recovery and stabilization.** You've settled into your new environment, and you're focusing on the job you were trained to do. You may push thoughts of your family off into a neat little corner of your mind so that you can focus on your job. At the same time, you're trying to keep in touch, and you're increasingly confident that you'll all make it through the deployment okay. Back at home, your wife is feeling confident too, and proud that she's handling all the extra responsibilities she's had to take on. (One toilet plunged? Check! One cat saved from drowning? Check!)

♦ **Stage 6: Anticipation of homecoming.** Starting a month or so before your scheduled return home, yet another period of mixed emotions will kick in. You're really looking forward to going back home, but you're worried about what it will be like. Will they be happy to see me? Will my kids even remember who I am? Your wife will be going through something similar, practically unable to contain her excitement that you're coming home, but worried about what you'll be like.

♦ **Stage 6.5 (sometimes): Deployment extension.** What can we say about this one? Delays happen, missions change, and there's nothing you or your family can do about it. Hey, if the military behaved in nice, predictable ways, they'd be the Girl Scouts, and you'd be out selling tasty mint cookies.

Phase III: Post-deployment

You return home and begin the process of rejoining and reintegrating into the family—which is not nearly as easy as it sounds.

♦ **Stage 7: Honeymoon.** The first few days will be glorious, filled with hugs, kisses, and catching each other up on life. There'll be welcome-home parties and maybe even a romantic weekend getaway for you and your wife, where you and she can tentatively rediscover sex.

♦ **Stage 8: Reintegration.** Once the initial excitement of your homecoming has passed, you may want to jump right back in where you left off, taking control of the things you were in charge of before. But your wife, who's been doing everything while you were gone, is now perfectly capable of doing them herself. And just as you feared, instead of jumping into your arms and asking you to read them bedtime stories, your kids may push you away and demand that Mommy do everything. Active duty personnel have to get used to life in the United States, while Reservists and civilian contractors have to put their nonmilitary life back together. Eventually things may return to where they were. Or your family will have to deal with a new "normal."

Working through the various stages of the deployment cycle isn't going to be easy for you, your spouse, or your children. Over the next two chapters we'll be focusing in detail on the predeployment phase. We'll talk about the feelings and emotions that may come up at various times, and the behaviors that may accompany them. We'll also discuss some strategies you can implement to help everyone cope, and explore tons of concrete steps you can take to create a system that will allow you to stay in contact with your family and remain an important part of their life. Let's move out!

2.

No Heavy Artillery in the Living Room

The Emotional Side of Predeployment

In this section, we're going to be talking about the emotional, psychological, and behavioral effects your impending deployment could have on you, your wife, and your children. (Your Monday-night bowling team will have to be covered in another book.) As you're reading this, keep in mind that nothing is set in stone, and not everyone feels or thinks or behaves the same ways at the same stage. Some people may go through the process in a few days, others may take months. Some may go through the stages in order; others may go out of order, or do two stages at the same time, or skip one or two altogether. You get the point.

That said, what I'm describing below is what *most* people go through. Regardless of your situation, I'll guarantee you that a lot of it will apply to you and your family.

What's Going On with You

Stage 1: Shock, Anger, Denial, and a Jumble of Other Emotions

♦ **Shock, anger, denial.** If you're serving on active duty, you knew perfectly well before you signed your contract that deployments are a normal part of military life and that one of these days it was going to happen. So the idea that you might be shocked, angry, or in denial about being deployed might seem a little odd. But it happens. A lot. Getting those deployment orders, while not really much of a surprise, is almost always a little jarring to everyone concerned—whether you're in the Reserve and got three days' notice to report, or you're on a regular combat deployment rotation and you've had your deployment date on your calendar for a year.

After the initial shock subsides, there's plenty you might be angry about. You might, for example, really resent that you're being taken away from your family—especially if you're a single parent or you and your

"LET ME GET THIS STRAIGHT..... YOU'RE LATE FOR THE WAR BECAUSE... YOU DIDN'T GET THE E-MAIL!!!?"

It's Undeniable

Long before actual orders are given and predeployment briefings are held, the air is usually filled with rumors. Because rumors are so often true, the pre-predeployment phase (the time between the rumors and the orders being received) can give your family some extra time to prepare. Too many service members wait until they have their orders in hand before telling their wife. They worry that they'll upset her, or they try to convince themselves that if they avoid the whole topic, maybe it'll go away, or they honestly believe that waiting until the last minute to break the news will somehow protect her and the rest of the family from the pain of separation. Unfortunately, as kind as these thoughts are, *not* telling her sooner usually makes things worse—especially if there isn't much time between the official notice and the actual departure. People, and by "people" I mean wives, appreciate knowing what's going on. Keeping them in the loop helps keep you out of the doghouse.

wife are both being deployed at the same time. You might be ticked off at your CO or the secretary of defense or the National Weather Service for not giving you more notice, or angry at the enemy, or even at yourself for having volunteered in the first place.

Given all that, it's easy to see how you might say to yourself, "This just ain't happening." But you'd be wrong. A good rule of thumb? If you have a uniform hanging in your closet, you can pretty much count on being deployed.

♦ **Fear.** Whether this is your first deployment or your fourteenth, you'll experience some kind of fear as the process unfolds. You might be afraid for those you're leaving behind, worried about how they'll cope with your absence; you may be afraid that your marriage or relationship with your wife won't survive, or that she'll have an affair while you're gone. (In a way, being deployed is like having a baby—it can make whatever is good in your marriage better, or it can make whatever's bad worse.) And of course, if you're deploying to a combat zone, the fear is never far from your mind that you'll come back a completely changed person or be physically or psychologically wounded—if you come back at all. Your fears might come up infrequently, like when you're reading a bedtime story to your child, or they might be a constant presence, gnawing at your stomach

all day long and sometimes making it hard to concentrate on anything else. Rest assured: however many fears you have, whenever they crop up, and whatever they're about, they are a completely normal and unavoidable part of the predeployment phase. And anyone who tells you he's not afraid of anything is lying to you.

♦ **Uncertainty**. We all want to have some element of control over our lives—even over things we know we can't. But since what happens during the deployment is largely out of your hands, it's completely natural to feel a healthy dose of uncertainty. If this is your first deployment, you really have no idea what you're in for. Sure, you've talked to the guys in your unit who've been there, done that. But hearing about someone else's experiences is very, very different from going through it yourself. If you are one of those more experienced guys, you definitely have a better sense of what will happen on the deployment. Still, every mission is different, and the list of unknowns and unknown unknowns (the things you don't even know you don't know) is long. You may not even know exactly when you'll be leaving and when you'll be home. Uncertainty—even in small doses—can aggravate your fears and take a real toll at home. You want to be strong for your family and reassure them. But you can't. The fact that big, strong Daddy seems unsettled and doesn't have all the answers may make them more afraid too.

It's a Little Different for Civilians

If you're a military contractor, don't count on experiencing as much (or any) of the shock, anger, denial, and uncertainty that your military brothers do. After all, you volunteered for deployment, and you have a very good idea of exactly where you're going, why, and for how long. Plus, you can go home pretty much whenever you want. If you're working in a security-type job, there's a good chance that you're ex-military or worked as a police officer back home, so you understand what your role is and what the price could be. That said, you can still expect to feel some fear and excitement as the deployment date approaches. All in all, it's like taking a working vacation, but without the vacation part.

Hopefully, you will have discussed all of this in great detail with your wife long before you go. Doing so will go a long way toward making the predeployment phase (and the deployment itself) quite a bit easier on your family. But don't delude yourself into thinking that they're not going to be affected by your absence.

♦ **Excitement.** As counterintuitive as this might sound, a lot of service members feel a strong sense of excitement when they first get their deployment orders. It's like getting called up to the big leagues after putting in a long time in the minors. The prospect of gearing up, going into theater (the combat kind, not the movie kind—it's important to know the difference before shipping out), engaging the enemy, putting all that training into action, doing something heroic, and earning a combat patch or maybe the Congressional Medal of Honor (and staying alive through it all) can be very invigorating. And as the excitement gets more and more contagious, you'll hear a lot of "Oh, hell yeah!" "Hooah!" (or "Oo-rah!" or "Hooya," depending on which service you're in) from the guys in your unit. At the same time, you may start feeling a little guilty about being excited. And that brings up something very important. Although I think it's a good idea to talk about all the other emotions you're feeling at this stage, you might want to consider keeping this one to yourself. It's pretty unlikely that your wife or children will understand why you're excited—they may even take it as a sign that you don't care about them. And even if they do get it, don't expect them to actually be excited *for* you.

Lagging Leaders

If you're in a leadership position, you may be so busy getting your teams mobilized and trained and seeing to their health and welfare that you won't fully experience all the emotional zigs and zags described in this chapter. At least, not right away. I heard from one commander with a number of deployments under his belt that the feelings didn't start hitting him until the deployment was already well under way—and sometimes not until it was time to start the process of demobilization to come back home.

Stage 2: Acceptance

♦ **Introspection.** You've just been called to duty, and the orders you got told you to report to your unit to begin preparing for deployment. They didn't say anything about your emotions or how you're supposed to deal with the feelings associated with the task at hand. But believe me, you're going to be doing a lot of thinking as you come to terms with this new phase of your life. You'll find yourself muttering under your breath about everything from, "What was I thinking when I signed up for this?" to "Man, I own a lot of socks. Should I bring them all?"

♦ **Sadness and regret.** You know your kids will never again be the age they are right now. You know you'll miss the holidays, birthdays, anniversaries, baseball and hockey games, recitals, and graduations. And you know you'll never get those memories back—even if someone captures them on video. Besides events, you're going to miss day-to-day life: the family bike rides and movie nights, those lazy Sunday mornings hanging out with the kids, helping them with their homework, seeing your ninety-seven-year-old grandmother, who you worry might pass away while you're deployed, the Wednesday-night poker games with your buddies, and everything to do with your wife. You'll even miss some of the boring stuff—there are no leaves to rake in Afghanistan. As you realize the extent of what you're going to miss, you might have another brush with denial, trying to convince yourself and those around you that nothing's really going to change. That's the wrong thing to do (we'll talk more in the next chapter about not making promises you can't keep), but it's a natural response when you're trying desperately to reassure the loved ones you're leaving behind.

Great Expectations

If your wife is pregnant and your baby will be born while you're on deployment, you can add "missing my baby's birth" to your list of regrets. And you can add "my wife's health" to your list of things to worry about. Many commanders understand just how important it is to you to be with your wife when your baby is born, but their job requires them to put the mission first. If that commander knows you, he should be able to tell whether you'll be able to perform your duties safely and effectively while your wife is in labor five thousand miles away. If he's got a heart (and believe it or not, many do) and the unit can spare you, he may pull some strings to get you home to meet your baby and give your wife some support—even if it's for only a few short days. But heart or not, if he's got twenty guys whose wives are all expecting babies at the same time, there's no way he'll let you all leave. And no, he's not going to fly her and the new baby over so the three of you can be together. Good try, though.

♦ **Guilt and jealousy.** The flip side of sadness and regret at the things you'll miss is feeling guilty that you're somehow letting people down by not being there, leaving the most important people in your life, the ones who depend on you so much. At the same time, you may feel incredibly jealous that your wife will be there to experience all of it, and the most you'll get is a story, some pictures, and a lot of, "Oh, you really should have been there."

♦ **Pride and patriotism…or ambivalence.** I remember one of my drill instructors trying to give us a lesson in military race relations: "There's no black and white in my Marine Corps," he announced. "Only green." Well, we may all be green, but let's face it: not all of us join the military for the same reasons, belong to the same political party, or feel the same way about our leaders and our foreign policy. You may feel that there's nothing more patriotic than serving your country, and getting the chance to represent the United States of America abroad in a peacekeeping or a combat mission might very well leave you with damp eyes next time you hear the national anthem. But if you don't fully support the mission, the war, or the president, you're going to have a tough time getting excited about packing your bags and shipping out.

♦ **Bonding.** As the deployment approaches, you'll be spending an increasing amount of time training with the guys in your unit. Forming closer bonds with each other, becoming a cohesive team, and preparing your team to work together with others is critical to the success of the mission. This intensive period of predeployment training also serves as a warm-up, giving you and your family a small taste of what it's going to be like after you've left.

♦ **Tension.** Unfortunately, your time is a zero-sum game, and as you begin spending more with your unit, you'll have less for your wife and children. For some families, this is a time of increased closeness, when you all want to spend as much time with each other as possible, making every second count, building up a reserve of memories and emotions to last you through all those months when you'll be separated. But for many families, it's a tense time, as each person finds a different way to begin adjusting to the coming new reality. So don't be surprised if you and your spouse argue more. And be prepared for things to get even more tense and the arguments more frequent as you get closer to departure.

Stress

Take some shock, add a little denial and anger, mix in some fear and uncertainty, and you've got the perfect recipe for stress. In everyday situations, stress is an unavoidable and—in small doses—a very important part of our lives. Without it, you'd never have been able to ask your high-school sweetheart out on that first date or pull an all-nighter before a final exam. You couldn't beat out an infield single, your heart wouldn't pound while watching a horror movie, and you wouldn't feel the slightest joy at the birth of your child or buying a car. In some cases, stress can actually save your life. For example, if you're in a dangerous situation, your body gives you a jolt of adrenaline and goes into "fight or flight" mode. Your pulse races, you focus intently on the problem at hand, and blood rushes away from your face and body and out to your arms and legs so you can protect yourself or get away from whatever it is that's threatening you (that's why people who are frightened are often "white as a sheet." No one knows, though, why sheets themselves are white).

In the days, weeks, and months before your deployment, you'll have to deal with all sorts of small stresses every day, like increased training schedules, pressure from your wife and children to pay attention to them, and having zero time to yourself. Your body responds to these small stresses in pretty much the same way as it does to larger ones. Fortunately, in most cases—when the immediate stress or danger has passed—your pulse slows down, your muscles relax, and you can get on with your day. Sometimes, though, the pressures of daily life pile up, and your fight-or-flight response never fully shuts off, causing your body to stay in a stress mode longer than it should. This is not a good thing.

Stress has been linked to a number of very serious health concerns, including high blood pressure and heart trouble, diabetes and ulcers. We'll talk about how to cope with long-lasting feelings of stress in the next chapters. But for now, let's leave it at this: Do not give into the temptation to self-medicate with drugs or alcohol. This "solution" has been tried many times, by many people. And it never works out well. Actually, it usually works out really, really badly.

Stage 3: Detachment and Withdrawal

♦ **Physical and emotional distance.** As your departure gets closer and closer, the bonding-with-your-buddies process that began just a short while ago continues, with the intensity and pace picking up as you approach mission readiness. You may have extra training sessions, some of which might involve even-longer-than-usual-hours and days at a time away from your family. As if that weren't tough enough to cope with, even when you *are* home, your mind will be elsewhere, and that will create *emotional* distance. This isn't something you'll do on purpose—it's one of those things that just happens as you become more focused on and energized by your mission.

In the middle of talking with your wife or playing with the kids, for example, you'll find your mind wandering—back to your training, your buddies, your fears, and the dangers and unknowns you'll face. Or you'll want to talk about your unit and your mission all the time (assuming you're allowed to). As you can probably guess, this is a real problem: your wife and family are trying to maximize the time they have left with you,

"Permission to speak freely, sir!"

Coping with Sudden Deployment

If you're one of the unlucky ones who gets just a couple of days notice before shipping out, don't think you can escape the three stages of the predeployment phase. Oh, no. You'll still go through the shock, denial, anger, fear, uncertainty, excitement, acceptance, regret, and all the rest, but it'll be a *Reader's Digest* condensed version. Instead of having a lot to do and very little time to do it, you now have a *huge* amount to do and zero time to do it. Just thought I'd let you know.

Sudden deployment can have both positive and negative effects on the entire family, according to Janet Paulovich, chief of services of the Fleet and Family Support Center at the Naval Air Station North Island. She found, for example, that sudden deployment...

👍 Can strengthen a marriage as spouses manage on their own and then reunite and share experiences.

👎 Can upset an already shaky relationship.

👎 Can stress one or both spouses if serious family issues are present.

👍 Can give the spouse at home more confidence in his or her own abilities.

👎 Can cause stress for extended family members (parents, siblings, and so on).

We'll talk about how sudden deployment can affect your children on page 75.

and they crave your attention. Physically, you're still with them, but it's getting awfully clear that psychologically, you're on your way out.

If you're in a command position, it's unlikely that your wife will find any humor in the irony that although your predeployment pressures and preparations have made it hard for you to stay connected to your family, you're always there for the service members in your command. But try to keep your sense of humor handy—you're going to need it. Borrow one if you have to.

♦ **Busy, busy, busy.** According to the National Military Family Association, many service members describe their predeployment phase workload and stress levels as *triple* what they were before the deployment orders came through. Besides all the training and bonding you'll be doing, you'll also be trying to put your family's (and your own) affairs in order and get

them as prepared as possible for separation. You'll have a mountain of paperwork to fill out (not literally, of course. Most stacks of paperwork are under a meter in height. Unless there are special circumstances. Like you're living on Earth. And you'll spend hours going through your predeployment checklists, drafting a will and powers of attorney, packing your bags, and buying any special items you'll need while you're away. At the same time, you're inadvertently adding to the pressure by scrambling around trying to take care of as many household projects as you can (everything from cleaning the gutters and putting a new set of tires on the car to setting up online bill paying) to spare your wife the hassle of having to do them while you're gone. As one service member interviewed for

Hey, There's Some Good News Too

I know I've been focusing a lot on the tension and strain that you and your wife may experience in the predeployment phase. And I know it may sound like deployment is a death sentence for your marriage. Fortunately, it's not. In a lot of cases, it's like running a marathon for your marriage: it takes planning, focus, and sweat, but at the end, you have something to be proud of. And a T-shirt.

A recent RAND Corporation report, *Families under Stress: An Assessment of Data, Theory and Research on Marriage and Divorce in the Military*, found that not only does deployment *not* increase the chance of divorce, it might actually *strengthen* marriages. This isn't to say that deployments aren't tough on couples and marriages—they definitely are. But there are some benefits as well. According to the RAND researchers, these benefits include:

- Higher earnings from combat pay and certain service-related tax breaks.
- Potential for career advancement.
- Other forms of support (such as health care, child care, and housing subsidies) that offset some of the negative effects of stress.

You may also develop some excellent skills at sending R (or X)-rated e-mails to each other.

Interestingly, these positive effects are much more significant when the service member is male. In addition, female service members are more than twice as likely to file for divorce as men. I'm not sure which of those two sentences is the chicken and which is the egg. But they do seem to be related.

Other studies have shown that families who have experienced hardships or challenging situations often develop coping skills that benefit them in the long run. I wouldn't go quite so far as to say that deployment and being away from your family is good for your family, but you may find it somewhat comforting to know that with a little bit of work and guidance, your family will come out stronger in the end.

Hoping to Get Some? Yeah, Right.

The first casualty of your deployment could be your sex life. You may want to have as much as humanly possible, knowing you won't be getting any until you get back. Meanwhile, your wife may have started emotionally preparing for the separation by putting any thoughts of sex out of her mind.

This works the other way around too. Your wife may be horny as hell while *you're* just not in the mood. Not many guys will admit it, but it definitely happens. Finally, all the tension and fighting may have left you *both* feeling a little less-than-romantic toward each other.

Single and Double

As tough as deployment is on ordinary married couples, it's even tougher if you're a single parent or are in a dual military marriage where you and your wife are being deployed at the same time. For ordinary couples, being deployed is plenty stressful, but in most cases, the service member himself can leave feeling confident that his children will be well taken care of by his wife while he's gone. If you're dual military, there will be no other parent at home, which means that besides the emotional craziness we've already talked about, you'll have the extra burden of having to find someone who will be able to basically run your life and take care of your children until you get back.

If you're a custodial single parent and your ex is still in the picture, you can hopefully take some comfort in the fact that your children will be with their mother. If you're a noncustodial parent, you may be worrying about whether being deployed will jeopardize the visitation you currently have and how you'll be able to rebuild your relationship with your children when you get back home. Please be sure you have completely filled out a Family Care Plan. At the very least, having an FCP in place can give you a little peace of mind. And see "Going It Alone," on pages 86–87, for more.

a RAND Corporation report put it, "*Doing* the deployment is better than *working up to* the deployment."

♦ **Even more tension than before.** The pressure builds as you try to cram in as much as you can into your last few weeks and days at home. You know your wife and kids need you to spend more time with them, but you find yourself wanting to stay at the office or to hang with the guys. You tell your wife that you've got a lot on your mind and need some space, and when that doesn't go over as well as you'd hoped, you feel terrible. Then, in an attempt to smooth things out and make her and the kids happy, you promise to be around more. But something work-related comes up and messes with your plans, and that just makes the tension worse.

All this tension—along with the accompanying anger, resentment, and pain—can lead to *a lot* of arguments. Any problems you had in your marriage may get worse, and new ones may develop. You may start wishing you were already gone, and she may be thinking the exact same thing. The good news is that being at each other's throats at this stage is extremely common and completely normal. Play nice.

♦ **Confidence.** Being well trained for your mission and getting to see your peers and your commanders function in a realistic training situation is a definite confidence booster—especially if not everyone in your unit has worked together before. But that's not all. Service members who feel fully prepared for their mission say that their training made it easier for them to cope with the actual deployment later on.

What's Going On with Your Wife

Now that you've got a handle on how you're dealing with the news of your deployment, let's take a look at how your wife may be feeling and reacting—to both the deployment itself and your responses to it. Some of her emotions and behaviors will be similar to yours; others will be completely different.

Stage 1: Shock, Anger, Denial, and a Jumble of Other Emotions

♦ **Shock and denial.** Like you, your wife knew (or at least should have known) that there were risks involved with your being in the military, whether you're on active duty or in the Reserve. Even though she secretly or not-so-secretly hoped you'd never have to be deployed, the news that you're leaving could still come as a shock.

That initial shock is often followed by denial—after all, these things are supposed to happen to *other* people, aren't they? Well, no. But that won't keep her from thinking or saying (or believing) things like, "There must be some kind of mistake," "I absolutely refuse to believe this is happening," or "You are so *not* leaving!" or "I'm calling the president and see if he can't do something about this!"

♦ **Anger and resentment.** The next item on her emotional smorgasbord is anger. She could be furious at the president, Congress, and every other government official she can think of for getting us into a war, at the country as a whole, at the terrorists who attacked us, and at your unit for getting deployed. She may resent you for having joined the military in the first place, or because you let slip that you're actually excited about the deployment.

She may be angry that (in her mind) you love your job more than her, and she may resent you expecting her to take care of the children you had together—and everything else—by herself. And if she's pregnant and will deliver the baby while you're gone, she may be mad at you for getting her pregnant and forcing her to have the baby on her own. Very few of these reasons are rational, but that doesn't mean they're any less real for your wife. She's just trying to find her equilibrium in a very tough situation, and that's not easy when her favorite husband is shipping out and she has no idea when you'll be back.

♦ **Fear.** There's no shortage of things your wife could be afraid of. She might, for example, be worried that she's not good enough, strong enough, resilient enough, or resourceful enough to do it without you (what "it" means can include everything from parenting the kids appropriately and keeping up with household chores to coping with loneliness). She's definitely afraid that you'll be killed or that you'll come home physically or psychologically scarred (this is true whether you're going into combat or are taking part in a peacekeeping mission. Sadly, some of the latter turn into the former). She's also focused on how all this will affect *her*. She's probably been talking with other military wives and knows that combat changes people. Will she like the person you are when you come home? Will she still be sexually attracted to you? Will you still be attracted to her? Will the marriage be able to survive during your absence? Will you like the new drapes she picked out all by herself?

You may find her breaking into tears for what seems to you to be "no particular reason." When you do, resist the urge to dismiss her feelings as insignificant or unimportant (or as less significant and important than yours). This never helps, trust me. There's no question that if you are killed or injured, you'll be the one who bears the entire physical experience. But emotionally, she'll be suffering too. She may express her emotions differently than you do, but they're hers, so let her have them. No second-guessing, no pooh-poohing. You get to watch football and play poker—two things she many not understand—and she gets to cry at small things. It balances out.

♦ **Pride and patriotism.** Most military wives are proud of their deploying husband and feel a strong sense of patriotism. And most support their husband's mission. Some, though, don't. Not surprisingly, her level of support has a big influence over how well your entire family will handle the separation. If she believes in the cause, things will be a lot easier. If she doesn't or has some ethical or political objections, she'll have a tough time with the deployment, and that will make it harder on you and your children.

♦ **Uncertainty.** If this is your first deployment, you're in your twenties, recently married, or have young children, your wife is going to have an especially tough time coping with your absence. She's got a hundred questions and has no idea where to get the answers. She doesn't know when you'll be able to call or what your living conditions will be. She has no clue whether you have everything you need, and she doesn't know how often you can get mail, when she'll hear from you, or how she can reach you if there's an emergency. The less she knows, the more helpless and out of control she'll feel. This is especially true if you're in the Reserve. Because most of your day-to-day life revolves around civilian activities, neither you nor your wife will be familiar with the military culture and

Out of Sight...

As we mentioned earlier, separation has a tendency to magnify whatever's wrong with a marriage and make it worse. For some families, however, the forced break gives each person a chance to step back and focus on the big picture, and enables them to reunite with each other with renewed passion and commitment.

Unfortunately, for some wives, their husband's deployment becomes a "trial separation" of sorts. They wonder what it would be like to be single again, and sadly, some use this time to experiment. Our advice is to do your best to resolve as many issues as you can before you leave, and agree not to discuss anything that's a potential hot spot while you're on opposite sides of the world. Having an argument by e-mail is like skiing through a revolving door: neither fun nor effective.

By Julie Negron, daughter of CMSgt John A. Moore, U.S. Air Force (RET),
and wife of Maj. Angel M. Negron, U.S. Air Force

support systems. Fortunately, your wife will be able to tap into a network of older, more experienced military wives who can help her resolve some of these basic issues. They're also a handy shoulder to cry on and a pair of ears to complain to.

But even if she's been through this a dozen times before, there are still plenty of unanswered—and sometimes unanswerable—questions. And unfortunately, these questions are the ones that most accurately predict how well your wife and your family will cope with your deployment.

Hey, What about the Reservists?

Families of Reservists and Guardsmen often complain that they don't get the support they need predeployment. And they're often right. (What? The military is a huge bureaucracy? Why didn't anybody tell me?) In many cases, unit commanders don't have enough staffing to make the family support readiness group programs (see page 88) as effective as they are in active duty units. This creates a distinct lack of communication between deploying units and service members' families. Not knowing where to turn or whom to ask for help can make the deployment even more stressful than it needs to be. Get involved. Get answers. And get used to it.

Researcher Walter Schumm and his associates found that families really want a fixed departure date so they can plan their lives. In addition, "the extent to which spouses believe they will be able to cope successfully with a deployment varies by how long they expect the deployment to last, with longer deployments perceived as more difficult," according to the national Survey of Army Families. "Open-ended deployments (i.e., those of unspecified duration) pose the greatest challenge." Again, the answers to those or other similar questions are very hard to come by.

How well your wife deals with the uncertainties of your deployment has a lot to do with how independent she is and how good she is at rolling with

In Her Shoes

Here's a story one military wife told me. "My soldier-husband creates a distance between us at about three weeks before deployment. He becomes less willing to spend time with us and seems to want to catch up with friends. I, on the other hand, become clingy and want to store up all the time I can with him before he leaves. It seems the more I try to close the gap, the faster he retreats. I learned that this is his way of lessening the pain of departing from us, and once I called him on it, it seemed to diminish. Sometimes deployed guys simply aren't aware of what they're doing or that they're acting differently."

the punches. If she's an anxious type, relies on you for everything, and likes to have every detail of her life blocked out and organized, it's going to be a rough ride. The big problem here is that her anxiety may make her demand more of your attention—at a time when you've really got a lot of other things to be worrying about. It will also make it hard for her to attend to your children's needs before and during deployment. If her stress levels get too high, she may want to talk with a therapist. In some cases, a short course of anti-anxiety medication may help.

If your wife is more independent and relaxed, she'll still be nervous and worried, but she'll do a better job of keeping her emotions in check. She'll tell you how anxious and scared she is, but she won't ask you to fix it. And she'll be able to put the kids' needs before her own. But no matter how laid-back she is, the lack of information and having things sprung on her at the last minute will make her feel out of control.

Stage 2: Acceptance

+ **Sadness.** As reality sinks in, your wife may begin a period of grieving— not because anyone's died, but because she knows she's losing you for however long your deployment is supposed to last, and that life as she knows it is changing. She tries to tell herself that nothing bad will happen to you, but that sometimes makes her feel even worse. She watches you playing with the kids and worries about how all of you will be affected by time and distance. She's sad that you'll miss so many important events in each other's life. And she's not looking forward to explaining over

and over and over where you are and when you'll be coming home. You could get some cards printed that she can hand out: "Yes, my husband is deployed overseas, and yes, I'm doing all the parenting on my own. Your thoughts and prayers are welcome, but can we please talk about something else?"

♦ **Excitement.** In the previous section we talked a little about the feelings of excitement the deployment may bring up for you. Well, now it's your wife's turn. While newlyweds and young parents find deployment anything but exciting, more experienced military wives have been through it all before, and they know they can get through it again. So, for the seasoned military wife, deployment is often a time to reconnect with old friends, write a book, have some "girl time," or perhaps take a class she's always wanted to take. If you're a stickler for things being done a certain way around the house, she may look forward to the deployment as a time to let things slide. Or maybe she'll see your absence as a time for her to redecorate the house or finally get rid of that stuffed moose head you've been schlepping all over the country. Of course, having all those thoughts of independence and freedom may make her feel guilty that she may actually be looking forward to your departure.

♦ **Overwhelmed.** There is much to do and so little time to do it. Not looking forward to augmenting her regular activities with everything from playing catch with your child to mowing the lawn, your wife may put together a twenty-seven-page "honey do" list of things she wants you to do or buy or take care of before you go.

By Steve Dickenson, son of MSG Charles H. Dickenson, U.S. Air Force

♦ **Conflicted.** On one hand, she may be clingy and want to spend every waking second with you. On the other, she may want you to "just leave already" so you can get the deployment over with as soon as possible. Thinking about all the extra work she'll be doing around the house while you're gone might give her a break from worrying about you. Or vice versa.

♦ **Confusion and helplessness.** Here's how your wife might see things: you have direct orders and a rigid schedule to follow. You know the system and where to turn if you need something. She has none of that, so all in all, you have it a lot easier than she does. Nothing in her life up to this point has prepared her for the process of helping herself and the kids cope with your absence. And to top it off, she really wants to make *your* life easier but has no idea how to help you get ready for this enormous change.

Stage 3: Detachment and Withdrawal

♦ **Feeling like an outsider.** This one is tough. She sees that you're getting more and more excited about the deployment, and she'd like to share that excitement. But she can't, largely because her fear, confusion, and anxiety have taken center stage. As a way of staying connected to you, she may encourage you to talk to her about the deployment, and she'll listen to all your stories about the mission, who did what, where you'll be going, and more. But the talk is interlaced with so many acronyms that it might as well be a foreign language. Sounds like a clear case of WDUTL: Wife Doesn't Understand the Lingo. So either get the translation of all the acronyms for her or take them out of your stories.

♦ **Emotional distance.** You're spending a lot of time away from home, working late, training, hanging out with the guys. Your wife craves your attention and wants to spend time with you, but even though your body is still here, it's pretty obvious that your mind is already elsewhere. It's frustrating, she's beginning to get a sense of how lonely she'll be when you're gone, and she may start feeling depressed.

♦ **Withdrawal and detachment.** As a way of preparing herself for your departure, your wife may withdraw from you emotionally and physically. You may hear her crying in the bathroom, but when she comes out, she'll deny it. It's almost as though she's trying to protect herself from the sadness of missing you by pushing you away—literally and figuratively (she may not want you touching her, so don't expect much, if any, sex).

♦ **Fighting and feuding.** The tension and all this distancing and tiptoeing around each other is occasionally broken by fights, misunderstandings, and arguments.

♦ **Wishing you were(n't) here.** Given that you've been psychologically absent for a while, she may be wondering what's the point that you are still around. Thoughts like those are usually followed closely by feelings of guilt for putting her own feelings ahead of yours.

What's Going On with Your Child(ren)

Helping your kids cope with your upcoming deployment is one of the biggest—and most important—challenges you and your wife will face. At the same time, though, hanging out and having fun with your kids can be a great distraction, helping you get your mind off some of the more challenging and depressing aspects of predeployment. Plus, in a roundabout kind of way, your kids may also be able to give you some valuable insights into how you and your wife are coping with things. I know that may sound a little strange, but here's how it works.

In stressful situations—and there's no question that Daddy going away for a long time is going to be stressful for a child—young children in particular look to their parents for cues on how to behave. So if you and/or your wife seem depressed, angry, or withdrawn, there's a good chance your children will start behaving the same way. In addition, some of the tension between you and your wife will affect the way you interact with your children, and that, in turn, can have a tremendous impact on their behavior.

All of this is generally a bigger issue *during* the deployment, when your kids will mirror their mom's behavior and respond to her overall mood and attitude. But it will also come up a lot in the predeployment phase, when tensions between you and your wife are high and emotions may be running a little hot. For the next few pages, we'll look at how children of various ages react to the prospect of a parent's deployment. In the following chapter, we'll talk about specific strategies you can use to help your kids better cope.

From birth to twelve months

Although infants don't have the intellectual capacity to understand exactly what's going on, they're actually incredible emotional barometers. By three months, your baby can follow your gaze and will look at what you're looking at. At about the same age, your baby can tell the difference between a fearful expression and a neutral one.

Researchers Jeffrey Cohn and Edward Tronick did some fascinating experiments with three-month-old babies and their mothers (this research was done in the 1980s and '90s, but even today, too little research is done with dads). Tronick had mothers act in a depressed way with their infants—speaking in a monotone, keeping a neutral facial expression, not touching the baby, and standing farther away than usual. Within just three minutes, the babies started fussing and went back and forth between wariness and disengagement. The babies actually tried to reengage the mother by making noises and bouncing around, and they stayed wary and disengaged for a while even after Mom resumed her normal behavior. That's a lot of stuff going on between naps.

By six months, babies adjust their behavior depending on caregivers' facial expressions and tone of voice. In one of my favorite studies of all time, babies were asked to cross a "visual cliff" (imagine two tables a few feet apart with a sheet of strong Plexiglas resting on the tables and spanning the gap). Mom was across the chasm, looking and acting either fearful or encouraging. Almost all of the babies who saw encouraging, happy expressions crawled across the chasm. None of the babies who saw a fearful expression would make the trip.

All of this comes under the general heading of "social referencing," babies basing their emotional reactions—to things as well as situations—on the behavior of the adults around them. They gather information from what psychologist Paul Renn calls "micro-behaviors," which include vocal inflections, body posture, and facial expressions—all of which can change greatly depending on your mood. Your baby relies on you and your wife for security and safety. So if one or both of you change, even temporarily, how you normally—emotionally and physically—interact with your child, she may respond with one or more of the following behaviors:

♦ Lack of interest in playing.
♦ Lack of interest in food.

♦ Sluggishness or withdrawal.

♦ Unusual fussiness.

♦ Unusual clinginess.

♦ Having a tougher-than-usual time separating from you or Mom.

♦ Tantrums.

From twelve to thirty-six months

Your toddler has a pretty flimsy grasp of time and distance, and even though she's the smartest baby in the world (and the best looking), she's not able to fully understand what the phrase "Daddy's going to be away for a while" means. At the same time, like infants, your toddler is amazingly adept at picking up—and responding to—your and your wife's emotional state. She knows something's up, and she's not happy about it. But her limited verbal skills make it almost impossible for her to articulate her feelings. As a result, she'll try to get your attention and will express her dissatisfaction in all sorts of ways, including:

♦ An increase in temper tantrums.

♦ Excessive crying.

♦ Unusual irritability or sadness.

♦ Withdrawal or anger.

♦ Restlessness.

♦ Moodiness.

♦ Hitting, biting, and pushing you away.

♦ Being more ornery and noncompliant than toddlers usually are—almost as if she's punishing you for going away.

♦ Being overly compliant—as if she's willing to do *anything* to get you to stay.

♦ Refusing to give up the remote, even when asked nicely. Oh, no wait. That's you.

Ages three to seven

Preschoolers and early school-age kids are old enough to be told what's going on, but not all of them will have a firm enough grasp of time or the intellectual ability to make complete sense of what you're saying and to figure out how to react to it. None of that will keep your child from experiencing a flood of emotions, including:

♦ Confusion. It's almost impossible for Americans of any age to completely escape from the media coverage of conflict and violence—whether it's

"O.K., kid. Busy man here. Quality time. Here we go."

war in the Middle East or a drug bust that went bad in your own city. Your child will try to put what you're telling her about your deployment into the version of reality she's constructed for herself.

♦ Guilt. Many kids will get the idea into their little heads that you're leaving because of something they did or didn't do.

♦ Fear. She's afraid that since you left, Mom will be leaving too. She may also develop other fears, such as that terrible things will happen in your neighborhood, that she'll be taken away, and more.

♦ Worry. She may become obsessed with the idea that you don't love her anymore.

♦ Anxiety.

As with toddlers, your three-to-seven-year-old will most likely *show* you how she feels instead of telling you. If she does decide to talk to someone about your plan to go away, it'll probably be one of her lovies, not you or Mom. Her avalanche of emotions can come out in a variety of ways, some positive, others less so. These include:

♦ Clinginess (usually to Mom) and a refusal to have anything to do with you.

♦ Restlessness and irritability.

♦ Anger and desire for revenge.

You, Your Kids, and Sudden Deployment

As we discussed earlier, if you find yourself being deployed with little or no notice, you're going to be packing a lot into a very short time frame. You'll be making travel arrangements, trying to work your way through as much of your predeployment checklist as possible, attending meetings with your unit, and negotiating your way through an emotional minefield. (Okay, there might be a better metaphor, but you know what I mean.) Oh, and did I mention that your kids, thanks to their uncanny ability to hone in on your busiest, most frantic moments, will demand more of your attention?

How they react to the whirlwind of activity and your imminent departure will depend on their age and maturity level and will be similar to the reactions of children whose dads have a much more leisurely predeployment phase. As with your own experience, your kids will be condensing a lot of things into a few days or hours. According to Janet Paulovich,

- Infants and small children may pick up on parental stress and/or tension and become fussy and clingy.
- Preteens and teens may become upset and worried, needing reassurances and clear communication.
- Some older children may withdraw and feel deep sadness or sense of abandonment.
- Others may be angry at the sudden deployment and need to talk it out.

It's going to be hard to fit everything and everyone into your predeployment craziness, but make an extra effort to set aside at least a few minutes of good, uninterrupted one-on-one time with each of your children. And with the dog.

- Acting out.
- Withdrawal and sadness.
- Regression (wetting the bed again after being toilet trained, baby talk, a sudden inability to do anything for herself or get anywhere without you carrying her).
- Sleep issues (insomnia, waking up in the middle of the night more often than usual, nightmares, sleeping far more than usual).
- Moodiness and whininess.
- War games.
- Irritability.

Ages eight to twelve

There's a reason kids this age are called "tweens"—they're in between the early school years and the teen years. Generally speaking, eight-to-twelve-year olds are far more mature and worldly than they were when you were a kid. But there is a huge range of what's considered "normal" for this age group. Some eight-year-olds will behave more like teenagers, and some twelve-year-olds will behave more like second-graders. What they all have in common, though, is that they still have trouble appropriately labeling their feelings, and it's still going to be hard to get them to talk with you about what's going on inside their heads.

Fortunately, you can get a lot of clues about your child's inner workings and how she's handling the news of your departure by paying close attention to outer workings—her behavior. (Plus, if you listen carefully, you just might hear her talking with a real or imaginary friend about the military, deployment, and wherever you told her you were going.) Here's what your tween may be feeling:

♦ Some of the shock, anger, denial, fear, and other emotions that you and her mom feel.

♦ Anger and/or sadness that you have to go.

♦ Isolation. Yes, tweens want to be unique and individual, but they also want to be with other kids who have or are having similar experiences. These feelings of isolation can come up for any child, but they're especially common in families of Reservists, where most of the child's friends are civilians, and may have no clue what she's going through.

♦ Empathy. This could be empathy for Mom—your child sees how your departure is affecting her, and wants to protect her—or for you, for similar reasons.

♦ Just about anything from the preschool section (above) or the teen section (below). Tweens are the chameleons of the parenting world—just as chameleons are the tweens of the animal world.

And here's how those emotions might play out:

♦ Lots of "what ifs" and questions about death, where you're going and why, whether you really have to go at all, and who's going to take care of them while you're gone.

♦ Angry outbursts followed by clinginess.

♦ Limit testing—way more than usual.

♦ Acting out at home and at school.

♦ Regressive behavior.

Ages thirteen to eighteen

Teens, as a group, are pretty darn savvy, and yours are no exception. She'll understand what you tell her about your job and how things will change around the house. She probably has a pretty good grasp of what war is all about, and the various conflicts and missions we're engaged in. There's only one problem: your teen is insane.

In his book, *Yes, Your Teen Is Crazy*, psychologist Michael Bradley talks a lot about the teenage brain and the recently discovered fact that although 95 percent of a child's brain is developed by age five, certain vital parts—in particular the ones that control impulses, advanced reasoning, planning and decision making, empathy, emotional regulation, and the ability to understand consequences—aren't fully baked until the end of adolescence or the early twenties. (If you've ever found yourself shouting, "What the hell were you thinking?" at your teen, now you know the answer: Nothing.)

That, in a nutshell, helps explain a lot of "normal" teen behavior: risk taking, impulsiveness, mood swings, insensitivity to others, and not taking responsibility for their actions. At one time, when my kids were sixteen, thirteen, and three, I made the startling discovery that the only real difference between the teens and the toddler was height. That, and the toddler did her chores with a lot less whining. Throw in a little puberty, peer pressure, and a rough transition from middle school to high school, and you've got a real nut job on your hands. And oh, yeah, Dad's going overseas for a year....

Depending on her age and maturity, your teen may express her feelings more like a tween or more like an adult. She probably won't (or can't) tell you this, but here's what she may be feeling during the predeployment phase:

♦ **Shock, anger, denial.** Like you and your wife, your teen may be stunned that you're leaving. Anger can be directed at all sorts of targets: at our country, the president, or the military for taking you away. And many teens will go through a period of denial ("Dude, this simply can not be happening to our family").

♦ **Fear.** Could be fear for you and your safety. Or could be fear of her own power. Say she blurted out, "I hate you and I wish you were dead," in the middle of a fight (which happens pretty frequently with teens), and then your orders show up a few days later.

♦ **Sadness at the anticipated loss.** She knows you're not going to be there to play catch, coach the team, come to the recitals, help with homework, fill out college applications, or go for driving lessons. A lot of boys are also sad that they won't be able to have private conversations with you about girls, puberty, girls, other guy stuff, and girls.

♦ **Uncertainty.** There are so many unanswered and unanswerable questions. Not "Can you help me with AP biology?" but rather, "I can't believe you're leaving before my driving lessons are finished. You just don't care about me!"

♦ **Indifference.** This is mostly feigned. Coolness often covers up for a lack of coolness.

♦ **Relief.** If you and your teen have a rocky relationship, she may feel quite happy that you won't be around for a while. Those feelings of relief are usually followed by feelings of guilt for having felt relief in the first place.

♦ **Acceptance.** As the departure date gets closer and closer, reality sinks in.

♦ **Pride.** Some kids may feel that they're glad you're there to protect them and our country. This is not very common, but it does happen.

♦ **Worry.** About everything and anything, but most commonly about how your deployment will affect them. (You have noticed that teens are more than a little self-absorbed, haven't you?) Will I have to do more chores while you're gone? Will we have enough money to live on? What will we do if you get hurt?

Here's how those feelings get translated into actions.

♦ **Changing tastes.** She may, for example, suddenly begin listening to a different type of music, watch different types of movies, or begin reading different books than she usually does. Those things are not necessarily bad—it could be her attempt to reclaim some sort of control in an otherwise uncontrollable situation. It's sometimes hard to distinguish between normal teenage strange behavior and abnormal teenage strange behavior. But please be on the lookout for symptoms of depression, giving up activities that used to be enjoyable, unexplained mood swings, sudden changes in diet, and/or a whole new group of friends.

♦ **Pushing you away.** She may stay away as much as you will allow in order to surround herself with friends and activities so she won't have to face head-on the changes that are coming.

♦ **Withdrawal.** She may pull away from you physically and emotionally as a punishment for your leaving, because she doesn't agree with the mission you're going on, or simply as a way to attract your attention.

- **Increased tension.** She might start arguments or fights with you. In some cases, she's just trying to express her anger. In others, she may be trying to push you away so she won't have to admit how much she'll miss you. She also may feud and fight more with siblings.
- **A slump in academic performance.**
- **Discipline problems at home and school.**

3.

Try to Leave 'em Laughing

Staying Involved Before You Deploy

With an avalanche of emotions and behaviors coming from everyone in the family (including the dog), and the stress of preparing for deployment, don't be surprised if you find yourself feeling completely overwhelmed. If you like that feeling and want it to last, just sit back and ignore everything that's going on around—and within—you. But if you want to make the time between now and D-day as enjoyable as possible, read on. For the rest of this section, we're going to focus on hands-on activities that you can do to help yourself, your wife, and your children (and maybe even the dog) better cope during pre-deployment. This is especially important because what you do now, and the systems you put in place before you leave, will have a huge impact on how you and your family handle those long weeks and months of the actual deployment. And your dog, who does not have access to e-mail. So be nice to her now.

Taking Care of Number One

Call it the "flight attendant school of parenting"—if there's ever an emergency on an airplane and those oxygen masks drop from the overhead compartments, you're supposed to put yours on *before* you help your kids, right? Well, the same logic applies here. If you aren't feeling relatively under control, there's no way you can be an effective caregiver, husband, or father. That's why we're starting with some things you can do for yourself (not including running away, although it may sometimes feel like it would be a lot easier if you did). Yes, some of these suggestions will seem a little self-indulgent, but that's okay. Go ahead, take a little "me time," or maybe more than a little. Just don't go overboard. We'll worry about everyone else a bit later. For now, though, it's all about you, and you need plenty of time to process what you're about to go through and to focus on everything you need to get done before you leave.

♦ **Crack open a new book.** If you like books (and given that you're reading this, I'm assuming you do), take a trip down to your local bookstore. Or, if you know you're not leaving for a couple of weeks, start browsing your favorite online bookseller. Some guys like to immerse themselves in military history, or the nonfiction stories of soldiers who survived combat. Others want a crash course on wherever it is that they're going—the people, the culture, the customs, and the language. And some prefer something that doesn't require as much concentration, like the latest hardboiled detective thriller. Doesn't matter what the book is, as long as you're pretty sure that you'll enjoy reading it.

Speaking of reading, take a few minutes to look into a great organization called Books for Soldiers (booksforsoldiers.com), which, as you might guess from the name, sends books to deployed military service members. You can sign up to receive books while you're deployed, or you can help others by donating titles you've already read.

I strongly suggest that you spend a little time on child development. There's no question that your kids, no matter how old they are now, will be doing some growing up while you're gone. Fortunately, children's development happens at a fairly predictable pace, so you can prepare yourself now and get your expectations under control. (There's nothing worse than coming back to a two-year-old you haven't seen in a year and being disappointed that he's nowhere near being able to catch a fly ball—even though you'd been fantasizing that he could.) It's wonderful to know what's happening with your children while you're gone, and to understand what you're going to see when you get home. Still, children—especially very young ones—can change a *lot* over the course of even a few months. If you're seeing them every day, you may not notice their gradual transformation, but if you're gone for a year, you may walk into a house full of kids you barely recognize. (Okay, if they're teens and they're having a party, your house actually *will* be full of kids you don't recognize. But that's rare.) We'll touch on some child development issues throughout this book. But for a more detailed dad-oriented ages-and-stages discussion, the other books in this series can be especially helpful. These include:

◊ *The Expectant Father: Facts, Tips, and Advice for Dads-to-Be* (also available on CD)

◊ *The New Father: A Dad's Guide to the First Year* (also available on CD)

◊ *Fathering Your Toddler: A Dad's Guide to the Second and Third Years*

◊ *Fathering Your School-Age Child: A Dad's Guide to the Wonder Years, 3 to 9*

◊ *Father for Life: A Journey of Joy, Challenge, and Change* (which has a number of sections on tweens and teens)

◊ *The Single Father: A Dad's Guide to Parenting without a Partner*

♦ **Sweat a little (or a lot).** Besides being one of the best stress-relievers ever invented, exercise has all sorts of other benefits, including weight management, reducing the risk of high blood pressure and heart disease, and improving your concentration and productivity at work. Exercise is also a mood booster—and that's something that can come in handy during those tense times around the house. And finally, exercise can be a wonderful way to spend some quality time with as many family members as you can convince to join you. But be sure to allow yourself some solo workouts too. Watching sports on TV—even professional ones—does not, however, count as actual exercise.

♦ **Have a salon day.** I know this doesn't sound like a very guy-like thing to do. But if you're going to be humping an eighty-pound pack for six months and taking group showers with a dozen other sweaty guys, the idea of getting in a forty-five-minute deep-tissue massage and a good, long bath before you go could sound appealing. If you're feeling especially brave, go ahead and toss in some scented oils or bubbles. (I promise we won't tell. After all, why do you think they call it a *man*-icure?)

♦ **Get back to nature.** Whether you're a Democrat, Republican, or Libertarian, believe in global warming or think it's a crock, I'm betting you'll agree that we live in a beautiful country. So take advantage of it while you can. If you find hunting, fishing, camping, shooting the rapids in a raft, or just going for a long hike relaxing, go for it. The great thing about outdoor activities is that you can do them with the family or you can turn them into peaceful, meditative alone time where you can unwind, relax, and think without interruption.

◆ **Clean out the garage.** This won't make many people's top-ten lists of ways to pamper yourself, but think about it this way: chances are you'll be hard pressed to find anyone else in the family to volunteer to help you, so you could end up with a couple hours of solitude when you can attend to those feelings and emotions that you might otherwise be ignoring or shoving out of the way.

◆ **Go through some old photos.** You can tell the family you're looking for pics of yourself that they can place around the house (and you might very well be telling the truth). But reminiscing over old times and favorite memories just feels good.

◆ **Talk to someone.** Whether you're devoutly religious or a confirmed atheist, you may want to spend some time talking with a chaplain, priest, rabbi, spiritual advisor, therapist, guru, pundit, radio talk show host, or good friend. Many service members who are about to head into a potentially dangerous situation filled with unknowns don't want to burden their family with their worries, fears, concerns, and other thoughts. There are a couple of problems with this. First, pushing down all those emotions and feelings won't make them go away. Second, allowing your family to see that you're feeling many of the same things they are will actually do far more good than harm. We'll talk more about that a little later. Still, it's often very comforting to be able to talk about life, the universe, and everything with someone you don't live with.

◆ **Play close attention to your own mood.** Are you finding yourself feeling depressed about the deployment, or worried that you won't be able to handle it? Are you slipping into unhealthy behavior patterns, such as having a couple of drinks first thing in the morning? If so, make an appointment to talk with your unit commander and see about getting some counseling. While it's normal to feel some depression or ambivalence, self-destructive behavior is not, and it's important that you nip it in the bud. On the most basic level, self-destructive behavior is, well, self-destructive—and you need to stop before things get really out of hand. Second, your mood and behavior have a huge impact on the rest of the family, and seeing you depressed or hurting yourself could make them feel worse than they already do. Yes, thinking about depression can be depressing. It's weird that way. Finally, from your unit's perspective, your mood has the potential to jeopardize the mission and the life of your buddies.

Staying Involved with Your Wife

As we discussed in the previous sections, your wife is a basket of mixed emotions, and she may not be handling your impending departure particularly well. If she hasn't totally withdrawn from you or had you diving for cover from an argument that came out of nowhere, you can take advantage of this time to create some positive, lasting memories that will sustain you through your separation. Go to a chick flick or spend an afternoon buying towels at your local department store.

Honest, open communication during this time may not always be easy, but it's essential that you spend some time talking and making plans for keeping your relationship strong while you're unable to give very much to it.

+ **Go on a date.** At the very least, try really, really hard to set things up so the two of you can have one mom-and-dad-only evening a week. (If you can swing it, see about going away for a weekend, or maybe just one night in a nice hotel. Get the hot tub suite—it's totally worth it.) If that won't work for some reason, wait till the kids are asleep, spread out a blanket in the backyard (or the living room if you have to), and uncork a bottle of wine. Don't get your expectations too high, though. If she's going through the process of distancing herself from you (see pages 70–71), you're not going to have sex. But she'll definitely be up for hanging out and holding hands. Talk about the old days, before you had kids, before wrinkles, before whatever. Reminisce about your happiest days together—your honeymoon, the birth of your children, or buying your first home. Remind each other why you're still together—and be sure to spend plenty of time talking about the future, what you'll do as a couple and as a family when you get back home. All these conversations will give you both a little fuel to keep things warm on those cold, lonely nights ahead. Roses still work wonders, soldier. Send 'em early, and send 'em often.

  If a date just isn't in the cards, consider trying to do some basic errands, like shopping and going to the bank, together. Or take a walk or a bike ride together. Sometimes just hanging out, doing completely mundane things (not including changing the cat litter), is enough to reconnect you with someone you love. The added bonus is that every one of these joint activities will surely help your wife. She really wants you nearby as much as she can have you, but knowing how stressed and overwhelmed you are, she may feel a little uneasy asking you to spend extra time with her.

The Privileges of Not Wearing a Uniform

Civilian contractors often have their own rooms, their own offices, or common areas where they can use their own computers and phones to keep in very close contact with their family at home. If you don't have it already, check into Skype or Oovoo. If you and the wife call each other "Snoogielumps" and "Mr. Wimpledimple," though, it might be best to wait till after your cubemates have left for the day before making calls back home.

♦ **Take care of business.** Block out a couple hours—preferably when you and your wife aren't feeling too stressed or angry at each other. Start by drawing up a detailed budget—how much money is coming in from all sources and how much gets spent. The purpose is to make sure that your wife will have enough money (including your pay allotments and bonuses) to meet the day-to-day expenses of running the house. Next, flip back to the predeployment checklists that starts on page 249 (you might want to make a photocopy so you can write on it) and make yourselves comfortable. Go over the list one item at a time, making sure your wife understands what's going to be expected of her, what automated systems you've put in place to help her out (such as online bill paying), household and automotive repairs that will need to be done while you're gone, and so on. Don't forget to go over the powers of attorney and lists of emergency contacts for every contingency you can think of. And don't just talk at your wife; give her as much time as she needs to ask questions.

♦ **Prioritize.** Once you've burned through the checklists and both of you are on the same page, so to speak, it's time to talk about the practical side of parenting—the extra child care she'll be doing, sports and other extracurricular activities, special needs, and general rules and expectations. As you work your way through all of this, try to agree on what's most important. The fact is that given all of your wife's new responsibilities, there's no way everything is going to get done. Also, be sure to devote some time to firming up household rules and limits for the children, things like chores and responsibilities, allowances, and consequences for not going along with the program. Setting these up now and communicating them to the kids will reduce the number of "But Daddy always lets me" comments your wife will have to deal with.

◆ **Do some contingency planning.** Although most couples try to put up a united front when it comes to raising their children, there are always lots of areas where they don't see completely eye to eye. When Mom and Dad are living in the same house, those little disagreements usually work themselves out—when you're with Mommy, there's no jumping on the couch, when you're with Daddy, it's okay. However, if you're half a world away, who's going to make sure that the things that are important to you will actually get done? Honestly, no one. Ideally, you'd explain to your wife why something is important to you and why you'd really like her to try everything in her power to make it happen. But chances are, if she is not committed to what you are committed to, you're out of luck. So you might need to have a backup plan. For example, if you want the kids to go to

Going It Alone

As stressful as deployment is for people in intact marriages, it's even tougher for single dads. If you're a custodial single dad—in addition to everything else you're doing to get ready—you've got the important task of lining up care for your children while you're gone. Who's going to get them up in the morning, make their lunches, and drop them at school? Who's going to pick them up at the end of the day, shuttle them to soccer practice or violin lessons, and make sure they get their homework done? Who will teach the importance of proper flossing? In a perfect world, you could ask your ex to step in. But the world isn't always perfect. While the military won't arrange for child care, they at least required you to put together a Family Care Plan (see page 33). So you should have a pretty good handle on the answers to the questions above.

If you're a noncustodial dad, you probably won't have to worry quite as much about finding extra care, since the kids will be with their mom. But you'll be facing longer-than-usual periods of not being able to see (in person, anyway) your children. The good news is that many kids are wise in the ways of the Internet and will be able to e-mail, chat, text, or add you to their Facebook friends. Well, maybe not Facebook. That might be too much to ask for.

Either way, your ability to maintain a relationship with your children depends on how often you're able to communicate with each other. And there's a direct connection between the amount of communication and your relationship with the person who's primarily responsible church and your wife simply won't do it, arrange for someone else to take them. The same goes for any activity you find important that your wife doesn't like or doesn't agree with.

♦ **Review. Again.** Your entire life is in order now, and your wife understands everything you want her to, right? (Okay, not everything, but work with me on this one.) She's agreed to back you up on things that are important to you, or you've negotiated a compromise, right? Just be sure you've taken good notes.

♦ **Show her around.** Introduce her to your other "family"—all those guys you're going to be living and working with while you're deployed. If you're active military, she probably knows most of them already. But if you're in the Reserve, she'll appreciate the chance to put faces with some of the

for your kids while you're gone (usually Mom). That puts you in the potentially uncomfortable position of having to be more reliant on—and trusting of—your ex than you may have been in a long, long time. While you're gone, she can do either what's called "stage setting" (promoting the father-child relationship) or "gatekeeping" (interfering with that relationship). So no matter how good or bad your relationship with each other is right now, it's essential that you do everything you can to make it better.

Try to get a commitment from your ex (or other caretaker) to come up with a regular communication schedule and stick with it. And try to get her to commit to keeping you up-to-date with everything that's going on in your children's lives. How you define "everything" is up to you. (Read Chapter 6 "Enough About You" on pages 177–90 for some suggestions.) It's extremely unpleasant to come home and hear about all sorts of things that had been kept from you during the deployment. Even boring stuff is good—Johnny got a cold today and sneezed on the cat....

Even with plenty of advance planning and written commitments from your ex, you're still swimming upstream. It's fairly common for ex-spouses to impose "intentional barriers to relationships with children during deployment," says Purdue's Shelley MacDermid. She adds that this kind of thing sometimes happens *even when there were no problems before the deployment* (emphasis mine). MacDermid also found that, overall, family members "worked harder to promote female than male [service members'] relationships with their children during deployment."

names she may have heard—or to simply meet the men and women who might save your life one day. (Of course, if you're being attached to a new unit, you may be meeting some of these people for the first time yourself.)

♦ **Check into your communications options.** Your unit commander will know (or will know someone else who does) about the types of communication that will or may be available during your deployment. Will you have access to computers, the Internet, e-mail, IM, or video conferencing? Does your unit have a Web site that's updated regularly for the folks back home? Will you be able to send and receive regular mail and packages? Will you be able to use your cell phone to make and receive calls or for texting? How frequently will you be able to be in touch with the family? Is there a way for them to reach you if there's an emergency? If possible, buy a webcam and get yourself hooked up with Skype (skype.com), Oovoo (oovoo.com), or another free video conferencing service. Both make video chats incredibly easy and give the kids a great opportunity to show off their artwork or model their Halloween contests for you in real time. If you have a webcam on your end, your kids will be able to watch the Dad Channel, although they may wonder where the commercials are.

Officers and special operations teams usually have access to more communications technology than enlisted service members. More and more military installations abroad try to have whatever it takes to keep service members connected to their families. But resources are usually scarce, and things have a way of breaking down. That, as you might expect, takes the ample stress service members are already feeling up a notch. You may be able to buy some communications equipment of your own while you're deployed, but the quality is often very iffy, and tech support is nonexistent. Oh, and if you're shipping out to any desert locations, understand that sand- and dust storms are common and have a nasty habit of knocking people off line.

♦ **Check into support services.** Civilian wives often feel isolated and helpless during their husband's deployment. "Young spouses in new marriages, spouses living overseas, and foreign spouses were seen as at high risk for isolation and poor functioning during deployment," says Shelly MacDermid, director of the Military Family Research Institute at Purdue University. Fortunately, the military offers a wide variety of resources designed to help your wife and children, and you should encourage your wife to start doing a little research now. To start with, just about every military unit, whether active duty or Reserve, has its own family support network. In the Army it's called the Family Readiness Group (FRG), which they define as "an officially command-sponsored organization of family members, volunteers, and soldiers belonging to a unit, that together provide an avenue of mutual support and assistance, and a network of communications among the family members, the chain of command, and community resources." The Marine Corps' version is called the Key Volunteer Network, the Navy's is the Ombudsman program, and the Air Force's is the Key Spouse program. These organizations are a great place for your wife and children to connect with other families going through similar experiences. In addition, depending on your branch of service, your wife should be able to get information and support from one or more of the following:

◊ Navy Fleet and Family Support Center (nffsp.org/).

◊ Marine Corps Community Services (usmc-mccs.org/).

◊ Airman and Family Readiness Center (afcrossroads.com/). Each Air Force base has its own AFRC and Web site.

◊ Army Community Service Center (myarmylifetoo.com).

◊ Military OneSource (militaryonesource.com). Operates twenty-four/seven and is available to every active duty, Guard, or Reserve service member and family.

Unfortunately, though, despite the wide variety of services and the very best of intentions, these resources often don't get used as much as they could and should be. On the military's side, unit commanders may be so busy preparing for the deployment that they don't have time to do much outreach to families. In addition, many family support organizations are staffed mainly by civilian employees and volunteers who also don't have the time or bandwidth to get the word out. And finally, there's a general shortage of programs for children, and there simply aren't enough other resources to go around. This is especially true for families of deployed Guardsmen and Reservists. "During deployment, when both the active and Reserve components are on active duty," writes MacDermid, "the disparities in support systems are striking (even at the reduced levels experienced by the active component)."

But even when commanders and family support organizations are completely on the ball, plenty of wives don't even bother to investigate the possibilities. According to MacDermid, this is because:

◊ Seasoned spouses perceive whatever the family support organization staff has to say as "old news."

◊ Junior spouses don't think they need it.

◊ Some perceive it as intrusive or an invasion of privacy.

◊ Some service members obstruct or prevent spouses from seeking help (e.g., by taking their ID cards away—I hope you're not one of these guys).

◊ Child care, transportation, or other resources may be lacking.

♦ **Plan ahead.** You probably don't know how long it'll be between when you leave and the first time you'll be able to check in with your wife. And depending on your mission, you could be completely out of touch for weeks or months at a time. So talk with family and friends and make arrangements for them to call your wife or drop by every once in a while to make sure she's okay. You could even have them bring flowers, from you. See—in one sentence, this book just paid for itself.

♦ **Go shopping.** If you don't already have them at home, you'll need to pick up some paper and envelopes for writing letters home (try to get a unique color or pattern—that way the kids will know, without even opening the envelope, that it's from you). Since you'll be sending your letters and packages from a military installation, you won't need stamps. And your family will pay only domestic postage rates, no matter where you are in the world. The Post Office may offer some discounted postage on items being sent to deployed military.

While you're out, pick up a couple of international prepaid phone cards. There's no guarantee that you'll have Internet access or that, if you do, it'll actually be working. So don't rely totally on the Internet for communicating. Buy international phone cards. Buy a video recorder, a voice recorder, and/or a computer webcam, so when the Internet is up, you can do a video chat with the folks back home—an especially nice thing if your wife is pregnant. Even if you can't set up a chat, you may still be able to send and receive audio and video clips, so you'll put the camcorders and voice recorders to good use. And finally, don't forget to buy a few extra batteries and memory chips, and maybe even a spare charger.

♦ **Record your thoughts.** Take a pack of index cards with you to work, and when you're sitting in a meeting or at a traffic light, jot down a few words to remind your wife that you love her, that you're proud of her, that you appreciate everything she's going to be doing, and that you know she's strong enough to do this. Just before you leave, hide these notes around the house, in places where she'll find them long after your side of the bed is cold. It will mean the world to her. You can also record audio or video messages, favorite poems or stories, and special memories, and leave them on CDs or her iPod.

♦ **Make plans for milestones you'll miss.** Chances are you're going to miss your wife's birthday, your anniversary, Mother's Day, the holidays, or some other significant day for her (or both of you). If you're gone long enough, you might miss all of them. Even if you're the most organized guy and have a memory like a steel trap, the pressures of your job or just the time changes could make it easy for a big day to slip by without notice. It's ten times better to call early than late for any important date. And in all of recorded history, there has never been a case of a woman forgetting her own wedding anniversary. So get out your calendar and make arrangements with a local or Internet florist right now to have flowers or gifts delivered. She'll appreciate the effort you put in, and you'll stay out of the doghouse.

♦ **Set up a family blog.** One more way of keeping in touch. This doesn't have to be anything fancy, just something everyone in the family can easily log into to post pictures, thoughts, audio or video clips, wild declarations of love, or whatever. You can do this for little or no money through services such as WordPress (wordpress.com) and Blogger (blogger.com).

Staying Involved with Your Child(ren)

As I mentioned in the introduction, this book is a little different from the others in The New Father series. In those books, the focus was on building close relationships and doing fun things with a child you can hug and who can sit in your lap. In this book, however, the focus is really on how to maintain close relationships with your children and on ways of staying involved when you're separated by distance and time. If you want specific ideas for activities to do with your children while you're physically with them, there's a complete list of all the titles in this series on page 82.

Fortunately, kids are amazingly resilient, and are able to bounce back from almost anything. With a little luck and a lot of planning, yours will make it through your deployment just fine. Now, it's on to some concrete activities that you (or you and your wife) can do with your children, and some systems you can put in place before leaving, which are aimed at enabling you to be the best, most involved dad you can be. There are, of course, lots of other activities you could add to the list. But I picked these because they've been field-tested and given a thumbs-up by deployed service members and their families.

I've arranged them by the age of the child, but because there's so much variety in children's emotional, psychological, and physical development, feel free to jump a section or two back or ahead and pick and choose the activities that are most appropriate for you, your family, and your child. If you've got any suggestions to add to the list, we'd love to hear from you. E-mail contact info is at the back of the book.

Predeployment Activities for You and Your Unborn Child

♦ **Talk to your baby.** This may sound a little off the wall, but fetuses are actually extremely responsive to sounds from the outside world. In one study, newborns whose mothers had regularly watched a popular soap opera while they were pregnant stopped crying when the show's theme song was played. Infants whose mothers hadn't watched the show had no reaction when they heard the music.

So why would you want to spend time trying to communicate with an unborn baby when you could be doing something a bit more adult? Simple. It's fun. Plus, it may be able to help you establish a bond with your baby even before he is born.

Lots of fathers get jealous of the immediate connections their infants have with their mothers. But a good part of that connection might have more to do with the mother's voice (which your baby will have heard every day for nine months) than anything else. If you can spend some time "conversing" with the baby now and follow the advice in the next bullet, there's a good chance he'll recognize and respond to your voice when he finally hears it in person.

Some researchers believe that prenatal communication stimulates babies' brains and triggers nerve cell development, which helps process information more efficiently. In other words, they believe it may make babies smarter. They also contend (though not everyone agrees) that prenatally stimulated babies tend to cry less at birth, have longer attention spans, sleep better, are less likely to develop learning disabilities, and turn out to be more creative and musical. (Naturally, your baby will be all these things anyway. But you could pass this advice on to your less fortunate friends.)

There's a lot of disagreement about the effects of prenatal stimulation or whether it even works at all (although no one says it can do any harm). So if you're thinking about giving it a try, here are few things to consider:

♦ **Take it easy.** While it's great that you want to talk with your baby, your wife has a right to a little peace and quiet once in a while. On the other hand, you may want to let her know that some researchers have found that women whose babies are stimulated before birth have shorter labors and a lower rate of C-sections.

♦ **Speak up.** So speak loudly enough so that someone across the room can hear you.

♦ **Keep it regular.** Put yourself on a schedule so that the baby will get to know that something's going to happen. Ease into it by patting your wife's belly before you start. And don't go overboard. Ten or fifteen minutes twice a day is plenty. Fetuses need down time, just like regular people.

♦ **Mix it up.** Playing the same piece of music or reading the same haiku every day is great, but throw in some variety too. Fetuses block out stuff that bores them. Besides, most babies prefer sonnets anyway.

♦ **Don't get your expectations too high.** A publicist for a company that makes prenatal communications devices told me recently that the manufacturer guaranteed that babies who go through their program will score 15 percent higher on their SATs. That one just about floored me. Fifteen percent higher than what? And how could you prove it?

And imagine you've gone through a program that makes lots of wild claims, and your wife delivers a perfectly healthy baby who's average in every way. You're going to be disappointed, and that's a terrible way to start off a life. Bottom line: there's no guarantee that anything you do will affect your baby in any way. But at the very least, it'll be fun. And honestly, talking to somebody's stomach for fifteen minutes is nowhere near the weirdest thing you've ever done, right?

♦ **Record yourself reading.** Pick out a couple of short children's books, something with a nice rhythm, like *The Cat in the Hat* or *Goodnight Moon*. After you leave, ask your wife to play them with a speaker near her belly at the same time every night before the baby is born, and to continue the routine until you can be there to take over the story-reading yourself. There's a better-than-average chance your baby will recognize your voice when you come home.

♦ **Don't take a shower just yet.** Right before you leave, wear a few shirts to bed and have your wife keep them around until after the birth. Young babies acquire a lot of information about their world through their sense of smell, and the hope is that if your baby is exposed to your smell, it'll be easier for him to bond with you when you get home. You also might want to check into a fun program called Blankets for Deployed Daddies (blanketsfordeployeddaddies.com). They send blankets to deployed dads who have newborns or very young children at home. You sleep with the blanket for a few nights, filling it with your scent. Then you send it home. Yes, I know this sounds strange, but your wife will probably sleep with that blanket too.

♦ **Strike a pose.** Have your wife or someone else take pictures of you doing your favorite things, eating your favorite foods, hanging out with your favorite people, and so on. Print out the best shots, laminate them, and get them bound together. This will give your child a chance to get to know a little bit about you—and gnaw on you—while you're away.

Predeployment Activities for You and Your Infant (Birth to Twelve Months)

♦ **Just hang out.** Aside from feeding, diaper changing, bathing, dressing, playing with, reading to, and loving, there's not all that much to do with infants. So do as much of that as you possibly can. It'll be good for both of you. Keep in mind that, as we discussed earlier, babies tune in to the moods and feelings of the adults around them, so how you behave is more important than what you actually say.

♦ **Keep talking.** Of course your baby won't understand a word that comes out of your mouth, but he'll definitely enjoy being the center of your world. It's also a great way for you to store up some memories of his sweet little face. This is a great time to practice your stand-up routines or Three Stooges impressions in front of an appreciative audience.

♦ **Keep reading.** For the first few months, it doesn't matter what you read. Make up a story, sing a lullaby, read the instruction manual for your M-16. The point is for the baby to hear your voice, your intonation, the rhythms of your speech. And if he ends up being able to field-strip an M-16 at age nine months, bonus for you.

♦ **Keep recording.** If you know how long you'll be deployed, select books that gradually get more complicated so you can keep up with—or slightly ahead of—your baby's development.

♦ **Keep smelling.** Oh, you know what I mean. See "Don't take a shower just yet," above.

♦ **Break out the camera.** Take lots of pictures of you with the baby, doing all the things you do together. Hang some of these pics around the house and have your wife show them to the baby and talk about you. Don't forget to take a couple of those pictures of you with the baby. This is especially important if you have older kids. It's really embarrassing to have two hundred shots of your firstborn and only one—a high school graduation photo—of your second.

Predeployment Activities for You and Your Toddler (Twelve to Thirty-six Months)

♦ **Keep hanging out.** Get down on your toddler's level and have fun. If that means getting into a cardboard box and taking a trip to the moon, painting your nails pink, or following a lizard outside on the sidewalk, just be there. Nothing serious is needed, just good quality time.

♦ **Keep talking.** Your toddler doesn't need any specifics about where you're going or what you'll be doing. Just tell him you'll be leaving for a while. He doesn't need a lot of warning, but he definitely needs to know.

♦ **Keep reading.**

♦ **Keep recording.** Get a list of books and read age-appropriate stuff. End each story with an "I love you" and "Good night," and while you've got your recorder going, make sure to get a few minutes of your child talking so you can take his voice with you. You can load those precious words onto your phone, your iPod, or even a digital picture frame. Imagine being three thousand miles away and being able to hear "I love you, Daddy" anytime you'd like.

♦ **Keep smelling.** You still know what I mean. See "Don't take a shower just yet," above. Your wife and pets may enjoy this too.

♦ **Keep taking pictures.** Lots of you and your toddler doing things together. Laminate some of the photos so baby can drool all over them.

♦ **Video of you playing with your child, or of you reading a story.** Kids this age love to see themselves on tape. Small child, big ego.

♦ **Good night Daddy.** Bedtime is especially hard for toddlers who miss their daddy. If your wife is playing the stories you recorded, your child will hear your good night. You can also buy one of those stuffed animals that have a mini voice recorder. That way, your child can snuggle up with a stuffy and be comforted by your voice as he goes to sleep. For something a bit more realistic, check into Hug a Hero dolls (hugahero.com). You send in a digital photo of yourself, select from several fabrics, and they'll send you back a mini you. Mini voice recorders are an upgrade.

No News Is...

I know it's hard to do, but try to keep your children away from the news. The emphasis on death tolls, explosions, and danger—and the general lack of positive stories—can be extremely frightening to young children. You may also have to do some damage control when your child comes home from school and announces that the other kids in his class told him that Daddy is going to get killed. All of a sudden you'll find yourself longing for those monosyllabic answers to "How was school today?"

The reality is that the majority of deployed service members aren't usually in imminent danger, and you should explain that to your child. If you *are* going to be on a front line, it's important to address the issue as soon as possible, in an age-appropriate way—it's far better that your child hear something from you than from his friends or a television news report. Of course, you don't have to give away state secrets or operational details. All he needs to know is that you've been training and practicing for a very long time, that lots of people have done the job you're going to do and have come home safely, and that you'll do everything you can to keep out of harm's way. If you don't know the answer to a question, it's okay to say so. Don't lie, and don't make promises you can't keep. This is one of these times when what you say isn't nearly as important as how you say it: if you're acting scared, worried, tense, or angry, that's the message that gets telegraphed to your kids.

As a way of countering the prevailing media images and the rumor mill, try to find some positive images of the military. If you need help, check out one or more of the following: Air Force Crossroads (afcrossroads.com), My Army Life Too (myarmylifetoo.com), Marine Corps Community Services (usmc-mccs.org), or Navy Fleet and Family Support Programs (ffsp.navy.mil).

Predeployment Activities for You and Your Three-to-Seven-Year-Old

♦ **Break the news—better sooner than later.** A lot of parents put off talking with the kids about deployment, hoping to spare them (and maybe themselves) some pain. But even if you haven't said anything, your child probably senses that something's up, even though he might not be able to articulate exactly what it is. "Surprise absences breed insecurity in young children as well as heightened feelings of anger and sadness," says psychologist Ann Rasmussen, author of *The Very Lonely Bathtub*. For young kids, a week or two's notice is fine.

When you're ready to have the conversation, it's best for you and your wife to talk to the kids together. Having you both there helps underscore the idea that you're a family and that you're in this together.

Kids at the young end of this age range still won't have much of a grasp on time and what "Daddy's going away" might mean. By kindergarten, though, your child will understand morning, afternoon, weekdays, weekends, holidays, and summer. For that reason, when you tell your child that you're leaving, give him a few more details, like when, what you'll be doing, and when you'll be back. But skip things like, "Daddy will be working every day to win the hearts and minds of the oppressed people of the region."

Then ask whether your child has questions. Some kids don't, some do, so don't read anything into your child's silence or nonstop questions. The most important thing is to listen carefully to the questions, and answer them in a respectful, age appropriate way. And don't assume that just because you briefed him once, you're done. Dad-going-to-a-place-not-here-for-a-long-time is a pretty big concept for someone who's just figured out the potty. You may very well have to bring the issue up two or three (or more) times in two or three (or more) different ways before your child has fully processed it. But remember what my grandmother used to say: "You've got two ears and one mouth because listening is a lot more important than talking."

♦ **Be reassuring.** Young children are still rather self-centered and tend to look at things through a how-does-this-affect-me lens. That's why it's so important to spend time reassuring your child. Tell him honestly where he'll be living, how his life will change, and how it will stay the same. And emphasize that he will be safe while you're away. (These will be especially big concerns if you're in a dual military marriage and both of you will be deployed at the same time.) Many children, along with their normal self-centeredness, have a somewhat inflated sense of their own power (fortunately, this lasts only till about age eighteen). As a result, your child may feel that you're leaving because of something he said or did. And that means that Mom will be next.... It's very important that you try to help your child understand that you're leaving because of your job and *not* because of anything he did. In situations like these, there's no such thing as too many words of encouragement, too many hugs, reassurances, or I-love-you's. Think of it as loading them up with a little extra for later.

♦ **Go to school.** Talk to teachers, aides, administrators, coaches, and any-one else who has contact with your child during the school day. Tell them as many details about your deployment as you can. Knowing what's going on in your child's life will prepare them for any changes in his behavior or performance and will help them give your child the extra support he needs. If you know you'll have Internet access, give them your e-mail and ask that they keep you in the loop about grades, homework, games, even field trips and school plays. If e-mail won't work for you or the school, leave some stamped, self-addressed envelopes so they can keep you updated by regular mail.

♦ **Don't take it personally.** Your child may say and do things that are really going to sting. Please remember that he's not really trying to cause you any pain—in fact, that's probably the furthest thing from his mind. Chances are he's just angry, afraid, or frustrated, and he's not quite old enough to express these feelings in ways that aren't as hurtful.

♦ **Show 'em around.** Take the kids to your home station, where you will depart from. There are usually plenty of fun things for the kids to do on and around a military installation (although your child won't be able to drive a tank around, no matter how much he begs). If you are not usu-ally active military, chances are they haven't been to very many of these sites, so make the most of it! Aside from a playground and swimming pools, there is usually a museum or at the very least a display of tanks, weaponry, or aircraft. Take them there and show them around. If possible, introduce them to some of the people you'll be living with, or take a tour of the plane or ship you'll be leaving on. As much as you can, try and relay to them what your job will be and the type of equipment you will use so they can begin to understand. While on post, pick them up something to remember the trip by, like a sticker or flag with your unit's insignia. This will help them feel that they're a part of the team.

♦ **Leave a little of you behind.** Preschoolers may still enjoy having a Dad-scented T-shirt or blanket. By six or seven, though, a lot of kids (especially boys) may find that a little weird. But they'll love wearing your favorite fishing hat, or playing with your baseball glove. And there isn't a kid out there who wouldn't love to have a T-shirt with a picture of Daddy on the chest, or a set of dog tags so he can keep something of yours close to his heart. Your dog might appreciate a set too. Similarly, if you have a military medal or ribbon, consider giving it to your child to keep while you're gone. "If you entrust your child to take care of something important for you while you are gone, that sends a powerful positive message," write Diane E. Levin, Carol Iskols Daynard, and Beverly Ann Dexter, coauthors of the *Sofar Project Guide*. From the child's perspective, "Of course my Daddy is going to return because I have his medal!"

◆ **Keep recording.** Before deployment record yourself reading books, prayers, poems, or jokes, songs, plans for the future, and anything else you can think of. Variety is nice, but so is consistency. Your kids will play these recordings over and over and over. You could end up as big a hit as Barney. Lucky you.

◆ **Tick tock.** Get two clocks and set one for your local time, the other for whatever time it is where you're going to be. You might want to make a special decoration for the "Daddy Time" clock. (While you're at it, pick up an extra travel clock for yourself that you can set to "home" time.) The Daddy Time clock will help your kids feel connected to you, and they might find it endlessly amusing knowing that when they're getting up in the morning and getting ready for school, you're just climbing into bed. And when they're going to sleep, you're brushing your teeth and getting ready to go to work.

◆ **Start drawing on the walls.** Kids love to see how much they grow. Pick a doorway or a wall someplace in your house where you can mark the kids' height and date. Have Mom measure every couple of weeks. When you get back, one of the first things your kids will want you to see is how much growing they did while you were away.

◆ **Count.** Find yourself a large jar with a tight-fitting lid, and buy some small treats with a long shelf life (M&Ms, Reese's Pieces, gummy bears, peanuts, and dried fruit are favorites). Decorate the jar with the kids and then count out, together, the same number of items for each child as days you'll be away. Explain to the kids that they'll be able to eat one treat every day, and that you'll be home when the jar is empty. Since Mom will be the one to keep this on track, make sure she's on board with it. If you don't like the idea of candy or treats, you can give your child a few rolls of coins and have him put one coin into the jar every day. When you get home, you'll take the money and either all go out to dinner or buy your child a special gift. Or you can write out a note for every day you'll be gone, and have your child pull one out every day. Because deployments sometimes get extended, you'll need to work with your wife to secretly add a few candies, coins, or notes to the jar if necessary (although most kids over about four won't be fooled). If you're not 100 percent sure that your deployment will last only as long as your CO says it will, you may want to consider skipping the "take-one-away-for-each-day" activities and doing the "add-one-for-each-day" ones instead. If you are sure, go right ahead.

◆ **Where in the world is Dad?** Get yourself a globe or good map of the world. With preschoolers, simply marking an X is a good enough way to show them where you are now and where you'll be. Leave the globe or map in a central location so the kids can look at it anytime they want and can show family and friends where you are. If you know you're going to be moving around a lot, put Xs on all those spots too.

With school-age kids, tell them the country you're going to and let them practice their map-reading skills by finding it on the map themselves. Then use pushpins instead of Xs and use a marker or tie string between the pins to show the routes you'll be taking to get where you're going. Talk about the country, provinces, cities, rivers, mountains, and everything else they're interested in.

◆ **Do a little research.** Does your child love weather, plants, insects, or animals? If so, have him find out what's native where you'll be. Or, better yet, learn about them together. Besides being a wonderful way to spend time together, having a chance to talk about the camels, spiders, scorpions, monkeys, and exotic plants you'll be seeing this activity will give your child a sense of being in control of a situation he feels very helpless in. Your child may also be very interested in how life where you're going is different from life here. What sports do kids play there? How do they dress? What kinds of foods do they eat? Do they go to school? Maybe even learn a few phrases in the local language: "Hello," "Good-bye," and "Where's the bathroom" are popular.

◆ **Let's pack.** You've got a packing list as long as your leg, and you know you've got to get going, but you'd rather be spending time with the kids. Well, here's a way to do both. Getting your children involved in helping you pack your bags helps them feel part of the process and gives them a special chance to ask you some of those tough questions that have been knocking around their head for weeks. Or you don't have to talk at all. Sometimes just doing something together in silence is as intimate as a deep conversation. Before you leave, though, check your bags for stray kids tagging along.

◆ **The art of deployment.** Get a pile of whatever art supplies you'd like to work with—paper, glue, markers, paint, clay, macaroni, sugar cubes, or whatever. Then come up with a topic, maybe a family picture, self-portrait, or depiction of what you'd like to do with each other when you get back, and so on. After you each create your masterpiece, swap. If the one you got from your child is too big or too fragile to take with you, snap a couple of nice digital photos and take them instead. If you have a sea chest or large suitcase, an interesting alternative is to jointly decorate the inside.

♦ **Music.** Similar to the above, except you gather a stack of your favorite CDs and make a special mix for each other. Get ready for Disney sound tracks. Lots and lots of Disney sound tracks.

♦ **Start shooting (pictures).** If you have several digital cameras around the house (if you don't, you can get cheap ones for under $20), hand 'em out to everybody in the family—including the kids—and create a family photo journal of an entire day. Turn the shots into an online slide show or print out a bunch of them and put them all over the house, especially at your child's eye level. Getting to see the world through your kids' eyes will be great for you, and participating in a "grown-up" project like this will give them a huge sense of satisfaction.

If the kids are too young to actually do the picture-taking, you can have your spouse do it, but you should print them out and place them around where the toddlers and infants can see you everywhere they turn. Be sure to place them at their eye level. Remember that the more the younger kids see your face, the easier it will be to recognize you when you reunite.

Just before you leave, give your child a framed photograph of you, which he can keep next to his bed. And ask your child to make a special drawing or give you a special photo that you can keep next to *your* bunk.

♦ **A taste of ham.** If you feel your kids are old enough, hand over the video camera or audio recorder, step out of the room, and let them channel their inner ham. The only two rules are that (1) you can't be there standing over their shoulder, and (2) you promise you won't watch it till after you've left.

♦ **Unchain your heart.** There are two types of paper chains. One involves linking together as many paper loops as days you'll be deployed. If you can write a short message ("I love you," "I think about you every day," and so on) on every one, so much the better. After you're gone, your child can tear off a link every day and read your special words. The other type of chain is one that the child makes while you're gone—a new link every day—and then hangs it up as part of the welcome-home decorations.

♦ **Do a little boxing.** Give each child a special box where he can keep all the letters and packages you send. You can also stock the box before you

No "Man of the House" Speeches

Don't say things like, "You're going to have to be the man of the house when I'm gone" (to boys), or "I'm counting on you to take care of Mommy for me" (to boys or girls). Yes, your dad may have said something like that to you when you were little, and it might seem like a funny thing to say to a kid or a way to "make a man" of him, but we know now that throwing too much responsibility at a child—especially responsibility he has no business assuming—will backfire. The last thing you want is for your child to take on the role of disciplining younger siblings and comforting or taking care of your wife and you. The bottom line is that dads and moms take care of kids—even when they're sad—not vice versa.

leave with some photos of you and your child, a few jokes, or anything else.

♦ **Hide**. Spend a few minutes every night after your kids go to bed hiding small gifts and special notes around the home. Make up maps and clues that you can mail or e-mail to your child every few weeks to help them find the hidden treasures.

♦ **Go flat out.** Make a flat daddy—a poster of you that your child can roll up and take with him everywhere he goes. Although be careful of this one. I've heard from several wives that the constant reminder of Dad actually made the feelings of missing him stronger. After a while they opted to leave Dad rolled up in the closet.

♦ **Give him a job.** Preschoolers and early grade-schoolers love to help out around the house (but just you wait till they become teenagers...), so give your child a special job to do while you're gone. Make it something simple and fun, like helping to feed the cat or water the lawn. Do *not* tell your child that he's going to be the man of the house (see above for more), or that he will have to take care of Mommy while you're gone. Grown-ups take care of kids, not the other way 'round.

♦ **Make plans.** Talk about the future and all the great things you're going to do when you come home. By encouraging your child to come up with ideas, you're giving him something to look forward to as well as a feeling of control over the situation. What are we going to do when Daddy comes home? We're going to Disneyland!

Predeployment Activities for You and Your Eight-to-Twelve-Year-Old

♦ **Keep listening—and talk if you need to.** At this age, children are very capable of talking about what they're feeling, and you should encourage them to do so as much as they need to. Don't judge their questions—sometimes they may seem silly to you, other times they'll bring a tear to your eye. The fact that they're asking questions at all is an indication that they trust you and that they feel safe with you. There is no higher praise. Give your child as much information as you think he can handle and plenty of time to digest what you've said. This is a great time to talk to the kids about OPSEC (operational security) and to explain that even though there may be certain job-related things you aren't allowed to discuss, you still love them.

♦ **Give him some coping tools.** It's essential that everyone in the family come up with some positive ways of dealing with the various emotions. Of course that will mean different things to each person, but activities like hammering nails, digging holes, smacking a pillow or punching bag, painting, listening to music, or just going for a long walk are great for coping with anger and sadness.

♦ **Show yourself.** On one hand, as we've discussed, your children take a lot of their cues on how to react to situations from you and your wife, so you don't want to completely fall apart in front of them. On the other hand, you don't want to push away your emotions completely. Finding the right mix isn't easy, but it can be done. The trick is to be honest about your feelings, but in a way that doesn't burden your children and doesn't make them feel responsible for making you feel better. It's fine to tell the kids you wish you didn't have to go, or that you're going to miss them. But unless the kids bring it up, stay away from talking about your fears of being killed. If it does come up, focus on your training and preparation and the fact that most people come back just fine. Or, if it's true, that your job is quite technical and boring, and that you won't be in any real danger.

♦ **Give 'em a job.** Now that your wife's list of chores and household tasks has doubled, isn't it time to teach your ten-year-old how to run the washing machine, fold some laundry, mow the lawn, help out with a younger sibling, or, gasp, clean an occasional toilet? I'm not suggesting that you turn your kids into indentured servants (although they will accuse you of doing exactly that)—the goal is to get them to help Mom by stepping up and taking on some additional responsibilities. In most cases, having an extra job or two around the house actually makes kids feel more grown up and important. And if they're doing something you used to do, it's also a way of staying connected to you. Sure, your whites may come out pink every once in a while, but that's a small cost to pay for free help.

As a rule, you and your wife should come up with a list of chores she may want help with and that the children are actually capable of doing. Next, have a family meeting and discuss the list with everyone concerned, emphasizing that you and Mom are in agreement about what needs to be done and by whom. Then, do some training. You can't just announce to your child that he's got kitchen duty three nights a week if he's never loaded a dish into the dishwasher in his life. If you want him to do the job right, you're going to have to show him how. And your wife may have to get used to "kid clean," which is just like "adult clean," except for the clean part.

- ◆ **Do a little learning.** This is a wonderful time to learn about the history and the culture of the region or country you'll be going to. If you're heading for the Middle East, your child (and you, for that matter), may appreciate knowing the difference between Shiites and Sunnis, between al-Qaeda and the Taliban, who the Kurds are, and so on. It's also a great opportunity to talk with your children about the differences between life in the United States and life in other countries. What is freedom? What is equality? What is democracy, and how does it differ from what's available elsewhere? If you want to show off a little bit, you can quote Winston Churchill: "Many forms of Government have been tried, and will be tried in this world of sin and woe. No one pretends that democracy is perfect or all-wise. Indeed, it has been said that democracy is the worst form of Government except all those other forms that have been tried from time to time." One wonderful resource to explore with your child is Deployment-kids.com, which has all sorts of downloadable activities, time-zone charts, distance calculators, and more. At the very least, this will give your kids a real leg up in geography class.
- ◆ **Continue packing.** You may find it easier to have serious conversations (especially with boys) when you're both engaged in a project than when there's nothing to do but look at each other and read too much into one another's facial expressions.
- ◆ **Go shopping.** Pick up a few birthday, holiday, and just-because-you're-a-great-kid presents now and have your wife save them for the appropriate time. And hey, dude, buy yourself something nice. You're worth it.

- **Watch the news.** As your children move toward middle school, keeping them away from the news is going to be impossible. Your only line of defense is to watch with your child and talk about what you're seeing. Is the coverage accurate? How does it make you feel? Also watch some cartoons or a good sitcom and laugh together. Let's not make this too much like work.

- **Keep planning for the future.** See page 102.

- **Stay in school.** Ask your child's teacher if the class would be interested in "adopting" some of the single guys in your unit. (You can probably get the names from your CO.) Married service members and those who are parents tend to get a lot more communication and packages from home, and guys without families often end up feeling very lonely. Helping to organize a pen-pal drive or putting together care packages to send to the guys in your unit will make your child overflow with pride. It's also an incredibly kind thing to do. Think chocolate-chip cookies.

- **Make some introductions.** Take the whole family to some meetings of your base Family Readiness Group/Key Volunteer Network/Ombudsman/ Key Spouse program. Some kids may insist that they have no interest in meeting anyone they don't already know, or that any other kids who are there are losers. But deep down inside they understand that hanging out with other kids who share a painful experience will help them feel better and more connected to you.

- **Keep recording.** Yes, your children can read just fine by themselves, but there's something about being read to that most children (and lots of adults) find very comforting. Popping in a CD or DVD of you reading a chapter of a book or telling a story will always be a highlight of your child's day. And it'll probably make your wife happy too. Yes, you are allowed to do silly voices and your Elvis impersonation.

- **Keep shooting.** You take pictures of the kids, they take some of you, and you find someone else to take the group shots. You can frame them, laminate them, put them on T-shirts, cups, or mugs, make a home calendar, or make them into wallpaper or screen savers for your computer or cell phone.

- **Break out your calendar.** For the younger kids, just being able to X out passing days can be a visual reminder that each day brings you closer to coming home. For older ones, sit down and go through everything you will miss. Show them the holidays, birthdays, graduations, vacations, and other special times. This will give all of you a chance to talk about how it feels to know that you'll be apart.

Ask your child to use the same calendar to write down a few words about the events of the day. When you get back, you'll be able to flip through the calendar and ask for a little elaboration on "Shot my first rattlesnake."

Predeployment Activities for You and Your Teenager

♦ **Get out the calendar and have a heart-to-heart.** Are you going to miss your teen's school play, the entire basketball season, high-school graduation, college application deadline, or any other major event (understanding that what's "major" to your teen may not carry the same importance to you)? If so, talk about it. Ignoring it will not make the problem go away. Your teen can read a calendar as well as you can, and he knows what being gone means. What he may not realize, though, is that you're just as disappointed to be missing those big days—and all the ones in between—as he is. Let him know you'll do everything you can to stay involved in his life despite the distances that separate you. And remind him that keeping those lines of communication open will be good for both of you.

♦ **Keep being there.** In case you haven't noticed, your role as the father of a teenager has changed from "Dad-the-authority-figure-who-knows-everything" to "Dad-the-coach-who-gives-his-opinion-only-when-it's-asked-for." So if you want to have a relationship with your teen, you'll have to do it on his terms. Whether it's listening to his music, playing a video game together, watching YouTube videos, or helping him with homework, take a genuine interest (force yourself) in what he likes and shelve your own judgments. But don't back away. He may give the impression that he doesn't care whether you're around or not, but he still needs you to be there.

You may find that spending time together engaged in some activity makes it easier to talk about difficult topics. There's something about not looking at each other that takes the pressure off.

♦ **Be understanding.** Looking at your teen, it can be hard to remember that although he may look like an adult and may demand to be treated like one, he's still a kid and needs your support, encouragement, and love. Some fascinating recent research has found that the brain continues to develop throughout the teen years and into the twenties. In fact, the brain grows more quickly during the teen years than at any other time, except the first year. Bottom line? His brain won't be fully baked for another few years—and that goes a long way toward explaining some of his wacky behavior.

As he moves into his late teens, your child may become sullen, sarcastic, and self-centered. He'll want to hang out with his friends more, and will probably be more interested in borrowing your car and a few bucks than spending time with you. And you'd better get used to seeing a lot of the you-are-the-dumbest-human-alive-and-I'm-so-embarrassed-to-be-seen-with-you face. But be firm and insist that he endure a couple of dinners per week with the whole family.

♦ **Ask for a little compassion.** Teenage brain development aside, it's important that you give your child a sense of the pressure you and your wife are under as you get ready to deploy, and explain that you need his understanding and support. I'm not suggesting that he become your therapist—far from it. But expecting a little empathy from your child is not unreasonable. "Parents who disclose (1) what the deployed parent will be doing, and (2) their own deployment-related concerns, will assist the adjustment of their adolescents," write Angela Huebner and Jay Mancini, researchers at Virginia Polytechnic University. "What and how much is disclosed should be adjusted by the parent according to the adolescent's age and maturity."

♦ **Bite your tongue.** Teens often see the world in very black-and-white terms, and yours is likely to have some very strong opinions about politicians, the military, the country you're going to, the justness (or lack thereof) of your unit's mission, your job, and the kinds of clothes you wear. Odds are, your child will take a position that is 180 degrees away from yours—even if he secretly agrees with you. For most teens, part of growing up and establishing one's independence involves rejecting the influence, opinions, and sometimes the very existence of the adults around them. And that means you. Don't let your teen bait you too much. And come to terms with being wrong all the time. A friendly discussion and exchange of ideas is one thing; letting it escalate into an all-out, screaming, door-slamming fight is another.

♦ **Do research together.** Aside from investigating the language, climate, and culture of the place you're going, ask your teen to help you locate the best local restaurants and sights to see, or to use Google Earth to capture a few close-up images. This may seem a little too much like school for some teens, and others will be too cool or busy with life to want to do this, but it's well worth a try. Some teens may rudely reject your suggestion, but show up a couple of days later with a file folder full of fantastic information.

+ **Get ready to play.** There's a dizzying array of games you and your teen can play online, ranging from old standards like chess and checkers to fantasy, adventure, strategy, sports, puzzles, and war (like you need more of that…). Do a little research on your own to find out what's available. But ask your teen to find a few that he'd be willing to play with you, and go with one or more of his choices.
+ **Take plenty of pictures before you go.** Teens grow like weeds, and although you may be taller than your child right now, you might come home and find yourselves seeing eye to eye (physically, not politically).
+ **Read together.** Although some teens may still want you to read to them, most won't. But that doesn't mean you can't read *with* them. Ask your child to put together a list of books he's reading at school or for pleasure. Then suggest that you have a dad-teen book club, where you both read the same book, then discuss it via e-mail, over the phone, or any other way. And get ready to explain to the guys in your unit why you've got the whole forty-book set of *The Adventures of Nancy Drew* with you.
+ **Set him up for success.** Teens, better than anyone else, understand that that they're stuck—not a kid anymore, but not a full-fledged adult either. And they know that many privileges of adulthood are earned. So encourage him to look into opportunities to demonstrate responsibility. The possibilities are endless: he could take a babysitting certification class through the Red Cross, get a driver's license if he doesn't have one, do a little meal planning, help out with younger siblings, do volunteer work in the community, and so on.

PART II

Deployment

During Deployment:
Boots on the Ground, Hitting
the Deck Running, or Haze Gray
and Underway

4.

A New Normal

The Emotional Side
of Being Deployed

Between all the extra training, putting together to-do lists, trying to get your family prepared for your deployment, and squabbling with your wife, you probably haven't had much time to think about anything beyond your actual departure date. But now that all the hugs and tearful good-byes are done and your deployment has officially begun, reality is sinking in, and those gears inside your head are going to start spinning.

The actual deployment phase can be divided into three (sometimes four) separate stages:

1. **Emotional disorganization**, which typically lasts from one to six weeks after you deploy.
2. **Recovery and stabilization**, which kicks in one to six weeks after deployment and can last until a month before you head home.
3. **Anticipation of homecoming**, which starts a month or so before you leave and lasts until you touch down at home.
4. **Deployment extension**. As we discussed in chapter 1, delays happen, missions change, and there's little or nothing you can do about it.

What's Going On with You?

Stage 1: Emotional Disorganization
Starting the day you leave, you'll be entering a period of emotional disorgani-

zation, which is just a fancy way of saying that your feelings will be all over the place—and they'll stay that way for anywhere from a few days to a few months. If you go directly from your home base to your new assignment or if this isn't your first deployment, you'll start getting your emotions under control toward the earlier end of the range. But if you made a bunch of stops along the way—maybe to pick up equipment and supplies, or to get some additional training—or you're a deployment virgin,* the disorganization will continue. In the meantime, here are some of the emotions you may be feeling.

- **Regret.** All the things you said and did—or didn't say and didn't do—before the deployment will be gnawing at you. Be nice to yourself. You were under a lot of pressure, and not everyone is on his best behavior all the time. But hey, at least you managed to kiss everyone goodbye, get your bags packed, and arrive in the right time zone.

- **Whew!** For the first couple of days you may feel some relief that all the good-byes and predeployment tension are over. That's often followed by a pang of guilt at feeling relieved. After all, shouldn't you be sad? Be patient—that's coming soon enough.

- **Missing your old life.** It's perfectly natural that you're going to miss your wife and kids and all those family-related activities. But you may also find yourself missing a lot more: your old routines, normal work hours, hobbies, Sunday watching NFL football, working on the car, your base softball team, and let's not forget about hanging out with friends. The whole thing can leave you feeling kind of empty inside, as though you've completely lost everything that used to define you. And you may find yourself missing weird things that you might not have considered: wearing jeans, riding your bike, throw pillows, umbrella drinks. Depends on who you are…

- **Out of sight.** Before your deployment, you and your unit probably enjoyed a lot of attention and support. Nice articles in the paper, discounts from local businesses, special family events put on by the military installation, and special deployment ceremonies. Felt pretty good, didn't it? But all of a sudden, you're not the center of attention anymore—you're just another guy in uniform. You may not have been able to make contact with your family back home. (In some cases, communications networks will be up and running within a few days after you arrive. In others, depending on where you're going, what your mission is, and what kind of facilities are there, it could take a few weeks before you're able to

---

* It's not as painful as it sounds.

Special Concerns for Guardsmen and Reservists

Deployed Reservists and Guardsmen often have a tougher time in the early days and weeks of the deployment than active duty personnel. As a Reservist, you may not have had as much training, and your unit may not be as well equipped. But the toughest part of all is social. Because you see the guys in your unit only for a weekend a month and a couple of weeks every summer, you don't know each other nearly as well, and you can't possibly have the same sense of camaraderie and connection as a traditional active duty unit. You're not nearly as adapted to military life or as good at working the system as they are. In addition, for similar reasons, your family back home is going to feel isolated too. They don't live on base, aren't as familiar with benefits, support networks, and facilities, and they may feel completely buried in paperwork and have no idea where to get help filling it out. And to top it off, there's very little you can do to help them from thousands of miles away.

check in with your wife and kids.) Being out of touch may make you feel abandoned, as though no one cares about you anymore, no one is thinking about you, worrying about you, or even missing you. It's lonely and extremely depressing.

♦ **You're not in Kansas anymore.** It's hard to think of anything that *hasn't* changed. You're struggling with the loss of family, friends, and routines. If you're still doing the same job, the rules and regulations in theater have probably changed the way you do what you do—and, of course, *where* you do it. The scenery is probably pretty different from what you left behind—unless you lived in Greenland or the drier parts of Texas. You may have to do most of your outdoors work at night in order to keep from baking to death during the day. You may be sharing tiny living quarters with four other guys and not a shred of private space. And unless you lived in a really, really bad neighborhood, it's going to be a little disconcerting to come under enemy fire two or three times a day.

♦ **Exhaustion.** A lot of newly deployed service members are surprised by the increase in the amount of physical exertion that's required to do their job in theater. Add in a much, much longer workday than at home and few if any days off, and you've got a guy who's working harder and getting less sleep then ever. Besides making you irritable, chronic fatigue can intensify many of the other emotions you're already experiencing. So don't

If You're a Civilian Contractor

As the U.S. military gradually becomes leaner, meaner, and more portable, civilian contractors play an increasingly important role. "From laundry services and catering to logistical support in the form of fuel transports or strategic airlift, civilian contractors have long kept Western militaries up and running when deployed in the field," write Rem Korteweg and Ulrich Mans in a terrific article on civilian contractors published by the Hague Centre for Strategic Studies. Civilian contractors have also been used to "construct schools, hospitals, bridges, roads, pipelines, factories. And to protect them as well."

There are a lot of similarities between the experiences of civilian contractors and military service members. For example, your living arrangements will probably be a far cry from the comforts of home. And your options for recreation, showers, special meals, communication with your family, and religious services may be very limited. It's kind of like going to an adult summer camp: dirty, primitive, and at the end you might get a nice certificate, suitable for framing.

But there are also some very significant differences. For the most part, active duty service members live and work together. Their wives and children know each other, and when they deploy, they go as a unit, which means a lot of built-in camaraderie. Back at home, there are all sorts of systems in place to support spouses and children. As mentioned on page 66, Reservists have very little of this. But civilians have even less, and the feelings of isolation can be pretty significant.

The military also enjoys a lot of support from the American people. Unlike the situation during Vietnam, the public today is solidly behind our troops, regardless of how they feel about the conflicts those troops are involved in. Contractors and their families have to deal with being thought of as mercenaries, in it only for the money. The fact that you're putting your life on the line (all you have to do is look at the casualty statistics) doesn't register.

be surprised if you find yourself more susceptible to sudden, drastic mood swings.

♦ **On edge.** In a recent study by the U.S. Army's Mental Health Advisory Team, about 12 percent of noncommissioned officers on their first tour in Iraq met the criteria for depression, anxiety, or acute stress. If this isn't your first deployment, you might think you'd be immune to those problems. Don't delude yourself. In that same study, 18.5 percent of those on second tours suffered from depression, anxiety, or stress, and of those on third or fourth deployments, it was 27 percent. Soldiers' mental health and morale were lowest during the first two-thirds of the deployment and picked up significantly in the last months.

♦ **And more.** Typical emotions during this period include fear (due to exposure to life-threatening situations), worry (about how well your family will be able to cope with your absence), anger (at the evil that caused your deployment in the first place or at the administration that sent you), and, as mentioned, loss, loneliness, and emptiness. Other changes to expect when deployed? Well, a lot more tanks than at home, and fewer door-to-door siding salesmen stopping by.

Stage 2: Recovery and Stabilization

After four to six weeks of wildly disorganized emotions, you'll wake up one morning and realize that you've adjusted to most of the differences between your old life and your current one. You've gotten comfortable with the idea that there's only so much you can do to change things, you've overcome most of the feelings of loss and emptiness, and you've settled into your new routines, new hobbies, and new work procedures. (On the downside, though, some of the initial chaos has been replaced by boredom.) Congratulations. From here on out, your deployment is going to be a lot more predictable and tolerable. That doesn't necessarily mean, however, that it will be easier. Here are some of the issues you may face:

♦ **Feeling out of touch.** When you were home, you could communicate with your family anytime you wanted. Now, it's a bit more complicated. To start with, there's the huge time difference between you and your family.

Trouble at Home

Israeli researcher Zahava Solomon found that the soldiers who are at greatest risk of experiencing combat stress reactions are the ones who are also dealing with "home-front issues" such as marital problems, family illness, or a close friend or relative getting injured or killed. These last two can be especially troubling to combat soldiers. After all, if it can happen to someone at home whom no one is deliberately trying to kill, it could sure as hell happen in an actual combat zone.

A lot of service members find themselves cutting back on pesky things like sleeping and eating so they can have a better chance of reaching the folks back home while they're awake. Then there's the problem of access to communications. If you're limited to pay phones and Internet cafés, understand that resources are limited and be prepared for long lines. Apparently, calling home is a very popular hobby among service members, second only to complaining about the brass. Cell phones give you the most flexibility (and the lines are a lot shorter). But there are some problems. Many commanders forbid personal cell phone communications during deployments for operational security reasons, not the least of which is that the terrorists use some cell phone frequencies to detonate IEDs (improvised explosive devices). If you're lucky enough to be able to use your cell, you'll find that those out-of-network—waaaay out of network—charges rack up pretty quickly. So you may end up keeping your calls short to save money.

♦ **Feeling out of control.** "The biggest complaint many military fathers have about deployment is the changes that they will miss in their children," according to the National Fatherhood Initiative. "They might miss the first steps, or the first words, or the first birthday." You're going to miss a lot of other things, too. Some good, some not so good. The net result is that you may feel completely out of the loop, with no real ability to influence anything that happens at home. All those problems the wife and kids used to ask you to help with? Now someone else is handling things. The upside? No middle-of-the-night wakeups, and no changing diapers.

♦ **Jealousy.** Everyone is at home having a good time, and you're over here getting shot at. This may be one of those cases where the grass really *is* greener (I know, you probably don't have grass where you are—but you know what I mean). It's also one of those times when you'll just have to get used to it.

♦ **Ongoing Stress.** Your everyday life and routines—even if you're far away from the actual fighting—may be filled with stressors, most of which fall into two broad categories: (1) annoying and inconvenient and (2) disturbing and terrifying. Don't forget—you volunteered for this.

The annoying and inconvenient

♦ **Harsh, extreme climate conditions.** During the day the heat may be blistering. And while those Kevlar vests and helmets are great for stopping bullets and shrapnel, they're also incredibly hot. And heavy. And remarkably unfashionable. Oh, and at night, desert temperatures can drop to below freezing.

- **Dirt and sand everywhere.** Yes, there too.
- **The chow.** Back in my Marine Corps days, nearly every meal in the mess hall reminded me of a joke about two older women who are complaining to each other about a restaurant they've just eaten in. "The food was terrible," says one. To which the other replies, "Yes, and the portions were so small."
- **Not enough sleep.** But on the plus side, the bunks are uncomfortable too.
- **Long hours with little time off.**
- **Constant noise** from trucks, generators, incoming and outgoing shells, and so on.
- **The smell.** Don't you love the odor of latrines in the morning, or in the evening, after the contents have been baking all day?
- **Limited access to showers, laundry, and decent toilets.**
- **Few options for fun.** Depending on where you're deployed, there may be severe restrictions on your behavior, travel, leisure activities, ability to have a beer now and then, and sex life (which you shouldn't have much of until you get home, anyway).
- **Feeling isolated and lonely** (see above).
- **Little or no privacy or time to yourself.**
- **Not enough information.** Where are you going? What will you be doing when you get there? How long will you stay? When you get home, will you be there for a while, or will you be deployed again right away? What does the *i* in *iPod* stand for, anyway?
- **Too much information.** Rumors, media distortions, and inaccuracies.

The disturbing and terrifying

- **Challenges to your way of thinking.** Your fundamental beliefs about good, evil, and your own mortality may have to change.
- **Spiritual challenges**. What you've seen on your deployment may cause you to reevaluate your spiritual and religious beliefs.
- **Whipsawing between long periods of boredom** punctuated by moments of sheer terror. And, often, vice versa.
- **Exposure to war:** the sights, sounds, and smells of battle, like destroyed villages and burning flesh.

- **Constant exposure to danger**—IEDs, snipers, ambushes, mortars, bombs, and terrorist attacks.
- **High risk of seeing actual combat.** Service members in today's military are the most battle-weary in our history. In World War II, about 18 percent of soldiers engaged in combat. In Vietnam, it was 30–40 percent. Today, nearly 70 percent of service members deployed to Iraq and Afghanistan have seen combat. And in a recent study, 77 percent of the troops in Iraq said they had shot at or directed fire at the enemy. Nearly half reported being responsible for the death of an enemy combatant.
- **Guilt at having killed.** Even in self-defense or in the service of the mission. Especially if you've killed a noncombatant.
- **High risk of witnessing death and destruction.** In a study of Iraq and Afghanistan veterans, Charles Hoge and his associates found that 86 percent of soldiers in Iraq reported knowing someone who was seriously injured or killed, 68 percent reported seeing dead or seriously injured Americans, and 51 percent reported handling or uncovering human remains.

It's not all bad news

As challenging and stressful as deployment is, many service members find some good aspects of it too—and it's more than the cool uniforms and sexy haircuts. Testifying before Congress, Marine general H. P. Osman explained some of the steps the military has taken to improve morale and reduce deployment-related stress on service members. "We have Tactical Field Exchanges, phone service, free Internet service and expedited mail service…gyms, swimming pools, recreation centers and a movie theater…electronic equipment (such as televisions and computers with DVD players), and leisure items such as playing cards, games, books, and magazines. Finally, education opportunities are also available in-theater through distance learning sources."

In addition, many of the service members surveyed by Anita Chandra and her colleagues at the RAND corporation said that:

- The work they do is "fulfilling and leaves them with a sense of accomplishment."
- They feel they've contributed to a larger cause.
- They developed a strong connection to their buddies, and their unit "often becomes like a family."
- Being deployed offers a "chance to take on additional responsibility and participate in challenging, fulfilling missions."

Relationship Magic?

"All in all, I would have to say that after all the hurdles and tears and anger about the situation, after 10 years of marriage we feel closer now than we did before he left. We were able to reconnect on a mental level, and so many things were said that never would have been said if it hadn't been for all the hours logged in on the computer. I have grown to be more independent, sure of myself, and confident that I can do anything. Also while he was gone I lost almost sixty pounds and I'm a whole new woman. I can't speak for him, but he told me at one point that being over there made him realize just how important the little things are and how much he really did love his family. He even told me that 'I didn't realize how big a part of my life you are, but you are my life.' Wow that brought the water works on."

—Laura Huey, wife of a civilian contractor

You may also return home with a fine set of six-pack abs, which depends on how much physical work you're doing and how many actual six-packs you consume. Besides making your abs stronger, some service members have told me that the deployment made their marriages stronger too, by forcing them to come up with strategies for dealing with stress. It's kind of like working out: you put yourself through the pain, but in the end you're stronger for it.

Deployment can also help by giving you and your wife some time away from each other—sometimes absence really *does* make the heart grow fonder. Of course, deployment is not going to solve all of your pre-existing issues—in fact, they're almost guaranteed to re-surface after you comes home. But having some time apart can give you the break you both need to put things into perspective, understand what each of you wants in life, and then make a renewed commitment to each other.

Finally, a number of financial incentives may make up for some of the less pleasant things about deployment. These include the family separation allowance, hostile fire/imminent danger pay, the combat zone tax exclusion, hazardous duty incentive pay, and other tax deductions. Over time, these incentives can really add up. Some families are able to use this extra money to improve their long-term financial position by paying down debt or building up savings. Others may rush out and buy something big on credit. The problem is that the monthly payments may continue long after the cash windfall ends.

Can Being a Committed Father Save Your Life?

It just might. In fact, it did just that for a lot of dads who served in World War II. In her book *Parenthood: Its Psychology and Psychopathology*, Therese Benedek talks about how these soldiers' thoughts and fantasies of their children helped them overcome hardships and deprivation, and made them more resourceful when they were in actual danger. Each of these fathers knew he might not be able to see his wife or child again for years, if ever. But his sense of responsibility for his family kept him going. I get e-mail and letters from soldiers in Iraq, Afghanistan, and other places. What I find fascinating is that more than sixty years and dozens of wars after World War II, the contemporary military dad has the very same concerns. If he were to die, who would support his wife and children? Would his children remember him? Would he have made a difference in their lives?

Stage 3: Anticipation of Homecoming

Well, it's finally happened. Your deployment is wrapping up, and you're feeling pretty good about yourself—as well you should. You've shown tremendous courage, endured hardship, overcome significant obstacles, and served your country with honor. After all that, coming home to a loving wife and kids should be a walk in the park, right? Guess again.

One of the most important things to understand about coming home after deployment is that it's not a single event, something that happens once, and that's it (at least until the next time). It's a process, one that starts while you're still away, and can last for a year or more after you get back. In fact, author Karen Pavlicin, in her book *Life After Deployment*, suggests allowing yourself and your family a day of recovery for every day you were away. That could be a lot of days. Here's what you may be thinking and feeling as you prepare to return home.

- ♦ **Working hard.** In some ways, the last month of deployment will be a lot like the predeployment phase—lots of long hours and hard work to get your equipment and yourselves ready for transport.
- ♦ **Feeling better...or worse.** As mentioned above, the U.S. Army's Mental Health Advisory Team found that service members' morale drops and mental health issues increase in the first two-thirds of a deployment. In the last couple of months, the trend reverses—mental health problems decrease and morale improves as members get psyched about heading

home. However, the team found that even with all that optimism at the end of a fifteen-month deployment, three times as many soldiers reported mental health problems as had reported them after one month.

♦ **A little jittery.** If you don't feel at least a little nervous and anxious about seeing your family again, I'd be surprised. Most returning service members experience a combination of excitement (at seeing everyone again), hope (that life will get back to normal quickly) dread (of walking into a volatile situation or of people making too many demands), fear (that you won't fit in, or that they won't love you), euphoria (it's finally, finally happening!), frustration (at the constant date changes and uncertainty), and more. And then there are all the gnawing questions: Will my wife and kids be proud of me? Do they need me anymore? Will they understand what I've been through? Have my deployment experiences scarred me? What's changed since I left? Who's changed since I left? Will I ever be able to adapt to civilian life?

♦ **Fantasizing and planning.** Your mind is constantly wandering as you build expectations of how your life is about to change—how great everything will be when you return, how happy your family will be to see you, and how thrilled they'll be to have you helping out, and how all the problems that may have come up during the deployment will have been magically resolved. How hard could it be? Just hop on a plane, walk in the door, have sex with your wife, give everyone a big hug, have sex with the wife again, and pick up your life right where you left it before shipping out. Sounds like a great plan—especially the sex part. Except for one thing: even though everyone—military and civilians alike—would like to believe that homecoming is going to be nothing but bliss, it rarely is. We'll talk a lot more about the differences between expectations and reality in the next chapter.

Stage 4: Deployment Extension

You're down to fourteen days and a wakeup, and you're excited as hell to be heading home. There's only one problem: your deployment just got extended. There go all your plans. Unfortunately, this kind of thing has been happening a lot over the past few years, so even though it may seem as though you've been singled out, you're not alone. Fortunately, the Army, which has the longest deployments, has realized that fifteen-month deployments (twelve plus a three-month extension) are incredibly tough on service members, and recently said it would try to avoid them as much as possible. Don't hold your breath. As you know, the Army often says one thing, then, well <insert colorful expression for anger here> you....

Anyway, the problem isn't whether the deployment is six or nine or twelve months—it's the shock of having the deployment extended beyond the scheduled return date. That's what causes problems for service members and their family.

When you first get the news about the extension, you may go through a mini version of the predeployment phase, with all the negative emotions flooding back—especially anger. Anger and betrayal—"But they promised…" You may also find yourself feeling guilty. After all, you probably made promises too, to your wife, kids, friends, and coworkers.

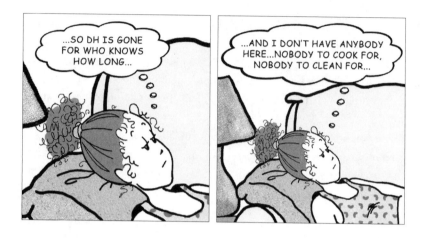

Deployed service members and their families often rely on hope to keep them going. Knowing that there's an end to the deployment and that you'll be home on a specific day can make some of the harsh realities of the deployment a lot easier to tolerate. However, when that date moves around, the foundation for that hope disappears. When that happens, the natural result is depression. In most cases it'll pass fairly quickly—just like it did over the first month of the deployment. You made it this far, so you can obviously hang on for a little while longer. The danger is if you start feeling apathetic, as if you just don't care. You may find yourself communicating less with your family (why bother anyway—no sense in getting their hopes up again) or taking unnecessary risks (what difference does it make—I'm never going home). If you find yourself feeling like this, or you're having any other kind of difficulty coping with the extension, talk to your CO. There is help available, even in the field, and it's important that you get some.

What's Going On with Your Wife?

Stage 1: Emotional Disorganization

In the first month or so after you deploy, your wife—whether you're in the military or a civilian—will experience many of the same emotions as you—plus a few. Some will be continuations of what she was going through in the predeployment phase. Others will be new. She may be sad, angry, relieved, afraid, lonely, and overwhelmed—in any order, in any combination, sometimes all

at the same time. With all that running around in her head, it's no wonder so many military wives have trouble sleeping after their husband deploys. Let's take a closer look.

♦ **Loneliness and sadness.** It doesn't matter where you're going or what your mission is—just about every spouse of a deployed service member feels lonely. Ninety-six percent of spouses of soldiers deployed to Somalia for Operation Restore Hope experienced loneliness at least once a week. During Operation Desert Storm it was 84 percent, during Operation Joint Endeavor (a peacekeeping mission to Bosnia), it was 87 percent, and in the current conflicts, the number is about 84 percent, according to sociologists Bradford Booth, Mady Wechsler Segal, and D. Bruce Bell. In their book *What We Know about Army Families*, they write that spouses report missing the companionship and intimacy they normally share with their deployed spouse. "And many regret their [service member] being unable to share in once-in-a-lifetime events that may occur during deployment (e.g., a first Christmas together, a child's birth, a baby's first steps)." Or the Cubs winning the World Series. Hey, it could happen.

Interestingly, only about a third of spouses say they do a good job of managing their feelings of loneliness. And it doesn't seem to matter how long the deployment lasts. That one-third number is consistent whether the service member was away one month or twenty out of the previous thirty-six.

One factor that does seem to help combat loneliness is kids. If she's like many mothers, your wife may throw herself completely into taking

On the Home Front

Leah McDermott, author of the children's book *Hurry Home* (hurry-home. us) wrote me about her experience during her husband's deployment.

"We have had cars break down, water heaters blow up and many other things. I have called on family and friends to come alongside and help me find the right help for these things. There have been some really great things in the community like a weekend oil change and car wash from a huge group of mechanics in the area. With military ID they hosted an event all day helping the women who were alone to change our oil, inspect our cars for needed repairs and then they washed them for us. We sat under tents and had breakfast while we waited to make sure our cars were in good shape in the middle of deployment times. You sometimes have to put yourself out there and ask for some extra help. I hire a lawn service in order to avoid the extra stress of yard work until he gets home."

care of your children as a way of taking her mind off the giant hole you left in her life. On a short-term basis, this is a pretty effective coping strategy. But eventually she'll have to face her loneliness—which is a lot easier to do if she's got a network of friends who are going through the same thing at the same time.

♦ **Breathing easier.** Don't take this personally, but there's a good chance that your wife will be relieved that you're gone (don't be too critical— you may be feeling the same thing right about now). Think about it this way: during the predeployment phase, your wife had to deal with a lot of uncertainty, and she may have worked herself into a tizzy worrying about how she would take care of the kids, pay the bills, and keep the household running while you're gone. Your body was taking up space in the kitchen and bedroom, but your mind was elsewhere, and the two of you probably spent a lot of your time together angry at each other.

♦ **Fear and anxiety.** If your wife is a worrier, she'll have plenty to keep her mind occupied. Her biggest fear is that you'll be killed or seriously injured. Other common fears include not being able to handle all the additional responsibilities that you left behind, worry that there won't be anyone to protect her and the kids while you're away, and not knowing how she'll handle the kids' negative reactions to your being gone.

Moving On

Families that know they're going to suffer financially from the deployment (and even those that aren't worried about money) sometimes consider having the wife and family move—usually to be closer to relatives or friends who can help out with child care or provide other kinds of support. This is a big, big decision, and you and your wife should think long and hard before you pull up stakes. Here are some of the pros and cons.

PRO

- She'll get a well-deserved break from military life.
- She could save a ton of money. If you're living off base now, she'll continue to receive your BAH (basic allowance for housing). Living at home would allow her to pocket all or most of that allowance.
- She'll have a familiar community of friends and family.
- Getting child-care help could allow her to get a job or pursue an educational program.
- If she's pregnant or you have children under five, it's not that big a deal to change routines.
- Not being so close to the base may help her take her mind off of worrying about you.
- She also won't have to worry about maintaining the house, mowing the lawn, repairing a broken water heater, or snaking out clogged shower drains.

CON

- You'll have to pick up all the expenses of moving both ways. The military will not pay for any of it.
- The housing allowance you get right now may not be enough to cover your family's expenses wherever they go.
- If you had on-base housing and your family moves out, you may lose your spot and have to reapply when you come back home.
- She'll be further from all the base services: commissary, exchanges, recreational facilities, chaplains, family support organiztion, medical care, communication facilities, and so on.
- It will be harder for her to connect with other wives who are going through the same thing. Civilians don't always get it.
- If the children are five and up, moving will probably require taking them away from their friends, putting them in a new school, and upsetting their routines.
- If you or your wife need to reach each other in an emergency, it's easier to do it on base where they're set up for that kind of thing.
- You won't have a "home" to come back to.

♦ **Depression.** We all want to have some degree of control over our life, and in many ways we do. But when you joined the military, you voluntarily gave up a lot of control. At this point, you've been at it for a while, and you're pretty used to following orders. But your wife isn't. Even when you're not deployed, she has very little to say about where you live (she may be able to lobby for on-base or off-base housing, but the city, state, and country are up to the brass). And of course she had no control over when your deployment would start, when you'd be back, whether you'd be engaged in combat or not, or anything else. Even though she intellectually knows that this is her (and your) life, all that being out of control can lead to a feeling of hopelessness and depression. In several studies of children whose dads were deployed, the kids often reported that their mother became very absentminded, daydreamed a lot, or slept much more than she used to before the deployment.

Another area your wife will have no control over is when she'll hear from you. For that reason, many spouses turn to the TV and Internet—where they can get news in real time. While that sometimes satisfies the need to hear what's happening where you are, it can add a huge amount of stress and increase fear levels because of all the things that aren't reported. In the early days of the deployment, a majority of military spouses become obsessed with news, watching eight hours or more every day. Interestingly, only a third of spouses—regardless of their husband's rank—say they're satisfied with national media coverage; in their view, local media does a better job. As time goes on and communication from you becomes more regular, your wife will be able to shake her news addiction (although she may replace it with an addiction to the Home and Garden channel).

♦ **Anger.** As we talked about in the predeployment chapters, your wife may be angry at the military for taking you away, at you for having joined the military in the first place (or for having stayed in when you had the chance to get out), at foreign governments for not being able to handle their own problems, and more. Interestingly, some wives don't experience much anger before the deployment, but once you're out of the house and they have time to think, that anger will come bubbling to the surface. As if to prove the point, teens often report that their mother is much more snappy and quick to anger. What mothers report about their teens is fodder for another book altogether.

Looking for Support

Less than half of the families of deployed service members say there's a consistent level of family support during any phase of the deployment, according to the National Military Family Association's Cycles of Deployment survey. Seventeen percent found no support available at all.

This is especially hard on Reservists. As we talked about above, the wives and children of your active duty brothers are already plugged in to the military life. They've got a built-in group of people who are going through the same thing at the same time (or who at least know what it's like) and can offer support. They know what their benefits are, how to shop at the commissary, where the base rec centers are, how to reach their loved ones in case of emergency, and where to go for anything they *don't* know—which is a lot. Your family has little if any of that, and they aren't used to the demands the military makes. It's easy to feel isolated, frustrated, and overwhelmed. Those feelings can sometimes spill over into their relationship with you. The RAND Corporation study found that 44 percent of reserve wives experienced "difficulties in their relationship with the spouse," as compared to 35 percent of active duty wives.

Things are even worse (assuming that's possible) for the families of civilian contractors. Employers rarely, if ever, organize support groups, and the military generally offers no programs for civilians who live near installations. (Even if they did, the civilians wouldn't be allowed on base anyway.) Sometimes meetings happen off base, but that doesn't help. One woman I spoke with described how she'd been invited by an acquaintance to attend a meeting of military wives. But after the first meeting the facilitator told her she couldn't come back. Why? Her husband wasn't in the military. Most of the contractors' wives I spoke with were extremely dissatisfied with the level of support offered by the husband's employer.

♦ **Feeling overwhelmed.** Remember that big list of your former responsibilities that your wife is taking care of now? Imagine what would happen if the situation were reversed. You can see how easy it might be to feel completely overwhelmed by the sheer volume of tasks that need to be done. In *What We Know about Army Families*, Bradford Booth and his colleagues write that "compared to spouses of non-deployed Soldiers, spouses of deployed Soldiers have more difficulty with tasks such as arranging for

child care, working at their paid jobs, managing house and car maintenance, and having to quit a job or schooling." This was confirmed in a
recent study of wives of British soldiers. Eighty-seven percent said that
they expected that their husband's deployment would place additional
demands on them. A third of those women were worried about how they'd
cope with the extra work. Interestingly, 95 percent of the deployed husbands felt confident their wife could handle things. Wives of civilian contractors also have the same concerns.

♦ **Financial issues.** If you're on active duty, your family probably won't
run into many financial issues. In fact, as we discussed on page 118, you
may actually have a bit of a windfall (although your family may not be
as thrilled as you are with the danger vs. money tradeoff). That said, if
your wife is handling the family finances for the first time, she may not
be prepared to keep track of all the bills and bank accounts. As a result,
she may make some bad financial decisions or miss some payments. (Of
course, there's also a chance that she might do a better job than you did.

What's Most Important to Whom During Deployment

TASK	SPOUSE	YOU (SOLDIER)
Household repairs, yard work, car maintenance	#1 (63%)	#3 (53%)
Ability to communicate with spouse	#2 (52%)	#2 (56%)
Managing expenses and bills	#3 (40%)	#1 (57%)

But your puff pastries are waaay better, so it evens out.) Given that it can take seven years to get even the most minor black mark off your credit report, one tiny financial misstep could make it hard for you to buy a house, a car, or anything else that requires good credit.

The good news is that overall, most military families don't experience financial difficulties during a deployment. However, 30 percent of lower-ranking enlisted service members (E-4 and below), and 13 percent of higher-ranking members, do face challenges. For example, you could slip into a financial hole if you're in the Reserve and your military pay—even with all the bonuses—is lower than your civilian pay. Or, whether you're on active duty or in the Reserve, if your wife worked because your family needs the money, you'll definitely feel a pinch if she has to quit her job so she can handle all of the additional responsibilities that your absence has shifted to her.

According to Booth and his colleagues, for those families that have financial difficulties during deployment, the major contributing factors are "deployment-related purchases (e.g., supplies and equipment for the Soldier such as sunblock, insect repellent, uniform items, baby wipes); shipping costs; extra costs to communicate with the Soldier; and other unplanned expenses such as additional child care." Am I the only one who finds it weird that guys who are risking their lives overseas have to buy their own sunblock? Just doesn't seem right. And given that about 20,000 soldiers need sunblock in the same place at the same time, you'd think that somebody would open a kiosk or something.

Length Matters

Knowing that your deployment is temporary may be exactly the boost your wife needs to maintain all those adjustments she's been making. Up to a point. The longer the deployment goes on, the more exhausted, stressed out, frustrated, and dissatisfied she'll be. So how long is too long? As you might guess, the answer will be a little different for everyone, but in general, deployments of six months or fewer are the easiest. Six to twelve months is tougher, and the hardest of all are deployments in the twelve- to fifteen-month range. Long deployments to combat zones are especially difficult. Overall, families also seem to have a better time coping with a chain of shorter deployments than with a smaller number of long ones.

Stage 2: Recovery and Stabilization

As the emotional disorientation phase passes, your wife will start settling into a routine. This isn't to say that all the problems and stresses she was feeling will be magically solved. Not even close. It just means that she and the family have reached a point where they can better cope with the daily frustrations and inconveniences of your deployment.

Here's what your wife's new "normal" life might look like.

♦ **Communication.** The two of you have finally connected, and you're in regular contact, whether by phone, e-mail, text message, IM, blog, regular mail, or mental telepathy. Or all of the above. ("Regular contact" is a pretty fuzzy term encompassing everything from a few minutes or less per week to an hour and a half every day.) One of the factors that most accurately predicts how well a couple will cope with the deployment is the frequency of communication. We'll talk a lot more about this in the next chapter.

♦ **Responsibilities and routines.** As a matter of necessity, your wife has gotten used to being a single mom, and all of the household tasks you used to do have been redistributed. Hopefully, you were able to set up some systems to lighten her load—like automatic bill pay—and you were able to get friends, family, or even the kids to chip in too. Not with paying the bills, with doing the chores.

Your wife really misses having you around, and she may have come to appreciate the heavy lifting and all those other things you used to do that she never really knew about (you mean the oil in the car doesn't change itself?). How well she copes with her new workload will depend a lot on

How Well Will Your Wife Cope with Your Deployment?

FACTORS THAT INCREASE THE DIFFICULTY	FACTORS THAT DECREASE THE DIFFICULTY
♦ Your wife and family are living overseas.	♦ Your wife doesn't believe in traditional family gender roles (see above).
♦ Your wife is foreign born.	♦ This is not her first deployment.
♦ Your wife is young.	
♦ You have children under six (who tend to be more demanding).	♦ She has lots of community and social support.
♦ You're E-4 or less.	♦ You had a very strong marriage before the deployment.
♦ You have a disabled child.	♦ You're an NCO or officer.
♦ Your wife is pregnant.	♦ Your wife is or was in the military.
♦ This is your first deployment.	
♦ Your wife has no connection to your unit, and doesn't have access to or doesn't take advantage of support resources such as your family support organization, chaplains, and so on (especially true for Reservists).	♦ Your income goes up during the deployment.
	♦ Your wife is the daughter of a four-star general.
	♦ You're a four-star general.
	♦ You're deployed less than two miles from home.
♦ The deployment has hurt the family financially.	

her mindset. Women who have strong, traditional beliefs about who does what (Dad is the breadwinner/provider/protector, Mom takes care of the house) have a tougher time handling jobs that "should" be done by the man of the house. Women who can get past those stereotypes have a much easier time taking on the extra work. As far as family routines, there will undoubtedly be some changes there as well.

♦ **She's over it—well, some of it.** Many of those feelings of being out of control will fade with time. Sure, you're gone, and she may still not know exactly where you are or when you're coming home, but at least you're there and you're reporting that things are fairly calm (hopefully). She thinks about you every day, but not every single minute of every

Learning Lessons

A very nice Web site for wives of deployed military (deploymentlessons. org) did a survey recently and asked members what they learned during their husband's deployment. Here are some of the most popular:

- ♦ I have learned that you don't believe anything till the plane lands.
- ♦ I have learned that no matter what happens, I will survive!
- ♦ I have learned that our four-year-old son thinks that Daddy can't come home because Mommy has the car.
- ♦ I have learned that many women take for granted the fact that they have their husbands to drive them crazy. I want mine to come home and drive me crazy!
- ♦ I have learned that civilian friends do not always relate to the situations we face while there are empty boots left in our homes. Military spouses will become your best friends and help shop for new shoes to wear to the welcome home to put next to those boots!
- ♦ I learned that I actually am strong enough to handle a million things I never thought I'd be strong enough for: emotionally, mentally, and physically.
- ♦ I learned that there is a switch in my brain labeled "Auto-Pilot." I use it often.
- ♦ I have learned that my grandmother has amazing patience. She waited months for a letter when I can barely wait a day for an e-mail.
- ♦ I have learned that as soon as your husband leaves is when everyone in his family wants to tell you exactly what they think of you.
- ♦ I have learned that spouses of the United States Military are given the job because they are some of the strongest people on the planet.

day, and she's gotten past a lot of the anger she was feeling not that long ago.

- ♦ **Growth and independence.** One of the dirty little secrets about deployment is that it's often a time of great personal growth for the non-deployed spouse. It may take a few weeks or months, but eventually your wife will start feeling pretty darn proud of herself as she realizes that, yes, she actually *can* do it. (You go, girl! Or woman! Or male spouse of a deployed service person at home taking on both gender roles in a traditional house-

Deployed Mothers: When You're the Trophy Husband

No one knows exactly how many dads are at home while their wives are deployed, but it's definitely in the thousands. If you're one of them, your support for your wife is critical. Although much of what she's going through is similar to what we describe in the "What's Going On with You" sections—just reverse the genders—there are some military-mom-specific things to be aware of. To start with, there are the gender stereotypes about "acceptable" professions for men and women. While it's okay for men to provide and protect, a lot of people have trouble when the combat boot is on the other foot.

Society puts a lot of pressure on mothers to be the nurturing one, the primary caregiver, the one the toddler runs to with a skinned knee. And when a woman turns those expectations on their head, the reaction can be harsh. In an article that appeared in the *Agape Press*, journalist R. Cort Kirkwood takes on mothers serving in the military, questioning their patriotism, accusing them of being bad mothers, and demanding to know who the "military morons" are who think that allowing women to be deployed away from their families is okay.

It's tough enough to be away from your children for months at a time. Having to take garbage from idiots with a political agenda just makes it worse. Unfortunately, women are not the only ones who bump up against stereotypes. Because you, the guy, are "supposed" to be out there in the workforce, you may end up feeling extremely isolated. Plus, it's not easy to find an apron that fits a Big and Tall man. In the next chapter we'll talk about how to support your wife—and yourself—while she's deployed. I believe the politically correct term is "house dude."

hold!) And she's right. She can balance the checkbook, change the oil and air filter, do basic household repairs, get the kids where they need to go, bring home the bacon, fry it up in a pan, and still have time to get a work-out in. She may be losing weight, is putting away a little money, has built herself a nice little social network, and is enjoying the hell out of the free time she has—time that would have been spent with you. All in all, she's feeling competent, confident, and independent.

All this freedom and independence may come at a cost. Some women

feel a twinge of guilt that they're having a marvelous time doing whatever they want while dear hubby is over there getting shot at.

Trouble in Paradise?

Given the nice routines that have developed at home, it's tempting to think that the toughest times are over when your family enters the stabilization stage. Don't. Twenty-nine percent of spouses in a recent study by the National Military Family Association said that the middle of the deployment is more stressful than any other time. There are lots of reasons for this.

- ◆ **Media.** The inability to escape graphic media coverage can keep the family constantly on edge and worried about your safety. Avoid CNN. Spend some time on the nice, calming weather channel, or C-Span.
- ◆ **Stress**. For some families, it's the slow buildup of minor annoyances that never manage to get worked out (which isn't much of a surprise, since it's hard to discuss these issues when you're halfway around the world). A lot of the teenagers in a study by researchers Angela Huebner and Jay Mancini "attributed their mom's increased stress to her taking on more responsibilities, having concerns over money, and worrying more about dad." As a result, many of these kids said they weren't able to participate in as many of their usual extracurricular activities.
- ◆ **Depression**. Many of the teens in Huebner and Mancini's study described their mother as "being very emotional, more sleeping and being absent-minded or being 'off in another world' "—all possible signs of depression. Not surprisingly, the teens also said that while Dad was deployed, Mom wasn't as good about enforcing discipline as when he was home.

♦ **What's important to whom.** Something else that can contribute to ongoing tension during your deployment is a lack of alignment between your priorities and your wife's. Take a look at the chart on page 129, which shows the results of a Department of Defense survey of active duty military deployed out of the country for a month or more. As you can see, your wife's top concern is most likely household repairs, yard work, and so on. Number three on her list is family finances. For you, those two are reversed, which means that you may be pressuring her to do things that you see as critical but she doesn't. It's all very complicated—first you have to agree on what to disagree about. Then you can get down to the actual arguing.

Working Mothers

The most satisfied military families are the ones where the spouse works outside the home, according to a report by the RAND Corporation called *Working Around the Military: Challenges to Military Spouse Employment and Education.* The good news is that the majority of military spouses are, in fact, employed.

Like civilians, military wives work for all sorts of reasons: to feel productive, to keep from being bored, to stay current with new developments in the field, and of course for the money—to pay bills, pay off debts, build up the nest egg, or simply have a little extra cash to spend. Rarely ever for the snappy McDonald's uniform.

Unfortunately, military wives are three times more likely to be unemployed than their civilian look-alikes. And when they do work, they make a lot less.

"Tommy and Ben are like Green Berets, Dan and Jerry are Navy SEALs, and me and Scott are like private contractors."

On an hourly basis, "civilian wives earn about twice as much as Army and Marine Corps wives, while Air Force and Navy wives with similar characteristics earn about $3 per hour less than their civilian counterparts," according to the RAND report.

As unfortunate as that sounds, it actually makes some sense. Compared to civilians, military spouses…

- ♦ Are younger. About 70 percent are under thirty-five, versus only 45 percent in the general population. And being young, they may have less education and job experience.
- ♦ Are more likely to have young children at home. Fifty-five percent of military families have children under six, versus 35 percent for civilians.

Reserving Judgment

Children of Reservists and Guardsmen often have a harder time coping with their dad's deployment than those whose dads are on active duty. To start with, there's a lot less support for Reservists. Fewer resources, fewer programs designed to help families, and less access to base services and support. But from the kids' perspective, the biggest problem has to do with isolation. For the most part, their usual circle—friends, classmates, relatives, teammates, and teachers—have no real experience with deployment, and no clue what it means to have Dad be gone for anywhere from a few months to a year.

Overall, children of Reservists have less connection with people who understand military life, according to Anita Chandra and her colleagues. Only about 15 percent of these kids have the opportunity to spend time with other children from military families, compared to almost 30 percent for active duty kids. And only about a quarter of reserve kids say their teachers understand what life is like for them with a parent serving in the military, compared to 35 percent of active duty kids.

Interestingly, though, Chandra found that active duty kids are a little more likely to worry about their non-deployed parent and have more problems with schoolwork than reserve kids. Hey, no one said that kids have to be logical, consistent, or even make any sense at all.

♦ Move around a lot more. Only 10 percent of military wives stay in the same home for five years, according to a recent Department of Defense report. Many jobs come through social contacts, and those are tough to maintain if you're moving all the time. It also makes it harder to earn certifications or satisfy licensing requirements.

♦ Are twice as likely to have their infants dressed in camouflage diapers.

Overall, about two-thirds of the wives in the RAND study felt that the military lifestyle had hurt their employment prospects. And about half of them felt that their education had suffered too. The one bright spot in all this is that the U.S. Departments of Labor and Defense have recently created programs that are specifically designed to help military spouses get into more portable careers. If she's interested, have your wife check into the Military Spouse Career Center (military.com/spouse), Allied Schools (education4military.com), or MilSpouse.org for info on scholarships, online training, and educational opportunities.

Stage 3: Anticipation of Homecoming

I've heard several military wives say that they'd almost rather suffer through the agony of having their husband deploy again than endure the last month of deployment.

Like the period immediately before the deployment, the last month can be filled with mood swings and conflicting emotions. For example, your wife may be excited that you're coming home and frustrated that the days never seem to end, but in a panic that she won't get everything done that she'd planned to. She may be fantasizing about spending time with you, but also have fleeting thoughts that she'll have to give up some of her freedom. She's nervous and wants everything to be just right for you, but she's worried that you might not like the way she or the kids or the house look. She's proud of herself for managing things while you were gone, and she's worried that you might not like the new routines and the changes she made. We'll talk a lot about how you can help her through these and other emotions in the next chapter.

Stage 4: Deployment Extension

As hard as a deployment extension is on you, there's a reasonable case to be made that it's at least as hard for your family. You and your wife and kids will most certainly feel similar emotions—the same anger, betrayal, disappointment, frustration, and hopelessness. And, in some cases, the same depression and feelings of apathy, both of which can rub off on the kids.

There are two odd things that may also happen. First, in between outbursts of negativity, your wife may actually have a few brief periods of relief—now she has a couple more months to tie up all the projects she didn't finish. Expect many newly painted rooms. More than you might think one woman could manage alone.

Second, you may notice a drop in communication from your family. They may be punishing you for having broken your promises, or they may not want to be reminded of this "grave injustice," which is going to happen every time they make contact. I know, it sounds crazy—they're upset because they can't see you as soon as they want to, and so they choose this particular moment to stop communicating? Well, it happens.

What's Going On with Your Child(ren)?

As mentioned in the predeployment section, your absence is going to be tough on your kids. What that means, exactly, will depend on your children's ages. For the first little while, their emotional and behavioral responses will look a lot like they did before you left. As the new routines become more familiar and they get used to the reality of your deployment, your children—just like you and your wife—will stabilize, and things will get easier, at least until the last month of your deployment, when tensions will start to build again.

Many of the actual emotions children experience are, in name anyway, fairly similar, regardless of their age. The difference is in the way they're expressed.

Birth to Twelve Months

Infants are too young to have many sophisticated feelings, but they'll definitely know something's up. As early as three months of age, babies can tell the difference between the way Mom and Dad treat them. If you're like most guys and are more physical with your baby, he'll get excited when you walk in the room, as if getting himself ready to rumble. If you suddenly disappear (which is exactly what it'll feel like to your baby), he'll miss you. One of the great, unsolved problems of deployment is how to tickle your baby over the Internet.

At this age, though, the most important factor in determining how your baby will react to your deployment is your wife's mood and behavior. Infants whose mothers are depressed are often listless, fussier, and may refuse to eat. And in one fascinating recent study, David Schwebel, a psychologist at the University of Alabama at Birmingham, found that infants and toddlers whose mothers were depressed were almost three times more likely to suffer accidental injuries than same-age children with non-depressed mothers. The problem isn't the depression itself, but the lack of care babies get when their mother's mind is preoccupied. If, on the other hand, your wife is doing well, your baby will too.

One to Three Years

Toddlers' emotional range is still fairly limited, but they can certainly express sadness, anger, and loneliness. As with infants, toddlers take their cues from Mom (or Dad, if he's the one at home) and will often mimic her behavior. However, even if your wife is having a marvelous time, your toddler will still miss

playing with you and will notice a change in routine. As a result, he may cry more, be more irritable, throw tantrums, and become more clingy than usual.

Fears—of animals, thunder, vacuum cleaners (dogs and kids have a lot in common here), toilets, strangers, and more—may increase. Problems sleeping and a little regressive behavior (for example, wanting a bottle or pacifier after having given them up) are also common.

Three to Five Years

Preschoolers are pretty me-focused, primarily concerned with how whatever is happening will affect them. The change in his daily routine will be the hardest thing for your preschooler to handle. Your preschooler will *really* miss playing with you, and may express his sadness and anger at you for not being there by acting out aggressively toward his mother, friends, and preschool teachers, or by testing limits more than usual.

As with toddlers, preschoolers may exhibit some regressive behavior: bed-wetting or daytime accidents after being toilet trained, lapsing into baby talk, refusing to sleep alone, and so on—all ways of regaining the attention they feel should be directed at them instead of whatever Mom is focusing on.

Overall, preschoolers with a deployed parent display more stress, trouble concentrating, and behavioral and psychological problems such as depression and anxiety than their peers whose parents are stateside, according to a recent study by Air Force lieutenant colonel Molinda Chartrand and her colleagues. At the same time, their emotions are getting more mature and nuanced, so while your child may still be afraid of dogs and loud noises, he may also be

afraid that Mommy might leave him too, or perhaps that something bad could happen to you.

A new emotion that starts showing up at around this age is guilt. Because preschoolers still don't quite get time, they don't know what it means that "Daddy will be back in six months." So every day can be stressful as they wonder whether today is the day... For your preschooler, guilt is a sort of abstract feeling that you left because he did something to upset or disappoint you. This might seem absurd to you, but in the mind of a child who still thinks he controls everything in his world, it makes perfect sense. In his mind, there's a clear connection between your departure and that time he put jelly beans in the DVD player.

Six to Twelve Years

As your child gets older, his emotional life gets richer. He'll experience higher highs and lower lows and may swing back and forth between them. He may overreact (at least in your opinion) to minor things, be irritable, have trouble sleeping, seem to have no energy, and even lose interest in friends or favorite activities. He may also complain about feeling sick or having various bodily pains. Laura Huey, whose husband was a civilian contractor in Kuwait, said her nine-year-old daughter seemed to handle Dad's deployment pretty well for the most part, but "she kinda pulled herself into a shell and wouldn't talk to Dad on computer, phone, or send mail to him. We also had some real temper issues, and plenty of "Dad's-not-home-let's-see-how-much-we-can-get-away-with" days.

Your child may get hit with waves of sadness and loneliness in certain places or at certain times of day, say in the mornings if you were the make-lunch-and-drive-the-kids-to-school guy, or at a game or recital where you would have been sitting in the front row, video cam in hand. "Younger boys... said they missed their dads most as a playmate," according to researcher Angela Huebner, "someone who would go out, run around, and play ball with them...." Boys starting puberty are especially at risk for feeling alienated or lonely in this way. Your son may have questions that he'd rather talk about with you than his mother, but can't because communicating with you isn't as easy as he (or you) would like it to be. Getting boys to talk about their feelings is tough enough when you see each other very day. Getting them to talk about them to a guy thousands of miles away is, well, really, really, really tough. Well, maybe not that hard. But still, not easy.

If you and your wife are confused by your school-age child's behavior, imagine what it feels like to actually be going through all this. It can be pretty frightening. Usually, what kids this age really want is a hug and a few under-standing words. But since he may not be able to articulate his feelings, you're too far away to talk to, and Mom is preoccupied with everything else, he may try to get the attention he wants by acting out, misbehaving, testing limits, and being rude.

Those discipline problems may carry over to school as well. School-age children—especially boys—may be disruptive and impulsive, and their grades may take a dive. When he isn't wising off or being sent to the principal's office, he may have trouble concentrating, and his grades could suffer. This could be because he has less time to do homework, thanks to all the additional chores at home. But some kids' grades actually improve during the deployment, because they want their deployed parent to be proud of them. (Note: this is *not* a reason to volunteer for another deployment.)

Intellectually, your child is less self-centered and probably won't blame himself for your departure. As his empathy skills grow, he may get very upset at media coverage of war zones, worrying that you're in danger—even if you've explained to him that you're nowhere near the fighting. He may also worry about his mother. If she's still having a tough time coping, your child may feel that he has to step in and take care of her.

On the more positive side, some children this age find that their relation-ships with their mom and siblings improve during this time. Being forced to pitch in and work together helps them bond.

Thirteen Years and Over

Teens may have many of the same emotional and behavioral reactions to your deployment as any adult. How well your kid coped before you left will give you a pretty good idea of how he'll do while you're gone. He may become moody, irritable, argumentative, rebellious, angry, apathetic, and generally refuse to communicate in anything other than grunts and single-syllable words. But given that he's a teenager, it's tough to say how much of that is normal behavior and how much has to do with your deployment.

In extreme cases, your teen may actually do something to deliberately harm himself. Often, this is a way of getting attention, or of providing a reason for you to come back from your deployment. Or it could be a kind of self-punishment. For example, not long before you deployed, he might have screamed, "I hate you and wish you were dead!" Ordinarily, that's pretty standard stuff for a teen. But now you're actually gone, there's a possibility that his "wish" could really come true. In a recent study published in the journal *Psychological Medicine*, researchers found that 46 percent of teens had caused some kind of non-suicidal self-injury within the previous year. The most common types of injury were biting, cutting, burning skin, and hitting.

If you notice an increase in risky behavior (sex, drugs, alcohol, fast driving, and so on), a sudden loss of interest in friends, or a dramatic change in wardrobe (wearing baggy clothes, for example, is a classic attempt to hide self-inflicted scars), talk to your child's pediatrician right away.

One very common reaction among teens is to withdraw emotionally and spend more time with friends. Sometimes this is their way of trying to make sense of everything they're going through. Sometimes it's a way of not having to deal with their fears and worries about you. Other times, it's to protect their mother, who they think is already under enough stress. In some cases, teens will even withdraw from their friends.

There are all sorts of other contradictory things going on. Your teen may enjoy the new independence and extra responsibilities, but may resent the extra work or being put into the position of man of the house (for boys) or parenting your wife (for girls). He wants to be unique and different, but he may lash out at you and your wife for having made your family *too* different. He may resent having to take care of his siblings, but feel closer to them as a result. He may be furious at Mom for making him give up extracurricular activities (no time to drive him to practices), but spend more time with the family and actually enjoy it. He may try to distract himself by packing his days with as many activities as possible, or he may feel bored out of his mind. His grades may suffer because he's anxious about you, or they may improve because he wants to make sure you aren't disappointed when you get home and doesn't want you to worry about him, say Virginia Tech researchers Angela Huebner and Jay A. Mancini.

5.

Morse Code, Smoke Signals, and Wireless Internet

Staying Involved while You're Deployed

Looking out for Number One

"One cannot underestimate the important role a family plays in a soldier who has left them for a higher cause," writes Timothy Kerner, a retired military officer and an expert in mail systems. Aside from staying alive, staying connected with your family is the most important part of your well-being during your deployment. When you're in regular contact with your family, you'll feel like you're still a valued, needed part of your family. It'll boost your morale and keep your relationships with your wife and kids fresh. It can also help minimize the shock you're going to get when you come home to a family that's been through a lot of changes.

Exploring Your Options

You're going to be insanely busy when you first get to where you're going. But as soon as you can, do a little investigating to see what kinds of communication are available, and try to make contact with your family right away. They've been holding their breath since you left, and finding out that you've arrived safely will come as a huge relief. So even if you only have a few seconds to call, do it—"Hi honey. Plane just landed and everything's okay" is fine. Sneak in an "I love you" for extra points. There are three basic ways of making contact with your family: telephone, the Internet, and good old-fashioned U.S. mail. Let's take a closer look.

♦ **Telephone.** Being able to actually talk to your loved ones is wonderful—for you and for them. It's not always easy, though. Phones are often in short supply, which means lines can sometimes get very long. Phone calls can also be extremely expensive. In one recent study, 55 percent of army spouses say their family has had financial difficulties because of the cost of maintaining communication with their service member. So before you pick up the phone, spend some time researching your telephone options. A lot of people will tell you that you should take prepaid phone cards with you because calls from overseas can be prohibitively expensive. While there's definitely a place for phone cards, they're really the best option if you'll have access only to pay phones. But if you're someplace where high-speed Internet is available, a VoIP (Voice over Internet Protocol) service like Vonage or Packet 8 will be a lot cheaper. (A few years ago my parents took a trip to Bulgaria, and my dad brought his laptop and VoIP box. Calling them from the States was actually a local call.) In some areas,

A Brief History of Military Family Communications

"During World War II…home front America mailed approximately 6 billion letters to U.S. Service members overseas," write the authors of *What We Know about Army Families*. "By the time of the Korean war, Soldiers were using telegraph, radio, and telephone…. By the time of the Vietnam War, photographs and audiotapes were added. Vietnam became the first TV war…. In the 1980s, Soldiers called home from invasions in Grenada and Panama with international calling cards, and telephone use increased during 1990s peacekeeping missions. Faxes and voicemail first appeared during Operation Desert Storm." Now you can even do live video conferencing—just be glad smell-o-vision has yet to be invented.

cell phones or satellite phones might be the best way to go. In other places it might be cheaper to buy a cell phone from a local provider and use their network. Be sure to look into the difference between incoming and outgoing calls, though. In some places only the person making the call gets charged. In others, both parties get billed. So talk to some of the old timers at your base. They know where the best chow is, the cheapest way to call home, and which is the softest bunk (although they'll keep that one for themselves).

If you're bringing your own cell phone, make sure you check into roaming charges and international rates. If the rates aren't too high (you can sometimes get VoIP for your cell phone), make sure texts, including Twitter, are covered. Most services charge for inbound and outbound texts, so if you're going to do a lot of texting, get an unlimited usage plan. Keep in

mind that because you and the family will probably be in different time zones, texting isn't good if you want instant response. But it's a great way to send short messages like, "Woke up this morning and thought of you," "Good luck with the game today," "Saw a bug the size of my hand," and so on.

♦ **The Internet.** Unless you have to pay for time at an Internet café, just about anything you can do on the Web will be free. You'll be able send e-mail, chat, IM, and video-conference to your heart's content—as long as the line to use the computer isn't too long.

♦ **E-mail** is the most popular means of communication, but it doesn't allow the instant feedback that phone calls do. It's also a lot harder to get a sense of someone's mood in an e-mail. There's a limit to what you can get across with emoticons (those graphic smiley faces) or keyboard shortcuts like :) and : (. (Why are all the faces sideways, anyway? Are they lying down?)

Too Much of a Good Thing?

There are both advantages and disadvantages to being in close contact, as this chart shows:

Advantages	Disadvantages
♦ You can be more involved in everyday decision making.	♦ You could get so involved in household matters that you end up distracted from your mission. The last thing you need when you're on patrol in an urban environment is to be worried about how upset your child is that you're missing her first baseball game or that your pregnant wife is having trouble finding child care so she can make her doctor's appointment later that day.
♦ You'll feel more like you're part of the family.	
♦ You'll be a regular presence in each other's life, and you can help your kids with homework, school projects, and more.	
♦ Your family will feel better about you being deployed, which means that if you decide to re-up for another hitch, they'll be more supportive.	♦ Conflicts you had before deployment could get even worse, because there's never enough time to fully discuss anything.
♦ It just plain feels good to see and hear from your family. Even the dog.	♦ Your wife may be enjoying the opportunity to make decisions on her own and may resent you getting too involved.
	♦ Your family might worry about you more. An HR manager at a big civilian contractor told me that he often gets calls from wives who are frantic because they haven't heard from their husband in twelve hours.

Webcams and VTCs are an especially good example of technology that cuts both ways. On the plus side, as mentioned above, it's fantastic to be able to see your family in real time, to watch their faces when they open up presents you've sent, to admire how much the kids have grown and how well they play the piano. Several wives I interviewed (both military and civilian) told me that they sometimes have to turn the video off and just do the audio thing. Phone calls, e-mail, and any other non-visual way of communicating allows people to keep a lid on their emotions and put on a happy face—or at least a happy voice. But with video, all too often, that face isn't happy at all. Seeing the fear and sorrow in their husband's eyes was sometimes too hard for these women to deal with.

♦ **Video teleconferencing (VTC)** is the least used, but it's growing quickly. Naturally, there are some obstacles. To start with, since other people are nearby, there isn't much privacy. Additionally, the high demand for VTCs combined with frequent technical difficulties connecting or maintaining a connection often limits your air time to just a few minutes. And if it doesn't work at all, the whole family is in for a big emotional letdown.

VTCs are not always convenient or available to everyone. For example, if you're in the Reserves or National Guard and your family lives far from the nearest base, they won't be able to take advantage of VTC. And if your wife and kids moved back home with her parents to save money while you're gone, she—and you—are pretty much out of luck, VTC wise. But don't give up completely. If you're willing to think creatively, there may actually be some workarounds.

You may be able to work out an arrangement with a local business that has VTC capabilities. Local television stations have been known to coordinate video links between families and their deployed service members. The military has also recently been buying time on commercial satellites (instead of using only military ones), which may make it easier for your family to connect.

If you have access to high-speed Internet and a webcam, you can bypass the military's VTCs altogether. Just get signed up with one of the many free, real-time video services, such as Skype (skype.com), Oovoo (oovoo.com), camfrog.com, Freedom Calls (freedomcalls.org), and Google chat (google.com/chat). I've heard wonderful stories from service members who took advantage of video conferencing to watch the birth of their baby, see the kids in their Halloween costumes, or even participate in parent-teacher conferences. You could, I suppose, use this technology to keep an eye on what the roofers are doing during your remodeling project, too.

Other services, like TroopTube (trooptube.tv, which is a service provided by Military OneSource), allow you and your family to upload videos for each other to see. Blogs and Web sites are also great ways to keep in touch. They're usually cheap and easy to set up. The problem is trying to find something to say on your 127th entry.

♦ **U.S. mail.** In this day and age you'd think that something as low-tech as paper and stamps would have died out long ago. But there's something about mail, especially for deployed military, that may make it the best option of all. Hearing your voice and seeing you on a video screen is great, but being able to feel and touch something that you packed up with your own hands adds a whole different dimension to your communication. And although you may be able to print out an e-mail or a photograph, it's not quite the same as being able to reread a letter your wife wrote or hold a picture your child made just for you anytime you need a boost. "Receiving letters at mail call often meant the difference in motivation during heavy combat campaigns," writes Timothy Kerner. "Most of all, it represented a future for these soldiers outside of war that kept their drive and commitment during their tours of duty." Of course, because mail takes so much longer to get from place to place, you won't use snail mail for all of your communication needs. But until someone figures out a way to e-mail cookies, it's an essential add-on.

We'll talk about some specific ground rules for communicating with your wife and children in the next two sections, "Staying Involved with Your Wife" and "Staying Involved with Your Children."

Beyond Communication
As important as communication is, there are a number of other things you can do purely for yourself. Don't be shy about this—you deserve it. We all need a break now and then. That, and nice, comfy socks. Okay, comfy socks have nothing to do with communication, but with all the marching you're doing, boy, are they nice. Get two pairs.

+ **Routines.** No matter how much predeployment training you did, once your boots are on the ground, things will be very different. Do yourself a big favor and try to create some new routines as soon as possible. They'll help you work more efficiently, better plan your days, and retain some control over your life instead of simply reacting to outside demands.
+ **Free time and hobbies.** If you can bring a hobby from home, like photography or collecting stamps or coins, so much the better. If you don't have one, this is a good time to start. Aside from that, work out, hang with your buddies, watch movies, or find some other way to have a little fun.
+ **A little me time.** This is a tough one, since privacy is going to be in short supply. But try to carve out some time alone, even if it's only a few minutes. Go for a walk, get in some reading, or do some simple meditation (see "Relaaaaax," above). Hot air ballooning might be a little ambitious.
+ **Smile.** You don't have much control over where your body is stationed during your deployment, but you're definitely in charge of where your mind is. What I mean is that a large part of how you handle the deployment has to do

Relaaaaax

Doing some simple relaxation techniques during tense times can lower your stress levels and make the overall situation more tolerable. One simple method is to close your eyes and breathe. Inhale for five seconds, hold your breath for one, then exhale for five. Hold your breath for one and start again. If you can, focus on making your belly rise and fall instead of your lungs. Five to ten minutes of this every day, and you'll feel awfully serene.

with your outlook. No question, there are lots of negative things that could consume your thoughts each day, but if you spend all your time focusing on them, you'll be miserable. If, on the other hand, you're able to find some humor in your situation—and there's plenty of it if you look hard enough—the time will pass a lot more quickly, and you'll have a lot less to be stressed about. Stuck for a smile? Have your kids tell you a few jokes. Somehow they have a way of making even the oldest knock-knocks sound funny.

♦ **Have a friend.** No matter how hard you smile, you're still waist-deep in stress, most of which you won't be able to share with your wife, because of security requirements, limited communication, or her lack of understanding of military life, or simply because you don't want to worry her. That's why it's super important that you find someone to confide in and vent your frustrations to, someone who's going through what you are and who will understand what you're feeling. It's very comforting to know you're not alone. The ideal person is someone in your unit. But depending on your position in the chain of command and what you want to talk about, you may need to go outside (for example, if you're frustrated about how your unit is run or you're furious at individuals within it, you'll be putting your confidant in a tough spot, and you could end up creating unnecessary friction).

♦ **Be a friend.** Listening and being supportive to someone else can take your mind off your own worries.

♦ **Keep a journal.** Many people find the process of writing down their thoughts quite relaxing. Plus, it'll provide a wonderful record that you can show to your family when the time is right.

♦ **Get help if you need it.** Don't be afraid to utilize some of the support services that are available to you during deployment. Even if you are not religious, military chaplains can be great sources of support without pushing religion down your throat.

Getting Ready to Come Home

As you're packing your trunk, spend a little time thinking about how you've changed over the course of your deployment. Do a little self-interview and ask these questions: Who am I? What do I enjoy doing? How do I spend my free time? What makes me happy? What are my strengths? What are my weaknesses? If you've formed new habits, adjusted your diet, developed new fears, or anything else, understanding how you've changed will help you better prepare your family so they can adjust their expectations accordingly. It'll also save them a lot of heartache and time trying to figure out the answers to these questions for themselves.

When Your Deployment Gets Extended

As we discussed in the previous chapter, deployment extension happens. And when it does, it hurts. Here are a few ways of coping:

- **Recalibrate your mental timeline.** I know, it's easier said than done and may take some time. But the sooner you can get used to the new departure date, the sooner you'll be able to move on with life.
- **Don't get dragged into griping sessions.** The negativity that's bound to sweep through your unit will do nothing but harm. It's okay to vent your frustrations, but try to find something positive to focus on as well. Doing this can make a huge difference in your day to day life throughout the extension. Sometimes all it takes is few episodes of *The Three Stooges*.
- **If you're in the Guard or Reserves, contact your employer and let them know your new arrival date.** You may need to provide a copy of your extension orders. Under USERRA (see page 39 for more), your employer has to hold your job. Also contact your ESGR (Employer Support of the Guard and Reserve) representative or visit their Web site, esgr.org. ESGR is an organization within the Department of Defense that helps manage relationships between employers and service members in the Reserves.
- **Inform any and all creditors as soon as possible.** This will enable you to continue taking advantage of your protections and reduced rates under the SCRA (see page 38 for more on this legislation).
- **Find out about any other financial issues.** If your family bought non-refundable tickets for a cruise or put a big deposit down to rent a medieval

When Things Go Wrong at Home

There's never a good time for things to go wrong, but it's especially bad when your wife is half a world away and completely unable to do anything about it. Whether it's a life-threatening illness, the death of a relative, a natural disaster, a sudden need for child care, unemployment, bankruptcy, or something else, help is available. Each branch of service has a special relief organization that's devoted to helping its own, so contact the one that's right for you:

♦ Air Force Aid Society, afas.org

♦ Army Emergency Relief, aerhq.org

♦ Navy–Marine Corps Relief Society, nmcrs.org

If there isn't an office for your branch nearby, find the nearest one from any branch and/or the American Red Cross (redcross.org). In addition, contact your wife's unit's contact person and Family Readiness Group/Key Volunteer Network/Ombudsman program/Key Spouse program.

In all cases, your family will need to know your wife's branch of service and rank, social security number, home base unit, and the address where she's deployed, and you should have in hand a copy of your deployment orders and most recent leave and earning statement (LES).

castle to celebrate your return, you may be able to get a refund by providing a copy of your extension orders.

♦ **Take some solace in knowing that units that have been extended usually get special consideration in upcoming deployment scheduling.** Theoretically that means that if your unit is going to be shipped out again, you may get an extra few months added on to the normal twelve-month "dwell time" between deployments.

♦ **Take good care of yourself.** As we discussed in the previous chapter, you may get hit with a wave of complete apathy. Get some exercise, eat right, and try to keep up the routines you had before you got the bad news. If you find yourself sitting on your cot with a thousand-yard stare and a gallon of butter brickle ice cream, it's time to make some changes.

When Mom Is Deployed

If you're at home while your wife is deployed, be sure to read the "Enough About You" chapter that starts on page 177, and do as many of those things as you can. In addition, here are a few more suggestions.

- **Follow the "Communication Ground Rules" starting on page 157.** Resist the urge to fill your e-mails or phone calls with complaining or to tell her all about problems she can't do anything to resolve. You'll just frustrate her. It could also take her mind off her job, which could put her and others at risk. On the other hand, don't paint an overly rosy picture—she'll get suspicious that you're covering something up.

- **Don't forget those care packages.** Treats (gum, cake, sunflower seeds, and so forth), reading material, and drawings from the kids are great. And include a picture of Arnold Schwarzenegger before he got fat and became governor of California, but Photoshop your face on to Arnold's neck.

- **Keep your ear to the ground and ask for help if you need it.** Overall, spouses who stay informed and have a solid support network cope better than those who don't. I hate to bring up gender stereotypes, but there is some truth to the idea that men often have a harder time asking for help than women. Get over it. The base Family Readiness Group (FRG)/Key Volunteer Network/Ombudsman program/Key Spouse program will have workshops on various issues that can come up during deployment and will be able to tell you about social activities that exist for you and the kids. Be prepared: you'll have a tough time being welcomed into the network of military wives, which can be such an important source of support and information. But don't give up. Eventually, you'll probably be adopted by a group of women, many of whom won't be able to keep themselves from mothering you. Enjoy it, but not too much. And if you happen to be anywhere near Fort Bragg, North Carolina, check out a group called Rear D Dads, a volunteer-run organization that's designed to help guys with deployed wives get information about everything from job hunting and social events to navigating the military benefits programs. And as long as you're reversing gender roles, go ahead and bake cookies for your spouse's support group. Chocolate chip.

- **Keep your contact list current.** Make sure you have contact names and phone numbers for the family support organization and your wife's unit's rear deployment people. You should also have a hard copy of her deployment orders and most recent leave and earnings statement (LES).

- **Maintain a schedule.** Kids crave routines, so help them—and your-self—by giving them something they know they can count on. Every Tuesday night you go out for Vietnamese food; Friday nights it's pizza and snuggle up on the couch and watch a movie together; Saturdays are for field trips to museums, parks, zoos, planetariums, and so on; Sunday nights you get a sitter and go hang out with your buddies.
- **Volunteer at the family support organization if you're able.** Help-ing other at-home dads will do you and them a world of good. You may also pick up a few good parenting tips and contact info for some terrific baby sitters.
- **Help her celebrate.** If your wife is in the Army, which has deployments as long as a year, there's a better-than-average chance that she's going to be away for Valentine's Day, Mother's Day, *and* the winter holidays. If she's in one of the other services, which have shorter deployments, she'll miss at least one big holiday. So as the big days approach, grab your cam-era and start shooting. Take pictures of the kids when they come home with the special projects they created there. If you're making something at home, film the kids doing that too. And of course, include the finished product in your next care package along with any holiday-related para-phernalia you can stuff in—a mini Christmas tree and a stocking, some Hanukkah candles and a dreidel, a Halloween costume, or whatever.
- **Help her be an involved mother.** In 2008, when Air Force doctor Ginger Bohl's son was six months old, she was deployed to Afghanistan. Not one to let little things like a war, 8,000 miles, and ten time zones get in her way, Ginger took a breast pump with her and every other week couriered thirty to forty pounds of frozen breast milk back home. Bohl's

husband, Michael, then filled the cooler up with goodies and sent it back to her. The customs guys at JFK in New York initially thought that Bohl and her husband were running an Afghani breast-milk ring. Obviously, not everyone can afford to do something like this, but it just goes to show you the lengths to which people will go to keep connected to their family.

Staying Involved with Your Wife

There's no question that it's going to be a little tricky to ease your wife's stresses and frustrations and maintain a solid relationship with her across time and distance. But if you're both willing to put in the effort, it can be done.

The single most important step you can take toward that end is to communicate with each other. Remember back in the predeployment phase, when you were physically present at home but psychologically absent? Well, good lines of communication allow you to reverse that, so you can be psychologically present even while you're physically absent.

Communication Ground Rules

Because of the uncertainties of technology and military life, it's important to keep in mind the following ground rules.

- ♦ **Quantity is more important than quality.** Frequent, short contacts are much better than infrequent, longer ones, so be in touch as often as you can. Up to a point. See "Too Much of a Good Thing?" on page 149.
- ♦ **Be patient.** About 40 percent of Army spouses say they have had problems sending or receiving communication from their service member,

On the Home Front

"Letters are always nice and packages are always appreciated since many service members have almost no contact with the outside world. Sending enough to share with those who get little to nothing. One time I sent a package to a ship mate for my husband's birthday full of all Star Wars birthday stuff. His friend was great and took the time on his birthday to set up the wardroom with plates, cups, napkins, etc., for everyone. I even wrapped and made gift bags for the entire wardroom so everyone got a treat. They all got party hats and party favors and enjoyed a 'kid's birthday party.' It was a great way to break up the monotony of daily life on the ship and everyone was able to participate. It was a great laugh and of course everyone made fun of him but I wanted him to have a birthday even without us. The kids participated in preparing dad's birthday box and they loved that. We count out and eat an M&M every day to count the days so that is fun for the kids."

—Leah McDermott, author of *Hurry Home*, hurry-home.us

according to the authors of *What We Know about Army Families*. In most cases these problems happen in the very early stages of the deployment, before communications systems are set up.

♦ **Try to put together a communications schedule**. However, remind your wife that there are plenty of things that could interfere with that schedule. There may be power outages or no electricity at all, limited or nonexistent land-line or cell phone service, long lines to use computers or phones, or erratic postal service—or you could simply be out in the field. There may also be security restrictions that limit what you're allowed to talk about, or you may be on a mission and have to go dark for a while without being able to let anyone know in advance. It'll be hard, but they need to understand that a bit of silence on your end doesn't necessarily mean that anything terrible has happened to you.

♦ **Talk about the most important things first.** You never know when something will interrupt your call. Open with "I love you." Everything else is details.

♦ **Avoid making big decisions.** Steer clear of really serious conversations—especially any having to do with relationships—unless you absolutely have to. Too much room for miscommunication. Plus, if you happen to get cut off in the middle of the discussion, you'll be brooding for days.

♦ **Read e-mails and letters over a couple of times before you send them.** Make sure you're saying what you want to say. And nothing you may regret later, like closing with "You're almost as hot as Angelina Jolie."

♦ **Think security.** Don't post any information about yourself, your wife, your kids, where they live, where you're currently deployed, when you're coming back, or your mission *anywhere* on the Internet, even on your own blog or Web site. Once something gets out, you have absolutely no control over what happens to it, and you'll never get it back again. Ditto for you posing in less than full uniform, if you know what I mean.

Keeping Your Relationship Strong

DON'T FORGET ABOUT HER

Sounds obvious, but with all the attention you're paying to keep your relationship with your children strong, it's easy to forget that your marriage needs care and feeding as well. There's no reason why you can't adapt some of the activities from the "Staying Involved with Your Child" section and use them with your wife. For example, if you're making DVDs to send home, don't stop with the kids' books. Go ahead and record some poetry or a chapter of a novel you're both interested in reading. Send some love notes home (in sealed envelopes) to your children and ask them to hide them where Mommy will find them. Send her little things you think she'd be interested in. Or come up with something new, such as writing R-rated (or X-rated, if you're feeling brave) letters to her. Send presents or e-cards for holidays and special occasions—or for no reason at all. Remind her in as many ways as you can think of and as often as possible that you love her and miss her. The possibilities are endless. And think of the fun you'll have explaining them to the congressional subcommittee when you're nominated for a cabinet post in the next administration.

DON'T COMPARE AND DON'T CRITICIZE

Yes, you may be dealing with life-threatening situations every day. Meanwhile, back at home, your wife is going through some pretty intense battles too. The two experiences are apples and oranges, so any comparison is going to be unfair to one side or the other. It's easy to second-guess someone when you're not up to your ears in their world. Your wife probably has the good sense not to tell you how to do your job, so show her the same courtesy.

Mid-Deployment R&R? Hmmm

The idea of getting a paid break in the middle of a long deployment sounds great, doesn't it? You get a chance to reconnect with the family, get away from the stress you've been under, and maybe have a nice roll in the hay. Maybe. Or maybe not.

Mid-deployment R&R—especially one that doesn't count against your regular leave time—can be a welcome payback for all those long hours you've been putting in. It's a wonderful opportunity for you to see the family and how the kids have grown in person rather than through a phone or video feed. It's also great for the family to see that you're healthy and safe and to have Daddy back.

As terrific as that sounds, there are some potential disadvantages, the biggest ones having to do with upsetting your family's routines. They've just gotten used to you being gone, so adjusting to you being home again, and then having to go through another round of painful good-byes, is not easy for anyone. It can also be very confusing for young children and may dredge up those feelings of Dad-went-away-because-I-was-bad.

Seventy percent of the British army wives studied by researcher Christopher Dandeker and his colleagues felt that having Dad come home for a few days in mid-deployment was a positive experience for the children. They also said it was difficult for the children to say good-bye again. As for the wives themselves, 61 percent said they'd give up the R&R in exchange for a shorter overall deployment. But 100 percent of their husbands were glad for the chance to unwind.

SUPPORT HER

Your wife truly needs to know that you understand that life isn't easy for her right now. She also needs to know that you think she's doing a great job and that you support her 100 percent. So tell her often how much you appreciate everything she's doing.

ASK HER TO LIMIT HER MEDIA DIET

If your wife is one of those obsessive news junkies we mentioned earlier—watching TV for hours and hours every day and consuming every other kind of news story she can lay her hands on or click a mouse at—do everything you can to get her to cut back. This kind of behavior is usually an indication that your wife is highly stressed about your physical safety and is in desperate need

If you're offered a mid-deployment leave and you decide to take it, there are a few things to keep in mind.

- **Take it easy.** It's better for you and the kids to spend some quiet time rediscovering each other than to pack everyone in the car and head out for the nearest roller coaster. Besides, you want to unwind, not get your adrenal gland pumping. And don't be shy about taking an occasional nap.
- **Be understanding.** Very little children may not recognize you or might be scared of you. Everyone in the family, including you, will go through emotional mini versions of a homecoming reunion and predeployment preparations.
- **Don't make concrete plans.** Your ability to take leave will be based on the needs of your unit and can change anytime. Also, since your flights home will probably be on a space-available basis, you could be bumped. (Of course, if you've flown a commercial flight lately, you may already be used to this.)
- **Get your priorities in order.** It's tempting to spend all your time repairing leaky faucets, cleaning leaves out of the gutters, changing the oil in the car, and taking care of everything else. Don't. You came home to spend time with the family, so do it. Everything can wait till you're really back.
- **Get real.** Don't expect that you'll be able to solve all the problems that may have come up while you were gone.

of some reassurance. As guys, we often like to report how tough our living conditions are, or go through a bullet-by-bullet description of a firefight we survived. But some information is best kept to yourself. When you get back, you can share your war stories, although if you do, you're setting the stage for more obsessive behavior from your wife when the next deployment happens.

ENCOURAGE HER TO GET SOME SUPPORT

Whether you're asking for it or not, you're getting a lot of emotional and social support from the other guys in your unit. Each of you knows exactly what everyone else is going through, and sometimes just knowing you're not alone can be very reassuring. Your wife needs to find a similar support network. Fortunately, every unit has some kind of family support organization where wives

Watch Out for Scams

It never ceases to amaze me that there are always jerks out there who will try to make a buck off of other people's misfortunes. And when you're deployed, your wife may become a target. Here are a few common scams.

- Someone claiming to be from the IRS calls your wife and tells her that because you're deployed, your family is eligible for a big tax refund. All she has to do is cover the postage—with a credit card, of course. Although there probably should be, there are no special tax refunds for families of deployed service members. The IRS doesn't charge for postage, and employees never ask for credit card information, according to the National Association of Tax Professionals.
- In a variation of the one above, military families receive an e-mail about the refund, with a link to an "IRS" Web site where they're asked to provide all sorts of personal and financial information.
- Insurance agents may try to sell your wife ridiculously overpriced and unnecessary life insurance. Servicemembers Group Life Insurance (SGLI), which you get through the military, has the best deals available, so stick with that.
- Your wife gets a call from someone claiming to be from the Red Cross who tells her you've been injured and need treatment. But they need a Social Security number and other information to do the paperwork.
- Your wife receives an e-mail from a "U.S. soldier deployed in Iraq" who found a ton of gold during a raid and wants to send it home to benefit soldiers and veterans. All she has to do is pick up the fees. Note: people who have tons of gold do not generally need help with postage.
- There are work-at-home scams, which promise at-home spouses easy income. We'll just need a credit card number to cover the start-up kit...
- Your wife responds to an ad by a "soldier" who's about to be deployed and needs to sell his car quickly. It's a great deal, and for her protection she's instructed to send the money to an escrow account—which turns out to be fake.
- Your wife actually buys a car from a local dealer. A few minutes after she drives away, she gets a call telling her that the loan was

denied and that in order to keep the car, she'll need to agree to a new loan—which just happens to have terrible terms.

♦ And then there are all those check-cashing places that pop up like weeds around military bases and offer payday loans and cash advances. Borrowing money at these places is very, very expensive, with interest rates sometimes as high as 500 percent per year (meaning that if you borrow $100, you'll need $500 to pay off the loan).

♦ Oh, and that guy in Nigeria who needs to get $16 million out of the country and into your checking account? Um, no. He doesn't. And he's not in Nigeria either.

According to the Red Cross, there's an increase in scams like these around the holidays, when people need more money. They're so widespread and so successful that the U.S. Department of Justice has recently stepped in. They're concerned that the financial difficulties these rip-offs cause or aggravate may affect military readiness and stress soldiers, according to the Department of Justice.

Your wife is probably a very smart woman. But remind her that she should *never* follow instructions in an unsolicited e-mail or phone call. Don't return the calls, don't click on links or visit Web sites. As the old saying goes, if it sounds too good to be true, it probably is. If she's the least bit suspicious (which she should be if a stranger offers to enlarge any part of her or your body or wants to give you money out of the blue), she should visit one or more of these sites:

♦ The U.S. Securities and Exchange Commission's military page, sec.gov/investor/military.shtml, which offers information on legitimate investments and how to avoid scammers and identity thieves that target military families.

♦ Military Sentinel (consumer.gov/military), a project of the Federal Trade Commission and the Department of Defense. This site has lots of educational materials about scams and complaint forms that can be used to report suspicious offers.

♦ SaveAndInvest.Org (saveandinvest.org/index.htm) has information on how to avoid fraud and rip-offs as well as accurate advice on money management and other financial issues.

♦ In short, 99 percent of unknown phone calls and 110 percent of unknown e-mails are scams, although the actual number may be somewhat higher.

(or at-home husbands) can get together with others who share their experience. These groups offer everything from a safe place to vent frustrations to help with babysitting. Unfortunately, a majority of wives don't participate in Family Support Group activities. Some don't see the value or don't want to open up to strangers. Others, like the wives of Reservists, may not know the family support organization exists or may live too far off base to make it worthwhile to attend.

If your wife isn't taking advantage of her family support organization, encourage her to do so. If she's not interested, contact them yourself and ask them to reach out to her. One of the great benefits of getting together with other wives is that she'll have a chance to compare her emotions—and commiserate—with others. (Sometimes kvetching makes us stronger.) Some moms worry that what they're feeling is abnormal or wrong or a sign of weakness. Seeing that others are feeling that way will reassure her that she's not alone and not going crazy. If you're a civilian and your wife isn't getting the support she needs, encourage her to check out the *Civilians in Iraq* Yahoo! group, which she can find at groups.yahoo.com/group/civiliansinraq/ (Yes, that's the correct spelling). Your wife may also want to find some support outside the unit and far away from the base. Friendships with other military spouses may be reassuring, but she may need a break from all the deployment talk and other military stuff. Spending some time with people who *aren't* sharing her experiences and *don't* know what she's going through might be just the ticket.

Celebrating from Afar

Given that most deployments are at least four months long, there's a better-than-average chance that you're going to miss at least one significant family event. But that doesn't mean you have to miss out on all the fun. Short of being there, the best way to celebrate together is to set up a video conference or chat. Of course, with time changes, that means that one of you will be ringing in the New Year at 1200 hours instead of 2400, but that's a small price to pay. If you can't get a real-time chat going, take pictures or video of you and your buddies celebrating and send them home. Yes, your family misses you and wishes they could be there with you (or, more accurately, that you could be with them), but what they really want is to know that you're safe and having a good time.

Also, if at all possible, try to keep your family traditions alive—just modify them as needed. If, for example, you and your wife made a habit of helping others around the holidays, your family can still serve meals at a soup kitchen, and you can share some of the presents they sent you with one of the guys in your unit who has no family back home.

ENCOURAGE HER TO KEEP A POSITIVE OUTLOOK

But be very careful how you do this. Telling a woman who's overwhelmed, lonely, sad, and depressed to "cheer up" or "look at the bright side" won't go over well. It reminds me of one of my favorite cartoons. It's called "One-session psychotherapy," and the illustration is of a therapist backhanding a patient across the face while yelling, "Snap out of it!"

ENCOURAGE HER TO GET SOME TIME TO HERSELF

Downtime in our society is a hugely underrated activity. And a little goes a long way. A couple of hours off to take a yoga class or just a long walk alone could energize your wife for the rest of the week.

If She's Going to Have Your Baby While You're Away

What can I say? You want to be there, your wife wants you to be there, but Uncle Sam needs you somewhere else right now. Despite the distance, though, there are a number of things you can do to stay connected with your wife (and, later, your baby).

♦ Make sure your wife knows every possible way to contact you, just in case she needs to reach you quickly.

♦ Talk to your CO about whether you can get a few days off. The military does offer some paternity leave, but exactly how much is unclear. The good news is that it won't count against your regular thirty days' leave. The bad news is that it's trumped by the needs of the military, so there's no guarantee that you'll actually get it. However, just having made the effort shows your wife that you're committed to her and the baby and will boost your stock in her eyes.

♦ Check into whether you can set up a real-time phone or video conference for the delivery. Its not the same as being there, but in this case, close counts for a lot. It'll be tough to get the timing down, but it has happened.

♦ Read as much as you can about what's left of the pregnancy—how the baby is developing, and what your wife is going through. When you get close to the due date, start in on a book that covers childbirth and infancy. Again, you want to understand as much as you can about what's happening with your wife and baby. And don't forget to think about yourself too. You may not be able to see or hold your baby, but fatherhood is changing you too, and it's nice to know how. The more up-to-date you are on where everyone is, the easier it will be for you to plug into the routines when you get home. My books *The Expectant Father* and *The New Father: A Dad's Guide to the First Year* will walk you through everything you need to know.

♦ Send presents, love notes, jewelry. Flowers may seem like a complete waste of money, but send some anyway.

♦ Reread "Predeployment Activities for You and Your Unborn Child," on pages 92–94. If you didn't have a chance to implement those strategies, it's not too late. Just to hit the high points:

◊ Burn a CD or DVD of you reading some simple children's books. Before the birth, ask your wife to play them near her belly. Once the baby is born, she can play that same CD/DVD, plus you can record new stories, songs, poems, or whatever. This will help the baby recognize you—well, your voice anyway—when you come. If you need help getting any of this set up, check out United Through Reading (unitedthroughreading.org).

◊ Ask your wife to put up lots of pictures of you and to talk to the baby about you.

◊ Send home a T-shirt you've worn. Babies learn a lot about their world through smell, and getting a whiff of you (within reason) may help her recognize you. You may want to do this again right before you come home. (Send one for the dog, too. Your cat couldn't care less.)

♦ Ask your wife to send things to keep you in the loop. Before the birth, this could be an ultrasound picture or a recording of your baby's heartbeat. After the baby comes, photos, worn outfits, and a full-length cutout of the baby are nice. If someone videotaped the birth, she may want to send that along too. But think about whether you really want to see you wife in incredible pain that you can't do anything to stop.

♦ Send more presents, flowers, and a gift certificate for a spa day. Poetry, even bad poetry, is appreciated.

♦ Ask a friend to take the childbirth class with your wife if she hasn't already lined someone else up.

♦ Ask friends to help. And make sure they understand what you mean. Most people define help as holding the baby for a few minutes, cooing, then giving him back. Your definition of help should include laundry, shopping, meal preparation, or reroofing the garage.

Anticipation of Homecoming
ANOTHER ASSIGNMENT
In the previous chapter we talked about "interviewing" yourself. Now let's turn things around and interview your family. Ask them some of the same questions

you asked yourself: What do they enjoy doing? How have they changed? What have they been struggling with while you were gone? How do they think that could be resolved when you return? How do they spend their leisure time? Who are their friends now? What do they do with their friends? What foods do they like to eat now? Any new family members I should be aware of? In the same way that understanding yourself will help you prepare your family for your return, understanding *them* will help you prepare yourself for the situation you'll be walking into. Far too many returning service members skip this important step and have to learn all these things the hard way. These interviews don't have to be formal; you can gather the facts a few at a time in casual conversation. But however you do it, just get it done. You'll be doing your family and yourself a huge favor.

MANAGE EVERYONE'S EXPECTATIONS

Now that you've gone through the self-interview and have a good handle on how you've changed, it's time to communicate that to your family. You could come out swinging with something like, "I just want you to know that I've become a vegan, I only drink water now, I like to spend at least two hours every night watching movies and two more at the gym, and I'll be hitting the sack at precisely 2000 hours. Oh, and I won't stand for any whining." Or you might try something with a higher likelihood of success, like, "Life over here is a lot different than it was at home, and I've had to adapt to some new routines. There wasn't much else to do with our free time but watch movies, and I kind of got in the habit of watching one a night. The food over here was so lousy that I gave up eating any kind of meat. I think I'll be able to shake some of these habits when I get home, but it may take me a little while. You've changed a lot too, so let's agree to give ourselves plenty of time to get used to each other again. Things might be a little rocky at first, and they might never get back to exactly the way they were before. But I know if we work at it, we'll come up with a whole new way to be together as a family."

GET READY TO CELEBRATE

You know your family will be excited to see you, and you know they're planning some kind of welcome-home event. The big question is, Who's the celebration for, you or them? On one hand, it's obviously you—after all, you're the one who's been gone. On the other hand, it's your family—they're not only happy for you, they're happy for themselves too. Given all that, let them know your preferences, but try to come up with something that allows everyone to truly enjoy the occasion. That might mean a small, family-only party the day you get back, and something bigger for the rest of the world sometime after you've had chance to rest up, do some laundry, and take a few dozen showers all by yourself—something you may not have done for a very long time.

EXPLAIN

Getting notice that your deployment has been extended is a real game changer. You and your wife probably made all sorts of plans for things you were going to do when you got back. You may be able to put some things off, but some many need to be canceled. Your wife, understandably, will be disappointed—more about not having you back when she was expecting you than because of the changed plans. Aside from reassuring her that you're disappointed too and that you'll be back as soon as you can, there's not much you can do. So focus on the future. Make new plans, but this time allow for contingencies.

Staying Involved with Your Child(ren)

A lot of service members I've spoken with say that the toughest part of being away from their kids was all the changes and "firsts" they missed—things like a baby's first step, a first lost tooth, the first school play, the first base hit, the first violin recital, the first TD pass, first missed curfew, first speeding ticket, and so on. Unfortunately, there's no substitute for being there, and there's no way to make up for all those lost hugs, kisses, and playtime. However, staying in regular contact with the kids is a close second. Reread "Communication Ground Rules," on pages 158–59. Here are a few more important things to keep in mind when communicating with your kids.

PLAN AHEAD

The goal of any kind of communication—whether it's by e-mail, phone, video, or regular mail—is to connect. And the easiest way to connect is to find common ground. So after you've been through the obligatory "How're you doing?" "Fine" "How's school?" "Good" part of the conversation, spend a little time talking about something you and your child both care about. Could be music, art, a favorite sports team, weather, venomous snakes, or anything else. (Yes, you are expected to make conversation about video games, 5th grade dances, and playing Barbies. It's all part of being a Dad.)

Another thing you and your child have in common is that you both take pride in the child's accomplishments. Hopefully, you brought a calendar with you and you've got the dates of big events in your kid's lives—recitals, performances, games, graduations, and so on. If not, ask your wife to let you know as far in advance as possible when something big is coming up so you can be sure to bring it up at the appropriate time.

It's also nice to keep a mental (or written) list of other things to talk about with the kids. Try to keep it light—ask about life in general, friends, who's learned to ride a bike, what's on sale at Home Depot. If your family has a pet, ask about it too. Sometimes talking about the most mundane stuff can make you feel closer and more connected. Plus, keeping up-to-date on the little things that are happening will reduce the shock when you get home to a bunch of people who have changed.

REMIND THEM THAT YOU'RE ALWAYS THINKING OF THEM

A number of studies have shown that children whose dads are deployed have genuine concerns about whether Dad still loves them while he's gone and whether he'll love them when he comes back. Kids, especially young ones, need plenty of confirmation. Being in frequent contact, giving them a way to contact you if they want to, and not being skimpy with the I-love-yous and I-miss-yous will help a lot. (Scientific studies—and plain, old common sense—show that wives appreciate these phrases used frequently as well.)

CREATE A SCHEDULE

You already did this with your wife, but you should also talk with your child about how often and in what ways you'll be able to be in touch. Given your physical location and your mission, does every day work? Every other day? Once a week? Will you call? E-mail? Video chat? Mail? Whatever you do, don't make promises you won't be able to keep. (Kids may take two months to learn how to tie their shoes, but they never forget promises, and they ain't gonna fall for "I meant *next* Tuesday."

Remind your child that although you'll try to be in contact as often as possible, that may not always be possible. If she's waiting to hear from you and the call or e-mail never shows up, you're going to have one worried kid on your hands. Also, remind her that your not responding to an e-mail or being out of touch for a few days is *not* an indication that you don't care about her.

CORRESPOND DIRECTLY WITH YOUR CHILD

Asking your wife to kiss the kids for you or to tell them you love them isn't good enough (unless there's no alternative). When your child receives e-mail or packages addressed to her, you're reinforcing the all-important idea that you're thinking of her.

WATCH WHAT YOU SAY

Your kids (and wife too) want to know you're safe. They may ask what you're doing, but you do *not* have to go into a lot of detail. And you *shouldn't* if it involves near-misses or extreme danger—even if you came through the experience okay. With you so far away, your kids will feel completely helpless. Instead of reassuring them, your war stories will only frighten them and make them worry about you even more. So skip the descriptions of the dangerous patrols you were on and keep your answers short and casual. Tell them about the new CD you heard, what you had for dinner last night, how hard it is to sleep when monkeys (yes, real ones) are chattering and screeching all night, and how much sand you dumped out of your boots. This might help them get some of those frightening TV images of soldiers in combat out of their head.

HAVE THEM WATCH WHAT THEY SAY

Yes, you want to keep up with what's going on with your child, but some things are better left unsaid. For example, telling you about a serious problem that you can't do anything about could distract you from your mission. And that's not good for you or anyone around you.

LET THEM KNOW IT'S OKAY TO BE WORRIED

Whether they admit it or not, your kids are afraid for you, and it's important that they feel safe talking to you about it. Unfortunately, a lot of dads don't make that very easy. How many times, when you were home, did your child tell you he was scared to go upstairs by himself in the dark, only to have you say something like "There's nothing to be afraid of," or "Don't be silly." You meant well—we all do—but what your child has heard is that his fears, which are very real to him, are something to be ashamed of. So next time he won't tell you. He's not any less scared, just less talkative. Understand that for a lot of kids, worries about your safety are really worries about theirs. So encourage them to talk to you, and then reassure them that (a) you're okay and (b) Mom will do everything she can to keep them safe at home.

PRAISE THEM

Even though you're not there, your kids will still be trying to earn your approval. So tell them how proud you are of what they're doing—whether it's getting straight As or just raising some Cs to Bs; hitting the game-winning home run or simply making it through the season; helping Mom by making dinner once a week or taking out the trash more often. Never assume they know what you're thinking, so be specific with your praise and tell them often.

BE UNDERSTANDING

There may be times when your young child (say under seven) will refuse to come to the phone (or the webcam) when you've called, or she wants to get off after a mumbled "hi." It's hard not to take that personally, especially because it *is* personal—or at least it feels that way to you. But understand that kids sometimes pick odd—and hurtful—ways of expressing their feelings. Chances are your child really does want to talk with you, but she may be trying to punish you for not being there. Or she doesn't want you to hear the sadness in her voice (or see it on her face). Or she may simply not understand how a big guy like you got into a little phone. When this kind of thing happens, do *not* try to force your child to talk. It's reasonable to expect a civil "Hi Daddy," but punishing your child or trying to make her feel guilty about not wanting to chat will make the problem worse. Most importantly, don't "retaliate" by refusing to talk to your child when she finally decides to say a few words. She needs to know that you love her, regardless of how communicative she is. So whether you get an answer or not, keep on calling, asking questions, telling jokes, singing songs, and doing animal impressions. Eventually, she'll come around.

Fun Ways to Stay in Touch with Your Child

Not all of these activities are appropriate for every age, nor is it a comprehensive list. So feel free to modify them so they work for your child. If you've got suggestions for other creative ways to stay in touch, please send them to armin@mrdad.com.

♦ **Go low-tech.** Technology is great, as far as it goes, but it's no substitute for a good, old-fashioned package from Dad. Little things like a dried leaf from a tree near your barracks, a film canister full of sand, or a menu from a local restaurant are great ways to let your child know that you're thinking of her no matter where you are. They also give her a tangible sense that you're somewhere, in a real place. This is particularly important for younger children. It also gives your child an object she can pull out and

Staying Involved in Your Children's Education from a Distance

Children whose dads take an active interest in their education do better in school, enjoy it more, get involved in more extracurricular activities, and are more likely to graduate from high school and go on to college. But how do you get or stay involved from afar?

♦ Be aware that your child's academic performance might slip during your deployment. Whenever possible, communicate with your child about homework, projects, and grades. If you can get your schedules lined up, you may be able to set up a regular time when you can help your child with assignments. Some schools have Web sites where they post kids' assignments, progress reports, and grades. Ask the school for the log-in info.

♦ Keep your child's teachers in the loop. If they don't know about the deployment already, it's important that they do. It will help them better make sense of any behavioral or performance problems.

♦ Keep in touch. Ask the teachers to e-mail you with any concerns, and feel free to e-mail them with any questions.

♦ Send interesting things to the school—locally made trinkets for all the kids in the class, some information on the language and culture where you are, and maybe even a flag that flew over your camp. Your child will be unbelievably proud of you. Avoid sending any live scorpions or monkeys, though, despite what your kid thinks would be cool for show-and-tell. *Frass,* however, is acceptable.

♦ Depending on your child's age, you might also ask that the class adopt some of the single guys in your unit. You've probably been hearing from your wife and kids fairly regularly. But guys without families can get very, very lonely, and most will be grateful and touched to receive letters or packages from your child's classmates.

hold whenever she wants to feel close to you. If you aren't able to send home a Humvee, a set of dog tags will be a huge hit. Kids love 'em.

♦ **Go high-tech.** If you've got access to video conferencing, one of the nicest things you can do is read to your children. If you and your child have the same book, you get to see each other, laugh with each other, turn the pages at the same time. Everything but the good-night kiss. If you can't do video, visit United Through Reading (unitedthroughreading.org), a wonderful nonprofit that helps you make DVDs or videotapes of you reading out loud and sends the recordings home to your child.

- **Sing.** Do a rousing duet (or trio or quartet) of a favorite song on your next phone call or video conference.

- **Remember**. Ask your child to send you a memento from an activity she's doing—a recital program, photos or videos of sports events, and so on. Art projects are always good and easy to mail. Although it might be tough to find a refrigerator to post them on....

- **Draw.** Your kids will love to receive your drawings—even if you're not too thrilled with the quality.

- **Be a tour guide.** Use a video or still camera to give a virtual walk-through of where you are. Just make sure it's all G-rated, no gore, no violence, and nothing that could be upsetting. Seeing mess halls, showers, your bunk, guys washing trucks, and other mundane things will help reassure your child that you're safe. If possible, include some shots of you holding something that your child sent to you. Again, that reminds them that they're always with you.

- **Get creative.** Write "I love you" in pebbles, cookies from home, etched in sand, or drawn into the dirt on a filthy vehicle windshield. Then take pictures and send 'em home.

- **Play.** If you've got Internet access, there are all sorts of sites where you and your kids can log on and play chess, solve Sudoku puzzles, play video games, or even take an online class together. If you don't have Internet access, check out Kids Across Parents Down (kapd.com), which has several books of crossword puzzles designed to be done just like the name says.

- **Snip.** Write a letter, then cut it up into puzzle pieces so your child will have to piece it back together. For younger kids, you could cut up a photo. For infants, a one-piece puzzle will have to do.

- **Collaborate.** Make up a story together. You come up with the opening, then send it to the kids to add a paragraph or two of their own. They send it back and you add to what they did. You'll come up with some stuff.

- **Teach...and learn.** You're probably learning all sorts of really cool stuff, so share some of it with your children. And have them do the same for you. Believe me, you can learn something from kids of any age. Do you know what caterpillar poop is called? I had no idea until my four-year-old daughter started telling me what she'd learned in preschool. It's *frass*, by the way. I also had no idea that lady bugs came out of cocoons.

- **Surprise.** Send home a bunch of little notes and ask your wife to hide them around the house for the kids to find. Post-it notes are fun because you can stick them in all sorts of unusual places, like ceilings, dog collars, and inside lunchboxes.
- **Use telepathy.** Agree on a certain time of day when you'll stop what you're doing and think good thoughts about each other.
- **Visualize.** Carrying your kids' pictures in your pocket or tucked inside your helmet can help you feel connected to them. Update the pictures often so you can keep up with how they're changing. Talking about the kids with your buddies—preferably guys who also have kids—is another way to keep the images of your children fresh in each other's mind. (Of course, *you* have the brightest, cutest, most developmentally advanced kids in your whole unit—but listen to the other guys' stories anyway.)
- **Explain.** If your deployment gets extended, try to be the one to tell the kids. If that's not possible and your wife has to break the bad news, at least make time to talk with them yourself. Young children may think that you're not coming because of something they've done (this feeling will be aggravated if your child has been doing a lot of misbehaving lately, or your wife has made the mistake of telling her to "wait till your father comes home"). You need to reassure them—probably more than once—that the extension has absolutely nothing to do with them and that you're going to do everything you can to get back home as soon as possible. Explain that plans sometimes have to change.
- **Plan.** If the extension screwed up plans you'd made to do things or go places with the kids, go ahead and make new ones—it'll give them something happy to look forward to. Just don't be too specific about dates.
- **Keep your wife happy**. Yes, I know we're supposed to be talking about the kids. But as we've discussed throughout the book, Mom's well-being has a huge impact on your children. If she's depressed, they may be too. If she's feeling good, they will too. Supporting Mom every way you can is a great indirect method of supporting your children. (You might want to revisit the previous section, "Staying Involved with Your Wife." Oh, and don't forget the flowers.)
- **Ask a friend to fill in once in a while.** Your kids probably miss playing with you—whether it's throwing a baseball, watching TV, coloring, wrestling, or just being silly. Sure, Mom tries to step in, but a lot of kids really crave some guy interaction. Asking a male friend or relative to drop by and get the kids overexcited is a great gift to give to your kids. It may

sting a little to know that someone else is playing with your child, but you can take some comfort in knowing that no one could possibly replace you in your children's eyes. So what if he teaches them to ride a unicycle or change a transmission? He's just filling a gap while you're gone. Hopefully you'll have a chance one day to do the same for some other service member's kids.

6.

Enough about You

73 Ways Your Wife Can Help You and Your Kids Stay Connected

As you can imagine, keeping a family together during deployment isn't a very easy thing to do. Throughout this book we've given the deployed parent a lot of valuable information, tools, and strategies that will help him maintain close relationships with you and with your children. However, given the distance that separates him from the rest of the family, no matter how hard he tries, there's no way he can do it all himself. This is where you come in. (And by the way, thanks.)

Because you're with your children every day, you have a very powerful influence over the kind of relationship they'll have with their deployed parent—the more supportive and encouraging you are, the closer and stronger it will be. But helping your kids and their Dad stay connected isn't something you do only for them—there's plenty in it for you, too.

When the kids feel confident that Dad still loves them and that they're an important part of his life, there will be less for them to get upset, angry, or depressed about (and that's certainly a bonus for everyone). That may translate into less acting out and fewer discipline problems for you to deal with, which will make your life a lot easier. And when Dad feels that he's still an important part of the family and is up-to-date on what's been going on in his children's life, he'll be much better prepared to step into a family that's changed a lot over the months he's been gone. The emotional and psychological transition from deployment to home will go much more smoothly, and you'll be back together as a family more quickly.

In the pages that follow, you'll find seventy-three things that you can do to keep those father-child relationships as strong as possible. This is by no means a comprehensive list—feel free to add others and to adapt these suggestions to the age of your child.

Start with Yourself

We referred earlier to the flight attendant school of parenting. You know what they say: When the oxygen masks drop down, put yours on first before you help your child, right? Same goes for relationships. If you're not feeling particularly close to your spouse or your kids, it's going to be hard for you to really get behind helping them strengthen their own relationships. Putting ourselves first seems to run contrary to everything we think we know about parenting—good parents always put their children first, don't they? Maybe, but it's not always in everyone's best interests.

1. Take a close look at the "Staying Involved" sections in each chapter of this book. There are lots of field-tested strategies and suggestions that may help you strengthen and maintain your relationship with your spouse. Just reverse the genders where necessary.

2. Get some R&R of your own. Hire a sitter, call in favors, work out some kind of swap with another overworked parent—whatever you need to do to get yourself some time off, do it. You may feel a little guilty at first, but you'll get over it. And you might even get used to it. Remember way back when you and your hubby had a whole night to yourselves?

3. Have fun with the kids. Your life together may be a lot more hectic and stressful without Dad around, but many moms report that being forced to spend more time working together toward a common cause improved their relationships with their children. Besides, being silly and running around like a loon can be a good stress reliever for you too.

4. Get help when you need it—and even when you don't. The military has a surprising number of organizations whose mission is to help deployed service members and their families. They offer social, legal, spiritual, financial, and practical help. You may not think you need it, but do yourself a favor and look up the numbers. Also, take a look through the Resources section in the back of this book.

They're Waaaaatching...

5. Be a good role model. You may be feeling depressed, stressed out, angry, sad, and overwhelmed—and that's perfectly natural right now. However, while your spouse is deployed, it's very important that you model good, healthy coping skills for your children. The younger they are, the more they'll be taking their cues from you on how to behave. Allowing them to see that you're sad can be a good thing—it lets them know that it's okay to be sad. However, if you become so depressed or angry that you're not able to effectively care for your children's needs, they'll behave in pretty much the same way you do. Fortunately, help is available if you need it. So start by contacting the family support organization attached to your husband's unit.

Journaling

6. Having your kids keep a scrapbook or journal can help them better understand, express, and cope with their feelings about Dad being deployed. The format isn't all that important: it could be a simple notebook with blank pages, a fancier journal, or even just an empty box. Whatever it is, let your children decorate it any way they want and fill it with movie tickets, restaurant menus, photographs, drawings, thoughts, notes, recital programs, award certificates, and other souvenirs and mementos of things they did or places they went during the deployment. If the kids are up for it, add a multimedia component— give them a disposable camera or a cheap digital and let them take pictures of their day or make a photo journal of a fun weekend. The idea is that by recording things that happen in their daily life, they'll create something concrete they can show Dad when he comes home.

7. Ask your husband to keep a similar journal—complete with dried scorpions—so he'll be able to share his experiences with the kids.

Chronicle Their Growth

8. If your child will be born while your husband is away, send ultrasound pictures of the baby and/or mp3s of the baby's heartbeat.

9. For infants, take a picture every couple of days of the baby propped up in the same place, then send the series. You and your husband will both be amazed at how quickly babies change.

10. You can do the same thing for older kids, but you won't notice much change from shot to shot. Instead, mark their height on a wall and send photos of the wall.

11. Take an ongoing video or photo series of your baby doing all sorts of things—cooing, giggling, spitting up, taking a bath, rolling over, crawling, standing up, cruising, and more.

12. As your child gets older, keep those videos and pictures coming and include tooth brushing, playing with dolls, building towers out of blocks, sleeping, counting to ten, saying "I love you" to Dad, listening to some of the recordings Dad made, learning to ride a trike or bike, balancing a broom on his nose, and, if you have a teenager, learning to drive (make sure you're wearing your seat belt). Dads find everyday boring stuff like this remarkably charming.

13. Make occasional ink prints of your child's hands and feet. You can send them by snail mail or scan them and e-mail. But don't get so caught up in sending the prints that you let Junior walk on the new carpet with "ink feet."

14. Compile a list of your child's current favorites—toys, clothes, colors, foods, bedtime stories, and so on—and see how that list changes over time. Or not. Thomas is timeless, but Bob the Builder and Polly Pocket are soooo last week, Mom.

Mark Time

Kids under about six have only an abstract sense of time, and a month may seem like forever. That's why it's nice to have a visual way of tracking time—not only how many days have gone by since Dad shipped out, but how many are left until he comes home. We talk about many ways to do this in "Predeployment Activities for You and Your Three-to-Seven-Year-Old" on pages 96–102. In case you weren't able to get a few of them set up before the deployment, here are a few good ones to get you started:

"It really helps him deal with the deployment,...besides..., It's just a wall"

15. Mark an X on a calendar for each passing day. Instead of crossing off each day, older kids may want to write down a sentence or two about something that happened (caught a snake in the bathtub). Those short entries can be great conversation starters when Dad comes back. (You caught a what? In the where?)

16. Tear a page off the calendar for each day (or week or month). Get a book on origami and make a balloon or crane or some other figure out of each page.

17. Fill a jar with as many items as days Dad is expected to be gone—could be M&Ms, beans, coins, or anything else that won't spoil. (But do this only if you're really, really sure that the deployment won't be extended—not all kids will be fooled by adding items to the jar). A glass or clear plastic container is best because the kids can see how the level gets lower and lower over time. Take one object out of the jar every day. If you're using something edible, your child can enjoy a little treat. If you're using coins, collect the ones you take out for a few days or a week and let your child buy something as a reward.

18. Paper chains. There are two ways to do this. The first is to make a loop for each day of the deployment and tear one off before bed every night. The other

is to make a new loop every day and use the chains you make to decorate the house when Dad comes back.

Facilitate Communication

19. Read "Exploring Your Options" on pages 146–51 and do your own research.

20. If you know how, set up a family blog where you, the kids, and your deployed spouse can post notes, video, audio, etc. If you don't know how, ask your friendly neighborhood teenager.

21. Make sure the kids are there for regularly scheduled calls or video chats.

22. If the kids are too young to do their own corresponding, have them add their own notes to the end of yours. Even a nearly illegible "I Love You" written in three-year-old scrawl will be much appreciated. As will a jelly smudge from your infant.

Make Dad a Presence in the Kids' Life...

With Dad not there, it can sometimes be hard for young kids to keep an image of him in their head. Here's how to ensure that Dad stays top of mind:

23. While you're still pregnant, be sure to play those recordings of stories, songs, or poems Dad made before he left. If he didn't make any, it's not too late. He can burn some audio or video now, wherever he is, and send them to you.

24. After the baby comes, keep playing the CDs or DVDs he made before he left, or new ones.

25. Ask your husband to send home a T-shirt he's worn. Then put it in the crib (no, don't wash it first) with the baby. By exposing the baby to Dad's scent, you may be making Dad a little bit less of a stranger when he comes home. Do not, however, reciprocate. It might be kind of hard for him to explain to the sergeant why he has a lovely set of frilly lingerie in his footlocker.

26. Make a "Dad wall," which over time gets completely covered with photos, drawings, and other reminders of Dad.

27. Talk about Dad whenever you can. Play his favorite CDs, eat his favorite foods, and so on.

28. Track where Dad is on a large map or globe.

29. Get two clocks, and set one to your local time, the other to Dad's time. Schedule a minute or two every day when the kids will stop what they're doing and imagine what Dad is doing right then. Ask Dad to do the same on his end. This will also help kids figure out the concept of time zones—or how it can be "now" in two places at the same time, just twelve hours apart.

30. Have the kids put together a list of questions to ask Dad next time he calls, and have them answer Dad's questions too (see #40 below).

31. Encourage the kids to ask Dad for help with homework, a school project, or writing essays, or even discuss college selection with him.

32. Have the kids pick out a birthday, Father's or Mother's Day, card or gift for Dad or Mom.

33. Make sure the deployed parent has a calendar of important events— school plays, recitals, sport games, graduations, and so on. If you set this up using Google or Yahoo Calendar (calendar.google.com or calendar.yahoo.com), Dad can receive e-mail reminders far enough in advance that he'll be able to make a special call or send an electronic card.

34. Interview your children and send Dad a CD or transcript.

35. Make sure the children understand that even though the deployed parent wants to be in touch as often as possible, certain things, such as technology glitches, lack of cell reception or Internet service, time differences, and mission security, may interfere. They (and you) shouldn't take an unexpected silence as an indication that something bad has happened.

...And Make the Kids a Presence in Dad's

36. Send Dad audio or video of a few seconds of the baby's babbling (it's good to do this during a rousing game of peek-a-boo or some other activity that makes the baby laugh hysterically). If Dad makes the sound his new ring tone, imagine the commotion it'll cause next time you call.

37. Send Dad an outfit that the baby has worn.

38. Take a set of pictures of all the baby's facial expressions and of daily activities like taking a bath, crawling, standing up, rolling over, and so on.

39. Send video or photos of the kids' sports events, birthdays, games, recitals, plays, performances, or graduations, or simply of the family having fun. Other mementos of your daily life, like theater programs, restaurant menus, and parking tickets are great too.

40. Make sure Dad answers the kids' questions (from #30 above) and asks some of his own.

41. Put lipstick on a child (mostly likely a girl, although plenty of boys this age love to dress up) and have her (or him) send a kiss to Dad.

42. Send other kinds of tangible reminders, like a lock of hair from a first haircut or a piece of candy from Halloween trick-or-treating.

43. Have the kids correspond regularly via mail, e-mail, CDs, or DVDs.

44. Have the kids send drawings, report cards, artwork, term papers, science fair projects, and so on.

45. Encourage the kids to talk when Dad calls. As we discussed in "Staying Involved with Your Children" on page 172, it's not uncommon for young children to refuse to talk when Dad (or Mom) calls. Insisting that they say "Hi Daddy" is fine—even the youngest kids can learn basic manners. And if the kids are older than about seven or eight, it's okay to let them know how important it is to Dad to hear their voice and how hurt he may be when he doesn't. But don't punish them for not communicating. Eventually, they'll get over it. At the same time discourage the kids from telling Dad about problems at home that he can't do anything about.

46. Trace an outline of each child's body on butcher paper and send it to Dad.

47. Encourage Dad and the kids to start a book group, where they read the same book at the same time and discuss. Now there's an image: your warrior asking for a copy of *Elmo's Very Happy Day* at the base bookstore...

48. Have the kids give Dad regular movie or concert reviews or a summary of how his favorite sports teams are doing.

49. Have Dad and the kids do something together online. Play a video or computer game, take a class, manage a fantasy sports team, and so on.

50. Have the kids do a magic show, talent show, or even just read Dad a story. Send Dad a DVD or post the video.

51. Have the kids burn Dad a special mix CD of their favorite songs.

Keep Dad a Part of the Family

52. Read Dad's letters or e-mail at the dinner table. If there isn't an actual piece of correspondence, just talk about him.

53. Have a meal together. If Dad is on a base somewhere, he may have a regular chow menu. If so, you may be able to make the same meals on the same days: Mac-n-cheese Monday, Turkey Tuesday, Frankfurter Friday, Sushi Sunday... Having the same thing each night of the week makes meal planning easier. Just don't overdo it. No matter how well you market it, Broccoli Thursday is never going to be a big hit.

54. Make a cardboard cutout of Dad and take it with you on family outings. Take pictures of the family with the picture and send them to Dad.

55. Ask the kids to draw family portraits.

56. Create a running story. One person writes the beginning, then passes it on to the next person, who adds a couple of paragraphs and does the next handoff.

57. Send care packages. Cookies or some other favorite treat are always welcome. So are other things that may be in short supply, like soap, reading material, bug spray, sunblock, movies, and gum. With the edible care packages, remember to send enough for everyone. Besides being fun to get, care packages can be fun to make too. If one of the kids has a suggestion for something silly to include, go ahead and send it. Everyone needs a Slinky...

Limit Media

58. It's best to keep young children far, far away from media—especially television— coverage of war. And steer clear of any movies that deal with war or fighting. Little kids simply can't tell the difference between the war Daddy may be involved in and the one those other guys on the screen are. It doesn't matter whether your spouse is on the front lines, in a purely administrative post, or even in the same country they're showing on the news. In children's minds Daddy is a soldier, soldiers fight wars, and if soldiers are being killed somewhere, Daddy will be killed too. It's frightening as hell.

Generally speaking, it's never a good idea to lie to your child. However, it's important to reassure your child that his deployed parent is safe and will be back soon. No, there's no way to guarantee that, but telling the "truth" that Dad is in danger every day and in fact may *not* make it back will make your child even more frightened than he already is and could leave long-term scars.

As kids get older, it'll be harder and harder to monitor their media exposure—you never know what they're going to be watching at a friend's house. So if your child, starting at about age six or seven, seems interested in the news and war coverage, sit down and watch it with him. That way you get to encourage questions and give explanations of what's being shown instead of leaving it up to your child's imagination.

Routines

Children are creatures of habit, and they take comfort in routines. When some-thing changes in a big way—oh, say, a parent gets deployed and goes away for six months—it's a sign that something has gone very, very wrong with the world. That alone can be traumatic enough. If other things change in their life too, like house rules, extracurricular activities, and so on, they may blame Dad (those things wouldn't have changed if he hadn't gone away, right?). And at this point in their lives, the last thing your children need is another reason to be angry or depressed. Overall, kids tend to fare better when their parents offer as consistent an environment as possible, according to Frederic Medway, a professor at the University of South Carolina and an expert on separation issues. Their life has been turned upside down enough; what they need right now is as much stability as they can get. This is one reason why bedtimes, lim-its, and rules are important. The other is your sanity.

59. Whenever possible, keep bedtimes, chores, allowances, violin practice, homework, family game night, and everything else on the same schedule. I know this may not always be easy—you're already working double duty— but try.

60. Maintain discipline. Your child needs to know that even though Dad isn't here, the house rules and the consequence for breaking them are still the same as they always were. Sometimes moms let kids get away with more than when

Dad is there. This isn't a criticism: you're exhausted and may not have the stomach or the stamina for one more big fight, or you may be trying to cut your kids some slack because they're going through a tough time with Dad being gone. Makes sense, but try to give in a little less. Your kids really do need those boundaries.

61. Never, ever tell the children, "Wait till your father comes home." It sets Dad up as someone to be feared and will make it much harder for him to reconnect with the kids when his plane touches down or his ship docks.

62. Make sure you're on time for the carpool. Pickups after school and other activities can be a difficult time for some kids. They're already feeling a little abandoned by Dad, and if you're even a few minutes late picking up little Johnny, he might start worrying that *you've* left him too.

63. Establish new routines. Sounds like a complete contradiction to what I've just been saying, but hey, you've got to be flexible. What you want to do is create some new rituals for the new Dad-isn't-physically-here family unit. Maybe that means reading one of Dad's letters every night at dinner, taking a candy out of the counting jar, or something else. Or maybe you decide that you'll have dinner out as a family every Thursday night.

64. Celebrate. When it comes to the holidays—whichever ones you observe—try to keep your family's traditions alive. Or, if you need to, start some new ones. If, for example, you usually spend the holidays with family, this might be the time to make an exception. Even if you've avoided hanging out with other military families, it can be awfully nice to have people around you who know what you're going through.

Roles and Responsibilities

65. Give the kids some age-appropriate additional responsibilities. Having an extra chore, particularly one that Dad did, can make the kids feel closer to Dad and is a good way to build independence, maturity, and self-confidence.

66. However, be patient. Your child may need to learn a new skill or get some training in order to do the job. This is *not* the time to give your five-year-old the leaf blower.

67. Don't go overboard. Yes, everyone in the family is having to adapt to Dad being gone, and this will involve pitching in more around the house. But don't give them so many new responsibilities that they become a source of stress.

They'll resent you for dumping so much on them, and they'll resent Dad for creating the situation.

68. Don't lean on them too much. If you have teens or particularly mature tweens, it's tempting to confide in them, to be, perhaps a little too honest about the way you're feeling, your frustrations, your anger, your sadness. Remember, your kids are kids. You're supposed to be parenting them, not the other way round.

Help Them Cope

69. Give them a way to vent their frustrations. For some kids, kicking a ball, punching a bag or pillow, jumping on a trampoline, or some other physical activity can help relieve some of their pent-up frustrations and anger. (You might benefit from a kickboxing class, a power walk, or test-driving a Ferrari.) Other kids may need to spend a couple hours playing video games, IM-ing, talking on the phone with friends, or texting others. If you've got a teenager, it may be all of those things at the same time. Really.

70. If your children don't already have a pet, this may be the time to get one (assuming they're mature and responsible enough to care for it). Having something cuddly and alive to love and pay attention to can be therapeutic for people who are craving some love and attention of their own. Hamsters are a good choice. Pythons less so—unless the kids are tired of the hamster...

71. Encourage your kids to spend some time with other military kids. Children of deployed service members—especially Reservists, who tend to live much farther away from military bases—often feel isolated, as if no one understands what they're going through. Having a friend who's experiencing the same thing at the same time can really help kids adjust to the deployment.

72. Encourage them to focus on what they have and not so much on what they don't have. From October through December, the Marine Corps Reserve runs the Toys for Tots program (toysfortots.org), which collects toys and distributes them to needy children in your community. Consider making a donation and having your children join you.

73. Investigate options for fun. There are all sorts of camps and special programs designed for military kids. The Military Family Outdoor Initiative (MFOI) has a joint program with the Sierra Club that gets kids out in nature. Same goes for the National Military Family Association's Operation Purple Camp. These programs are designed to give kids some skills to help them better cope with a parent's deployment. They can also be a great learning experience: the American Institute of Research has found that children "gain self-esteem and personal responsibility" from outdoor experiences. Other research indicates that students' science test scores improve after a week-long outdoor experience. There may be something about sleeping on the ground, all that fresh air, and plenty of bugs that sparks the imagination.

PART III

Post-deployment

Okay, So Now What Do We Do?

"Honey, I'm home."

7.

Who Are These People and What Are They Doing in My House?

The Emotional Side of Being Back Home

If you thought your deployment ended the day your feet hit the ground back in the old U.S. of A., think again. In fact, coming home—and starting the process of rejoining and reintegrating into your family—is just the beginning of one of the hardest phases of the deployment. Just as a reminder, this phase is divided into two basic stages: *the honeymoon*, and *reintegration*. (What? Your recruiter didn't mention this?)

What's Going On with You

The Honeymoon Begins...and Ends
Your first few days at home will be glorious, filled with hugs, kisses, and catching each other up on life. There'll be welcome-home parties and maybe

even a romantic weekend getaway for you and your wife, where you and she can tentatively rediscover sex. It's no wonder it's called the honeymoon phase. Plus, you have the added bonus of not having to write wedding present thank-you notes.

But while the honeymoon is definitely a physical reunion, it may not be an emotional one. Either way, all honeymoons come to an end. When, exactly, that happens isn't easy to pinpoint. Generally speaking, it's when the excitement, novelty, and charged emotions have worn off. But that means different things to different people. You might, for example, feel that the honeymoon is over a week or more before your wife or kids do (or vice versa). The honeymoon phase is typically shorter after long deployments and longer after short ones. Other factors that get in the way of long, leisurely honeymoons include physical and/or psychological injuries, being in a relatively new marriage, a wife who didn't get much social support while you were gone, and preparing for a new deployment before you've even unpacked from the last one.

Great Expectations—and the Not-So-Great Letdown

The most challenging—and most important—aspect of the honeymoon period is keeping your expectations reasonable. In fact, there's no better way to shorten a honeymoon than to imagine a trouble-free reunion, full of nothing but smiles, hugs, and joy. The problem is that honeymoons are kind of like a sugar high. You'll have plenty of energy for a while, and then you crash. When it comes to the honeymoon, the severity of the crash is usually a function of the difference between your expectations (fantasies) and reality. The more unrealistic the fantasy, the bigger the disappointment when reality takes over.

You've probably seen how this dynamic plays out in other areas of your life. Take the holiday blues. Families enjoy weeks of happiness, celebration, giving, receiving, and all-around good cheer. Then, all of a sudden, it's over. The weather turns gloomy, the credit card bills start showing up, and it's time to go back to work.

For most military families, the post-honeymoon reality can be quite jarring. Facing the fact that the reunion and honeymoon weren't what you imagined they would be is tough. So is realizing that the family problems that existed before your deployment not only have not gone away, but may have actually gotten worse. (Plus, that litter box will simply not clean itself.)

This explains why post-homecoming adjustment problems are so common among returning service members. In a 2007 study of Marine Corps Reservists returning from deployment, 36 percent reported relationship problems

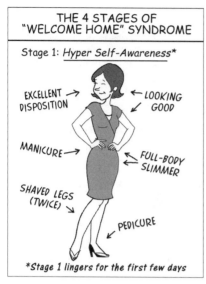

with spouse and children, and 43 percent reported problems with anger and aggression. Many veterans withdraw from family and friends and spend more time with the guys in the unit. Others try to cope with the aid of drugs, alcohol, or violent behavior. Bad idea. Still others consider the ultimate out, suicide. Much worse idea.

Bottom line: it's definitely great to be home, but you and your family need to prepare yourselves for the many challenges ahead. We'll talk about these in detail over the rest of the book. But, hey, congrats. Dude, you're home! Thank you for your service and sacrifice and welcome back to the wonderful world of wearing jeans in your off time, PTA meetings, and baby barf. Enjoy!

My, How You've Changed

There's nothing like being away from your family for a while to get you thinking about your priorities and how you're going to make life better when you get home. "I'm going to spend more time with the family; not get upset over minor things like spills on the carpet, clogged toilets, or idiot politicians; and get involved with the kids' homework." These are all great goals, and they can be accomplished. The problem is that the guy who made those resolutions (you) may not be the same as the guy who's going to try to make them a reality (also you). What I mean is that although things may look pretty much the same as they did before you left, being deployed has made you a different man. And for that matter, a lot of other things have changed too. In addition, some of the

issues you promised yourself (and your wife) you'd take care of when you got home may have been replaced by whole new ones. That carpet with that tiny stain? Well, there was a bit of a fire, and…

- ♦ **Friends change.** You just spent anywhere from a few weeks to a year with some pretty close friends. They may not have been your friends, or at least not that close, before you shipped out. But living through the same hardships, facing the same dangers, and providing emotional and social support to each other has brought you closer together. Breaking away from them isn't going to be easy. Your friends back home are great, but over the deployment you may not have been able to stay in touch with them all that often—even if you do have a Facebook page and you're on Twitter. And because they weren't deployed and may not really get what you've been through, you may find yourself thinking that you don't have much in common anymore.
- ♦ **Routines change.** While you were deployed, you probably had a fair amount of discretionary time. Your workdays were definitely longer, but when you were off duty, you could go to the gym, watch movies, read a great book, play cards with your buddies, or do pretty much whatever you wanted. No family to run home to, no kids to take care of, no lunches to make, no lawns to mow or carpools to drive. And while you may have had to share showers with a bunch of other guys, you still had a lot of personal space. Now that you're back, you'll be giving up some privacy, and you'll

have to get used to spending some of those former alone-time hours with your wife and kids.

♦ **Roles change.** One of the hardest things for returning dads to do is figure out how to plug themselves back into their family and assume their rightful role as head of the household (or as copartner of the household, as assistant manager of the Johnson family, or whatever the situation was before you shipped out). It's natural to imagine that you'll be able to jump right in and pick up as if you'd never left. Not so fast, buddy. That's a lovely thought, but a completely unrealistic one. In order to function during your absence, your family had to create new routines, new ways of communicating and making decisions, new approaches to discipline. This isn't to say they aren't happy you're back or that they don't need you. It's just that the new routines are the ones they feel comfortable with. Mom has been the primary decision maker in the house for the better part of a year, the kids have taken on some of your old chores, and no one may be terribly interested in making any changes. That might be okay if someone took over the lawn-mowing duties, but what if someone has taken to sitting in your favorite chair?

On one hand, you might be proud that your family came through your deployment in good shape. On the other hand, you may not be so sure you like what you're seeing, and you may be a little surprised—and, honestly, a little disappointed. After all, the logic goes, if they are able to thrive so well without you, what do they need you for? The answer is that your family *does* need you. A lot. They love you, too, and want you to be a part of the family again, to resume your duties as teacher, mentor, authority figure, fixer of all things broken, bad joke teller, and heavy lifting guy. It's just going to take some time. While you may feel comfortable with the old routines, it's doubtful that you'll ever get back 100 percent to the way things were. Instead, you, your wife, and your kids will end up creating a completely new routine, a hybrid that combines the best features of the predeployment and during-deployment ones. No, this does not get you out of doing dishes. Good try, though.

♦ **Even the pets change.** Having you back home could come as a bit of a shock to some household pets. All of a sudden, their routines are being changed, they may be competing with you for attention, and they may even resent having you sleeping on "their" side of the bed. So be prepared for some unusual behavior and some unpleasant "gifts" (cats are especially fond of punishing their owners for perceived slights).

"HUH"..... I HAVE LED THOUSANDS OF MARINES, COMMANDED ENTIRE UNITS INTO BATTLE, GIVEN ORDERS THAT HAVE STOPPED NAVY FLEETS......... BUT, AS SOON AS I GET HOME, I CAN'T EVEN TELL THE DOG WHAT TO DO!

♦ **Heck, the whole world seems to have changed.** The *TV Guide* is filled with television shows you've never heard of. Menus at your favorite restaurants may have changed—assuming they're still there at all. Ditto for the guest policy at your local gym. Changes like these—and there will be lots of them—will make settling in to your old/new life a bit harder. Unfortunately, there is no handy *While You Were Away: Important Things That Have Changed* handbook. You'll also have to get used to some of the things that *haven't* changed but that you got unused to while you were gone. For example, you no longer have to wait in line to use a telephone, and you're no longer limited to watching old, scratched-up DVDs on your base computer. Now, you can actually go to a theater to see a first-run movie, or get an almost-first-run movie from Netflix. And you can, gasp, actually watch live television (although you may not want to. How many crime shows do we actually need? Keep an eye out for *CSI: Peoria*).

While some of these changes are good, others may be a little embarrassing. For example, it's going to take a while for you to stop worrying that every car that pulls up alongside you might be a potential suicide bomber or part of an ambush. And it could take years before you're able to stop ducking for cover every time you hear a loud noise or someone slams a door. These things won't just affect you. It can be more than a little frustrating for your family to have you constantly worrying that you're about to be blown up.

Reaching Out...

Remember the old phone-company jingle, "Reach out and touch someone"? During your deployment you probably made good use of the phone and Internet to keep in touch with your family: phone calls, e-mail, texting, and occasional video chats, and "reach out and touch someone" was a lovely metaphor. Now you can actually do it—reach out and stroke your wife's face, push your kids on a swing, or pet the dog. You're also in a much better position to actually understand what people are really saying. Many studies have shown that only 7 percent of what's communicated in a conversation comes from the actual words. The rest comes from nonverbal communication—facial expressions, gestures, and body language (55 percent)—or tone of voice (38 percent). That means that you may have missed more than half of what your loved ones were trying to tell you in phone calls, and more than 90 percent of what they wanted to convey in e-mail or texts (even more if they were writing in teen-text). Now that you're home and you can see the people you're speaking with, your impressions of what happened in previous conversations may change. Also, because you haven't had the chance to watch your family's nonverbal actions for a few months, you might need some time to figure out exactly what their nonverbal gestures mean. One person's curled lip may mean something completely different than someone else's.

Through the Looking Glass

Several service members I've spoken with have told me that they felt that having been deployed made them more relaxed and helped them put things into perspective. (Finally, some good news). Spending quality and quantity time with the family moved up the list of priorities, and the need to be everywhere exactly on time slipped down a few notches. Compared to the daily mortar attacks, extreme heat, and pretty awful living conditions of Iraq and Afghanistan, getting a flat tire on a family outing paled in comparison. It was as if the important things in life suddenly became easier to identify and focus on.

What to Expect When Mommy Comes Home
from the War

If you've been the stateside parent while your wife was deployed, you have a very important role to play in helping her get reintegrated with the family. Because there's a lot of overlap between what male and female veterans experience when returning from deployment, your first assignment is to read the "What's Going on with You" sections in this chapter, mentally swapping the genders. This will give you a solid understanding of what she's going through, what she's concerned about, and the challenges she'll face.

Next, read the "What's Going on with Your Wife" sections and do the same thing, swapping out *she* and *her* for *his* and *you*. This will give you a good understanding of what *you* may be going through, and the special challenges you'll face. To save you a little time skipping around, here are a few of the high points.

♦ Your soldier wife has changed, and so have you. Life will not be the same as it was before—or as you imagined it would. It'll actually be much, much more interesting.

♦ You may be worried about whether she'll be happy with how the kids are doing, how you managed the household while she was gone. Interestingly, the better everything is, the worse she may feel. It's odd, but if you did a stand-up job, your wife might feel a little like a fifth wheel.

♦ You may be afraid that she'll be psychologically or physically scarred from her experiences.

♦ Although you and the kids may want to bombard her with questions and shower her with welcome-home gifts and surprises, she may need some time to herself to unwind or to take long naps.

♦ She may want to be pampered and taken care of, either by you or by getting a manicure and pedicure and soaking in a hot tub for two straight days.

♦ She may want to jump right back in and take over the responsibilities that she used to handle. You'll definitely be delighted to give up some of them, but you may not be so happy to say good-bye to some others.

♦ If she's been in or around combat, she may have experienced some very upsetting things. She may want to talk about some incidents but not others.

♦ She may be jumpy, irritable, tense, preoccupied, angry, isolated, and/or withdrawn.

♦ Sex may be a bit awkward at first—and maybe for a long time after that.

Overall, this is a good lesson. But understand that your newfound clarity and perspective will change the way you interact with your family—and that could come as something of a surprise to them. A nice surprise, yes, but it's one more new thing they have to get used to. Who would have thought that serving in combat could make you more relaxed and mellow?

Reaching Out...And Turning Off the Light

Aside from ice-cold beer and flat-screen TV, one of the things you probably missed most during your deployment was the intimate relationship with your wife—especially the sex part. Be careful not to confuse the two: sex and intimacy are *not* the same thing. For many men, sex can lead to intimacy. For many women, intimacy can lead to sex. That said, there's a good chance that after such a long time apart, you and your wife will skip the intimacy part and proceed directly to sex. But don't assume that the sex will be great when you return. It could be. That initial tear-each-other's-clothes-off-in-the-hallway episode will be spectacular, but after that, the quality (and quantity) of your sex life will depend largely how quickly you're able to rebuild the intimacy between you. It could take some time to get comfortable with each other, to

"And this one is for being faithful to my wife."

But Wait, There's More...

Here are some additional common thoughts and experiences I've heard from returning vets.

- **Will my family still love me?** What if I've killed people or done things they might find unforgivable?
- **Will they have any idea of what I've been through?** Could they ever understand?
- **What will work be like?** Do I even *want* to go back at all? Did they upgrade to Windows Vista while I was gone?
- **Who are these people, anyway?** Chances are you'll recognize your wife as soon as you get back, even if she's changed her hairstyle and lost a few pounds. But if you've got very young children, a year is a huge chunk of time, and unless you've seen pictures or video on a regular basis, you may not recognize your own kids. And believe me, that will definitely throw you for a loop. The same goes if you have teenagers, or are likely to acquire one while you're gone. See "What's Going on with Your Wife" and "What's Going on with Your Child(ren)" for more.
- **Will everyone just leave me the hell alone?** You may really crave some downtime, but with the wife, kids, and family all clamoring for your attention, solitude is in short supply.
- **Jealousy.** You might be jealous that your children seem to prefer Mom over you. (Several service members told me that they actually felt some resentment towards children who seemed to reject them in favor of Mom. Eventually they got over it, but it stung for quite some time.) Or you may be jealous that your wife has made all sorts of new friends and taken up new interests and seems to have had an all-around wonderful time while you were gone.
- **Did she...?** One incredibly common fear returning dads have is that their wife was unfaithful while they were gone. Sadly, this sometimes happens. A recent study by Paul Andrews of Virginia Commonwealth University found that 30 percent of married women have cheated—the same percentage as for men. The good (or bad, depending on how you look at it) news is that men's suspicions about infidelity are right 94 percent of the time (versus 80 percent for women). However, men are also more likely than women to suspect cheating when there isn't any. So be careful before you make any accusations (although if you've been gone for a year and you come home to a two-month-old baby, you're probably on the right track).

♦ **If you served in or near a combat zone, you may...**
◊ Be extremely sensitive to sounds, smells, and sights that remind you of your experiences.
◊ Be obsessive about safety, constantly afraid that your family is in danger.
◊ Have trouble concentrating or focusing on everyday tasks.
◊ Have disturbing memories, dreams, and nightmares.
◊ Feel irritable, angry, distracted, anxious, and/or emotionally numb.
◊ Blame yourself for a buddy's death, or have "survivor guilt," wondering why he died but you didn't.
◊ Be sick and tired of answering people's questions. Or you may want to talk about your experiences but don't want to burden anyone with your troubles.
◊ Be almost addicted to news about the war.
◊ Be worried about friends who are still deployed.
◊ Crave the excitement and adrenaline rush that only military combat can produce.
◊ Feel isolated and withdrawn, as though you don't fit in anywhere anymore.

truly feel close, to be able to communicate and trust each other. Eventually, though, it'll all come back to you. It's kind of like riding a bicycle—just with no clothes on.

What's Going On with Your Wife?

As mentioned earlier, your arrival at your front doorstep is just the beginning of a long process of reintegrating into your family. During the honeymoon phase it'll be nothing but rainbows and butterflies. But after all that rose-colored dust settles, you'll move into the Humpty Dumpty phase, where it'll be all about putting your family back together again. This is often followed by the Disney phase, where your kids will want you to watch every Disney DVD ever made. It's going to take a lot of effort and commitment on everyone's part.

Here's what you and your wife will have to do to make it work (we'll talk about some of these topics a bit later on in the chapter):

- (Re)learn to lean on and support each other.
- Decide whether you'll go back to your predeployment roles and responsibilities or create a new "normal."
- (Re)learn how to negotiate with each other and share in making decisions.
- (Re)learn how to co-parent.
- Renegotiate family rules and rituals.
- Respect and understand each other's need for independence.
- Respect and understand how your deployment experiences may affect your wife and kids.
- Keep expectations reasonable. And did I mention to keep expectations reasonable?

A pretty daunting task, don't you think? It's not surprising, then, that only about half of the spouses of returning service members rated the reunion as "easy," according to Bradford Booth, Mady Wechsler Segal, and D. Bruce Bell, coauthors of *What We Know about Army Families*. Put another way, 47 percent said it wasn't easy. Fifty-six percent of spouses said they needed more than two weeks to get used to having their service member back home (for many, the time was measured in months). The biggest problem areas for spouses were:

- Changes in soldier's mood or personality
- Communicating in the relationship
- Disciplining children
- Co-parenting
- Dividing up household chores
- Making decisions together
- Reestablishing marital intimacy

Spouses were more likely to express dissatisfaction with the reunion if they are married to enlisted service members, or had been in a strained relationship before the deployment. Interestingly, male spouses (the guys whose wife was deployed) were much more likely than female spouses to report the reunion as difficult. No one seems to have any idea why this is. If you were looking for a topic for your master's thesis in psychology, here you go.

Lest you think it's all bad news, let's get back for a minute to the 53 percent of spouses who had good things to say about the reunion. They tended to have had strong marriages before the deployment, to be married to officers, and to have had frequent contact with the service member during the deployment (phone calls and video conferences helped a lot, e-mail alone didn't). In addition, a number of the spouses in *What We Know about Army Families* said that the reunion and reintegration process helped them become more independent, made their marriages stronger and closer, and got their husband to participate more in making decisions and take on a greater share of household chores and child care.

Mom Has Changed

It can be very disconcerting to come back after months away from home to find that your beautiful bride has changed. Some of the changes will be superficial, like a new hair color or wardrobe, or a new favorite restaurant or TV program. Others will be more significant. For example:

♦ **Her friends may have changed.** She probably spends more time than she used to talking on the phone or getting together with friends. Who can blame her? You weren't there, and she was simply filling a void left by your absence (better that she spent the time with her girlfriends than with boyfriends). A lot of these friends will be new to you, and you won't like them all. But that doesn't matter. They provided a lot of emotional and social support over the last few months, and your wife won't be able to (or want to) break away from them cold turkey. More likely than not, the intensity of your wife's new friendships will fade over time as the two of you settle into your new life. The good news that girls' night out means… wait for it…boys' night out. Fair is fair.

♦ **The way she spends her time may have changed.** Maybe she's become a fitness nut and is taking yoga classes every day or training for a marathon. Maybe she's been taking art classes at the local community college and spends hours every day painting. Or maybe she's just learned some new skills and become more self-sufficient. The point is that although she was extra busy with child-related activities, she probably had a little spare time to herself—time she used to spend with you. She may be perfectly happy to give up some of her new pastimes—but not all of them. In fact, nearly one in three reunion moms report frustration with losing their personal time after the return of their husband.

Unfortunately, not every wife spends her free time in positive ways. Some don't do a good job of handling the stress of their increased responsibilities and worries about your safety. This can lead to depression, anxiety, and alcohol or substance abuse.

Now Here's an Odd One

Believe it or not, if you came back in one healthy piece, your wife may be a little irritated that you took care of yourself so well while deployed. You see, many wives like to think that they play an important role in your well-being—and most do, don't get me wrong. But what some wives don't understand is that the military does a fairly good job of taking care of its service members, especially while they're deployed. At the very least, you're guaranteed three meals a day, most of which are warm and freshly prepared. Depending on where you were deployed, you may have had surf and turf or something similar once a week. In addition, with no family obligations to distract them, many service members spend a lot of their free time at the gym. So in you march, the picture of health, well-fed, trim, and maybe sporting a tan from spending so much time in the sun. It's no wonder that the woman who pledged to take care of you for the rest of your life may feel a little displaced and resentful. She may also feel a little twinge of bitterness that—in her mind—you were having a good time with your buddies while she was pulling double duty at home. I'm not saying any of this is rational. It's just the way things play out sometimes.

The Department of Defensiveness

In an effort to reestablish their place in the family, some returning dads spend a lot of their time criticizing the way things got done while they were gone and generally trying to take over. This is a huge mistake. If you criticize your kids, they'll run screaming to Mom, who, like any mother bear defending her cubs, will come out swinging. And if you criticize your wife or start issuing orders, she may just turn around and bite your head off. She's been 100 percent in charge of things while you were gone, and she may not be ready to give up—or even share—her responsibilities. Thoughts like these will run through her brain and may even come out of her mouth: "You've been away for the last year, and you don't have a clue what it's been like here. You don't know what these kids have gone through. You don't understand what we've been doing, how we've lived our lives every day, what we do for fun, and how we relax." So watch out. You could be walking right into the middle of a power struggle that could make the combat you saw seem like a pleasant game of croquet.

Other Things She May Be Concerned About

- Will you still love her?
- Will you be proud of the way she managed things while you were gone? (If she asks, the correct answer is yes.)

- Are you okay? Has your deployment experience changed you?
- Have you been faithful? That's assuming you were deployed in a place where potentially available women outnumbered camels.
- Will you still be sexually attracted to her? (Yes, again.)
- Will you be interested in rebuilding your intimate relationship, or will you just want to have sex?

What's Going On with Your Child(ren)?

Children very often feel the same confusing emotions that the adults around them do: worry, fear, stress, happiness, excitement, and more. Exactly how *your* children react to your coming home will depend, in part, on their age and maturity level. Let's start with an age-by-age overview of what they might be going through and how their thoughts and emotions might translate into behavior. After this we'll dig a little deeper into the most important topics.

My intention here is not to frighten you with worst-case scenarios. I'm simply trying to prepare you for a wide range of possibilities and help you shape your expectations. This will allow you to discuss things with your wife ahead of time and give you a chance to start thinking about effective strategies for helping your child cope. You may see some, all, or none of these behaviors. Or you may see some, then none, then all of them in one week. Best to read up and be ready.

- **Birth to twelve months.** Even if she's met you before, your infant won't recognize you. When you hold her, she may cry, fuss, pull away from you, or cling to your wife or another more familiar caregiver. If she's upset enough, she may suddenly change her sleeping and/or eating routines.
- **One to three years.** Your child may not recognize you at all. If she does, she may hide behind Mom or some piece of furniture, be clingy, take a while to get used to you, cry when you're around, and possibly have temper tantrums. Some children this age may regress (start sucking their thumb after having broken that habit, or need diapers again after being toilet trained).
- **Three to five years.** Your child may show some guilt or fear about having made you go away and may be a little standoffish. As odd as it seems, some kids may wonder if they are the reason you were gone. Your preschooler may have all sorts of interesting and conflicting reactions. She may try to get your attention by acting out or testing limits, or she may

"Dad, here's that update on my childhood you requested."

hide and run away from you; she may seem angry and want to punish you for having been gone, or she may be overflowing with joy and excitement and chatter nonstop to fill you in on everything that's happened since you left; she may be afraid of you, or she may want to spend all day sitting in your lap. Children at this age may run around in their pj's all day or wear their rain boots in the house. This has nothing to do with you or your coming home—it's just something they do.

♦ **Six to twelve years.** Generally, your child will insist that you spend time with her and give her your attention. She may brag about you to her friends, but might still be angry at you for having left her in the first place. She'll have tons of art projects and other things to show you and will crave your recognition and praise, or she may be afraid of your discipline. Boys who've felt (or were told) that they were "the man of the house" may resent your coming back and taking over. Boys and girls may be anxious about how their role in the family will change now that you're back.

♦ **Thirteen-plus years.** Your teen may exhibit a dizzying array of emotions and behavior. She may, for example, be moody, aloof, excited to have you back, or excited but not want to show it. She may feel guilty about not

"That's my dad back when he was, like, militarized."

having lived up to your expectations, be concerned about how your being back home will affect some of the privileges she's earned (like driving the car), or worry that you're going to try to change her behavior or get rid of her friends (including her new boyfriend, Spike). She might act out in school, have academic or behavioral problems, be angry at you for having missed important events, and feel proud of you for being a hero. All at the same time. It's tough being a teenager.

How Kids Change

Just like you and your wife, children change too. Here are just a few examples:

♦ **Pastimes change.** You've got all sorts of grand plans—trips to the park with the kids, riding bikes, doing art projects, and snuggling up on the couch and reading to them. What you don't know is that little Jimmy doesn't like the neighborhood park anymore, and he's into inline skate-boarding instead of bikes these days.

♦ **Friends change.** Between you leaving and Mom working overtime to run the house, your children may have been feeling a shortage of emotional and social support. So they turned to their peers. Can you blame them? Now that you're back, you want to spend every available moment with your kids, but they're busy and won't want to break off those new friendships. Plus, with the blog, cell phone, IM, Twitter, and Facebook, who has the time?

♦ **Routines change.** You used to have the kids' schedule down pretty well. You knew when school started and when it let out, when their sports games and music recitals were, when they went to the library to do home-work, and generally where they were at all times. Chances are a lot of this has changed, and that will make you feel even more like a stranger than you already did. If you want to know the new routine, all you'll have to do is ask your kids—they'll know it cold. But can they remember to brush teeth two nights in a row?

♦ **Roles and responsibilities change.** Braden now takes out the trash and separates the recycling. Katie sets the table and puts the dirty dishes into the dishwasher. And Gabby wants to pour her milk and pick out her clothes by herself, thank you very much. Some of these changes were born of necessity: it was physically impossible for Mom to single-handedly manage everything, so the kids had to step up to the plate. Other changes are simply the result of your kids getting older and more mature and want-ing to take on more responsibility. And in some cases, changes in the kids' behavior are the product of a young child's attempt to protect herself. For example, before you deployed, Gabby may have really loved having you help pick out her clothes. Then, all of a sudden, you were gone. So now she's decided that she'll never again rely on anyone else, only to have that someone taken away. Like so much having to do with children, this is nowhere near rational, but it's the way they feel.

Hey, I Don't Have to Listen to You, Buddy

Imagine how things look from your kids' perspective. You've been gone for a long, long time. Yes, there have been some phone calls, and they've listened to the stories you recorded before you left and read (or had Mom read) your e-mails. Depending on their age, though, the kids might not recognize you at all. It's going to hurt, but in their mind you're a stranger. Even if they do recognize you, they may feel a little confused about who's in charge now that you're back. Or they might not accept you as an authority figure at all (rank means nothing to a five-year-old). Mom's the one who's been running the show,

Introducing the Newest Member of the Family...

Coming home to a baby who was born while you were deployed can be both exciting and terrifying. Of course, if this is your second or third or fourth child, you've already got a pretty good handle on what to expect and what you need to do. But if this is baby number one, you'll be stepping into a home that may look nothing like the one you left, and you may have no clue what to expect, what your wife will expect from you, and how you'll react to the whole thing. One of the great quotes I ever heard on this topic was from a woman who was asked to describe the difference between the way she heard becoming a parent was going to be and the way it actually turned out to be: "Simple—like the difference between watching a tornado on TV and having one tear the roof off your house."

One of the first things you'll probably feel is a conflict between wanting to jump in immediately and take care of your wife, and wanting to run away as fast as you can. No question it hasn't been easy for your wife to make it through the pregnancy and birth without you. But at least she had nine months to prepare. Your world is going to change in an instant. Sergeant one minute, daddy the next. Different uniforms, similar responsibilities.

Next, you'll start feeling guilty—in part for even thinking about running away, but mostly for not having been there for Mom and baby during the pregnancy and the birth. Get over it! The two of you knew that your being deployed was a distinct possibility, and there was absolutely nothing you could have done to change the situation.

You may also feel some jealousy at the closeness of the connection between mom and baby. Try to let that one go too. There's not much you can do about it, and you wouldn't want to even if you could. All you can do is jump in as soon as possible. Your wife will appreciate your being there to take on some of the parenting load. More importantly, you'll have a chance to start bonding with your baby. Don't worry about trying to make up for lost time—there's no such thing. Just do as much as you can and remember, (a) it's never too late to start, (b) the sooner you get involved, the stronger your relationship with your child, and (c) you're going to make a ton of mistakes. That's another wonderfully fun part of being a new daddy.

"_Wow!_, MARINES REALLY ARE BORN INTO IT!!"

and they'll keep on turning to her for permission, showing her their report cards, and running to her when they have a skinned knee or want a hug. Definitely not you. (Actually, some children may _want_ to start turning to you, but might feel guilty and worry that by doing so they'll upset Mom.) Eventually, you'll be able to assume the role of authority figure, but it's going to take some time, and you'll have to earn it.

It's hard, but try not to take this personally. Your coming back home is often a very confusing time for children, and it's not easy for them to sort out their feelings and emotions. And even when they do, they may not always express them in the most appropriate, nicest way.

Just Wait Till Your Father Comes Home

Aside from *The Great Santini* (if you haven't seen the movie, rent it now), very few dads truly want their kids to be afraid of them, but it's a pretty common occurrence among returning vets. A very young child who doesn't remember you might be afraid of your size, your deep voice, the funny clothes you wear, or all the noise you make clanking around the house. Slightly older kids might be afraid of the order and discipline they think you'll bring. That could be either because Mom didn't do much in the way of discipline while you were gone, or because she's been telling the kids, "Just wait till your father gets home." That would scare the hell out of anyone if it went on long enough. Kids who read the newspaper or get a lot of news from the Internet might have seen footage of combat and could associate that violence with you. And teens may be afraid of you, but also *for* you, worrying that you might come home with post-traumatic stress.

Stressed out

Chances are everyone in your children's world has been telling them that you're on your way back home and saying dopey things like, "I'll bet you can't wait to see your Daddy, can you?" or "Daddy is going to be so proud of you," or "When Daddy comes home, you're going to give him a big hug and a kiss, right?" Imagine how much pressure that puts on a kid. What if Daddy isn't proud of you? What if you don't really feel like giving him a kiss or a hug? What if you're really afraid of seeing Daddy after all this time? Even worse, what if Daddy doesn't love you? What if he's changed? What if you don't even know which of those guys getting off the plane is Daddy?

All the anticipation, uncertainty, unanswerable questions, and expectations can take a real toll on children. Their behavior at school and at home can suffer, and some experts estimate that as many as half of all children will become physically ill in the days and weeks immediately before and after Dad comes home, most likely from the stress of the readjustment.

Hey, get away from my mom!

For as long as you've been gone, your kids enjoyed their mother's undivided attention. Then, this guy they barely remember comes in and tries to boot them out of the center of the universe. And what does Mom do? She starts paying all sorts of attention to him! What an outrage.

Time heals all reunions

Although some of your children's reactions, thoughts, and emotions may annoy or hurt you, they are all a completely normal part of processing a very difficult situation. That said, within a couple of weeks after you come home, you should start to see a change in their behavior. Their harsh reactions will gradually fade, and they'll return to their normal selves. If, however, their hostile or extremely negative behavior continues for more than two or three weeks—or if they've had no reaction to your homecoming at all—it's worth getting some professional help from a child psychologist or family therapist.

8.

Daddy's Home

Getting (and Staying) Involved Now That You're Back

Looking Out for Number One

Making Time for Yourself

Homecoming is about spending time with family, right? Well, yes and no. There's no question that you all have plenty of catching up to do with each other. But you also need some time to yourself, to think about all the changes that are happening, to unwind, and to process some of the things you experienced overseas. The good news? You get to spend more time relaxing and a little more self-indulgent time. The bad news? You're going to have to get used to a different kind of life. Really different.

Everyone you know will want some of your time, and there'll be no shortage of social events, reunion parties, and activities to attend. The guys from your unit may want to get together for a beer. Friends and relatives you haven't seen for months may want to hang out. And let's not forget about your wife and kids, all of whom want you to themselves for long stretches of time.

As Abraham Lincoln said, "You can't please all of the people all of the time." So don't even try. For the first month or so after you get back, practice saying no. Prioritize, putting immediate family first, then family, friends, and coworkers. Go to the events you *want* to go to, not the ones you *think* you should. "Can't do it, sorry, I just got back" is a great excuse that works well for the first year or so. It's not nearly as successful if your deployment was back in the 70's.

Take Care of Yourself

Eat right, exercise at least thirty minutes every day, and manage your stress. Oh, and take it easy around alcohol. There probably weren't many bars where you were deployed, and even if there were, you probably weren't allowed to visit them. What this means is that even if you had only a couple of beers or cocktails a week, your tolerance isn't what it once was, and your buddies will find it a lot easier to drink you under the table.

Get Help if You Need It

On the battlefield, being tough, stoic, and not showing pain or weakness is essential to surviving. But back home, this kind of strong, silent behavior is dangerous. Stuffing your emotions may seem like the best way to cope with

Positive Coping Mechanisms

- Manage your expectations and expect change.
- Don't plan too much for your reunion.
- Rest and relax (easy enough, right?).
- Spend time with family (and friends, when ready).
- Maintain open, honest communication with your wife.
- Sleep in once in a while. Remember that one? Seems like a lifetime ago...
- Find a new hobby, or pick up an old one.
- Make contact with buddies to discuss your past deployment.
- Keep positive (try not to criticize each other).
- Have some fun and laugh a little. You're home.

troubling thoughts or behaviors, but eventually you'll explode, and you'll hurt either yourself or someone close to you. So read the sections on combat and post-traumatic stress and getting the help you need on pages 232-44. And if you think you need some help, or you just want someone to talk to, ask. Friends, clergy, your base family support organization, the VA, and all sorts of other organizations are standing by. And Military OneSource (militaryonesource.com) offers 24/7 phone consulting.

Staying Involved with Your Wife

Okay, so now that you know what's going on inside your wife's head and why she might be behaving the way she is, let's talk about what you can do to make the reunion as painless as possible and strengthen your relationship with each other.

- **Give her a little breathing room.** As we discussed earlier, your wife probably settled into a new personal routine while you were gone. Your return may require her to change that routine again, and she may not be too thrilled with the idea. As much as you might think she should want to spend all her time with you (even if you need some breathing room of your own), she needs a little space to ease back into the full family rhythm.
- **Don't overload her with reunion activities.** Your wife may see your return as a chance to relax and give you back some of those responsibilities she didn't enjoy over the past few months. Don't add to her stress

What to Do When Mommy Comes Home from War

Here are a few ways to help your deployed wife get reconnected to her family.

- Welcome her home. If you can, meet her at the airport or dock or train station or wherever. You'll probably do this with the family and friends of other returning service members, so you won't have to do all the organizing. A "Welcome Home, Mommy" banner is nice, but not essential. However, think flowers. Buy flowers. Bring flowers.
- Keep the first welcome-home dinner small and private—just you, Mom, and the kids. Having a large, loud party will be too much for her. Anyway, aside from giving you and the kids a couple big hugs, what she probably wants most is to go home and flop into bed, or perhaps take a bath. The kind with lots of bubbles and no kid interruptions.
- Give her plenty of space. The kids are going to be all over Mom, eager to tell her about every single thing that happened while she was gone, show her art projects, and give her presents. It's better to do the gift giving and storytelling a little at a time instead of all in one day.
- Show her the videos of what's been happening.
- Once she's had a chance to settle in, see about planning a weekend away for just the two of you—but not till she's ready to go.
- Don't spend all the money. Also, don't drink up the last of the coffee, run the tank below empty, or take the last cookie.
- Remember to start putting the toilet seat back down. Such an easy habit to get out of, so hard to get into… And while you're in the bathroom, unwrap a new roll of toilet paper when the old one runs out.
- Don't make major decisions for a while.
- Ask about her experiences, but don't push—she may not be ready to talk about everything right away.
- Understand that she may feel left out and unneeded, and may even be a little disappointed that you handled things so well. So do everything you can to help her fit in.
- Don't dump a lot of chores in her lap right away, just support her in gradually taking on the things she used to do. You may be so relieved that she's back that you're too eager to get rid of some of the less pleasant tasks you've been doing.
- Encourage her to talk and help her find resources for getting help if she needs it.
- Hugs, kisses, and smiles. Keep spares on hand.

Negative Coping Mechanisms

- Drinking excessively
- Drug use
- Gambling
- Frequent participation in risky/life-threatening activities (other than the ones that are part of your military job)
- Driving foolishly
- Starting fights
- Shopping or spending sprees

level by having her coordinate a lot of reunion parties. Enjoy some down time with her.

- **Close your eyes and jump back in.** Because she's been focused so much on the kids, you may sometimes feel like an outsider as she quickly attends to their every need without considering yours. Taking as much of the kid duty as you can will show her that you're serious about wanting to rejoin the team.

- **Go ahead and fight.** Even though you and your wife both want everything about the reunion to be perfect, it can be a tense, emotionally charged time. Expect arguments. Lots of them. About sex, money, roles and responsibilities, the children, and more. But when (not if) you do fight, at least agree to do it fairly. That means keeping focused on the issue at hand and not bringing up the past or dragging other people into it. It means making a firm commitment to finding solutions rather than scoring points. (This is good advice for your entire marriage—but you knew that, right?) And it also means that each of you has the right to call a time-out when the argument is becoming too heated or going down a completely unproductive path. Take a break, and finish the discussion when you're both feeling better.

- **Give yourselves time.** A recent study by the Military Family Research Institute found that a year after coming home, Reservists reported that the most difficult part of their reunion experience was learning how to be "inter-reliant with their spouse." That and understanding strange, made-up words like *inter-reliant*.

During your deployment, you and your wife became independent and learned to socialize and entertain yourselves without each other. So, take it

The Singular Sensation

If you had sole or primary physical custody of your children, you're going to be returning home to kids who have spent months and months building a closer relationship with whoever has been caring for them (in most cases, this will be your ex). Seeing how close your kids will have gotten to their Mom or other caregiver may make you jealous and hurt.

To top it off, you're not going to be able to just pick the kids up, take them home, and resume your life together as if nothing has happened. Abruptly severing ties between your kids and their soon-to-be-former caregiver can be extremely traumatic. Remember: kids crave structure almost as much as highly sugared breakfast cereals. And they love consistency—how else could they watch the same *Barney* video 100 times. Or more. So take things very slowly and have Mom or whoever help you with the transition. Talk to her about what the kids' routines were, what they watch on Thursday nights, what their favorite jammies are, their activities and interests, their health, their friends, their grades, and anything else you can think of. Engage the kids in this process as well. Talk with them about the difference between the household rules they've been living with and the ones that apply in your home. And don't be in a hurry to do an out-with-the-old-in-with-the-new thing. There's probably plenty you can learn from whatever the other caregiver was doing.

If you aren't a custodial parent, your kids' living arrangements didn't change much. What did change, though, was that you and they haven't seen each other for a much longer time than usual. So again, be patient: it may take some time for all of you to readjust to predeployment routines and visitation schedules. If you're able, spend some time with your ex talking about what's been happening in the kids' lives while you were gone.

easy on each other. It's going to be at least a couple of weeks before you both feel like a couple again and able to work out even the simplest things, like putting together a grocery list, deciding where to go for dinner, or picking out a movie to rent. Give in a little and agree to rent a chick-flick—who knows how many you missed while you were on base. Bigger decisions, like what kind of car to buy, personal space, bedtimes and allowances for the kids, and whether you should sign up for another tour, will take even longer.

This is one of the reasons why you should put off making any kind of major

"Agreed. We'll reduce our arsenal of insults, jibes and grievances by one-third but we will be permitted to stockpile them for use should the need arise."

decisions until you're sure you're feeling strong as a couple. When you do get around to the big ones, be sure you make them jointly. You don't want to be in the unfortunate third of service members whose wives report frustration at not being included in family decision making since Dad came back.

♦ **Just hang out.** After the initial lustful roll in the hay, a lot of couples aren't quite sure what to do with each other, how to get their relationship back on track. It's not really all that complicated. Start off doing low-stress activities that you know you'll both enjoy, such as going to the movies, bowling, having a picnic, playing cards, taking a long walk, reading, listening to (or playing) some music, or doing some kind of sport together. (It's a bit like dating again, only you already know she's a good kisser.) Plan some activities just for you and the wife (get a sitter if you have to), and do some as a family. For the first few months, keep the activities short. You want to feel comfortable with each other before heading off on that romantic weekend or planning a family vacation.

Show Me the Money

Between the combat pay, overseas bonuses, and tax benefits, you might have been earning anywhere from a few hundred to a thousand dollars a month more than usual. Some couples are extremely disciplined and sock away all that extra income for later. Some use it to pay down debt or for an emergency purchase. Others decide to blow the entire nest egg celebrating the end of the deployment. And in some unfortunate families, one spouse has made some major spending decisions without talking it over with the other, who may have had entirely different plans for the money. Often, this involves buying something big on credit based on the extra deployment income. Unfortunately, the bills often continue long after the income stream stops, and that can lead to some very serious problems.

This same kind of thing happens with civilian contractors. There are lots of stories out there of civilian contractors who were able to put aside enough money to pay cash for a new home. And there are stories of contractors who come home to no salary, no job, and a pile of bills they can't come close to paying. The only way they can dig themselves out of debt is to turn around and sign up for another overseas hitch. It's incredibly easy to adapt to a higher standard of living based on making two or three times as much as you used to. It's a lot harder to go back to living on the old salary when the windfall comes to an end.

Whether you're on active military duty, in the Reserve, or a civilian contractor, the advice is the same: talk with your wife about money. How much extra is/was there? How does that fit in with the budget? What assumptions are each of you making with regard to the money and how it should be spent? Do you really need a big-screen TV for the bathroom? Is private boarding school for the dog a reasonable expense? His and hers swimming pools, honey?

♦ **Limit the deployment stories.** Although you may want to get it off your chest, save the battlefield stories—especially the ones that involve violence or death—for when you get together with your buddies. A lot of guys do this instinctively, in an attempt to protect their family from the horror of war. Be careful about non-combat stories too. Remember, your wife may still be a little jealous of the freedom you had while you were deployed, and hearing about all the marvelous experiences you had will

just aggravate her. So instead, tell her about all the stuff you missed, like home cooking, having the kids around, and colors other than camouflage and dirt.

♦ **Show a little appreciation.** Your wife had a ton of extra responsibilities to handle while you were gone. No, she may not have made the same decisions or done things exactly the same way you would have. But keep your second-guessing and criticism to yourself (see "The Department of Defensiveness" on page 205 for more). Instead, keep smiling, and never pass up an opportunity to tell her what a great job she did and how grateful you are that she kept the household and everyone in it running smoothly.

And if family, friends, or anyone else lent a hand during your deployment, thank them too. Simple things like flowers, chocolates, a six-pack, or a bottle of twenty-year-old single malt go a long way. There has never been a recorded case of someone refusing fresh-baked chocolate chip cookies.

♦ **Watch your tongue.** The expression "having a mouth like a sailor" is hardly limited to the Navy. I've always considered myself relatively articulate, but when I was in the Marines I'd guess that four-letter words—in every possible combination and variation—accounted for a good third of the words that came out of my mouth on any given day. It's going to be tough to switch back to a G- or PG-rated vocabulary, but do try. Just think of all those adjectives you can rediscover. And while you're working on your vocabulary, make a special effort around your wife and kids to use real words instead of lapsing into military speak and peppering your conversations with acronyms and abbreviations.

Me! No, Me!

So, who had it worst during the deployment: you, your wife, or your kids? Each of you would probably vote for yourself. And, in your own way, you'll all be right. It's always much harder to meet life's challenges without the love and support of someone close to you.

We're just pointing this out because it's important for you to understand what everyone in your family is going through. *Do not*, however, get into a frustrating contest about who suffered the most. (I can guarantee you that losing this struggle to a five-foot-four woman is embarrassing. Been there, done that.) There's certainly a good case to be made that anyone who's been in combat, especially if that person has come home with an injury, has had the most traumatic experience. But if you try to argue the point, all you'll be doing is demonstrating that you don't understand the challenges your family faced and the sacrifices they made.

♦ **Know when to get help.** You've both been through a lot over the past few months. If you need help (see "Getting the Help You Need" on pages 235–38), get it—it'll be good for you and good for your relationship. If you think your wife needs help, make sure she knows how to get it.

By "help" I'm not only talking about getting therapy or medication. In some cases, spouses and children leave the base while the service member is deployed. This could be to save money, to have better access to employment opportunities, or to be closer to family and/or in-laws. Whatever the reason, understand that while being off base might have had its advantages, it also had the downside of taking your wife and kids away from the support systems the military has in place. It could take a while to get plugged back into your military "family."

♦ **Quit worrying about sex.** Hopefully, it's been a while since you had sex, and you're probably both really looking forward to it. But take it easy. Re-igniting a sexual relationship after a long break can be almost like having sex for the first time—but no parents in the next room this time. There's going to be some fumbling around, some tentative discovery of what works and what doesn't, and a lot of "I want this to be perfect" thoughts coming from both sides. There can also be a strong sense of trying to make up for lost time. Keep in mind that the more pressure you put on yourself to perform, the greater the likelihood that you'll be disappointed—either in your own performance or in the experience as a whole. So maybe set up a few "practice" dates before you have the official one.

♦ **Think of things from her perspective.** Let's face it, sometimes when we're hanging out with other guys, we're not as concerned with politeness as when we're in the company of women. That often means not being terribly concerned about loud burping or tracking dirt into the house. Now that you're home, try to leave all of that—including the muddy boots—at the door. Your wife won't find it nearly as entertaining as your buddies do. And, dude, remember: the kids will copy whatever you do, and it's only cute the first twenty or thirty times.

♦ **Talk, listen, watch, and listen some more.** Your wife will want to hear everything about your deployment—the good and the bad, the scary and the funny, the disturbing and the heartwarming. Most of all, though, she'll want to hear that you love her and missed her. She'll also want to tell you *her* stories.

Listen carefully and respectfully to what she says. After all, while you were away she was dodging bullets of her own, and she needs you to understand. And keep your eyes open. Remember the discussion we had a while back (see "Reaching Out..." in the first chapter of this section) about how 55 percent of communication is nonverbal? Her gestures, hand movements, facial expressions, and body language—all of which you haven't seen for a while—will give you a lot of important insight into how she's really feeling. Besides, its fun to relearn how beautiful she is.

Helping Your Family Help You

Your family may have all sorts of questions about your deployment. They may want to know what you did, whether you saw casualties or killed anyone, how successfully the war is going, and so on. Sometimes questions like these are the result of natural curiosity. Other times, they're a nervous attempt to make conversation. I suggest that unless you really want to talk about your experiences, you ask your family to hold off on the questions for a few weeks.

Even if you weren't in or around combat, you were still up to your ears in military activities and culture twenty-four/seven for months and months, and chances are you'd just as soon forget it for a while. Of course, you won't be able to—thoughts and memories will keep popping into your head at all sorts of odd moments. But you can limit the intrusions by limiting the conversations until you're ready.

At the same time, ask your family in advance for their patience. They need to know that it's going to take some time for you to transition from all-military-all-the-time to a workable blend of military and family (or, if you're a Guardsman or Reservist, to a completely civilian life). Your wife and children need to know that they may see some unusual behavior from you—sharp responses to the kids' acting out and testing limits, needing to be left alone, strange exercise and eating habits, just to name a few. ("You got up at oh-dark-thirty every day? For real? What is oh-dark-thirty, anyway?") They should know that identifying what needs to change, making a commitment to change it, and then actually making the changes isn't a process that happens overnight. But you'll do everything you can to speed it along.

Staying Involved with Your Child(ren)

♦ **Focus on the kids.** The moment you walk in the door your wife, your kids, friends, family, and other people will be competing for your attention. To the extent possible, spend as much time as you can focused on the children. (Understand, though, that your kids may want to do *everything* they missed right away, on your first day home—this is both very tiring and mathematically impossible.) If you do the opposite, and focus on your wife, the kids will be, understandably, angry and jealous that you're diverting Mom's attention away from them. You and your wife can hang out after the kids hit the sack. You'll be able to have better quality time then, anyway. Everyone else can be patient for a few more days.

♦ **Embrace reality.** Coming home after a long deployment presents you with a very Zen choice: bend or break. Accept that everything and everyone has changed and look for the positives that have emerged, or insist that everyone and everything should be just as you left them and spend all your time banging your head against the wall. I think you'll agree that the choice is pretty clear. Reuniting with your family is not about fulfilling all your preconceived plans. It's about sharing your family's excitement in their newfound activities and friendships. So instead of letting it get you down when the old family jokes and family activities don't pack the same punch as they used to, take comfort in the new activities and family fun you'll create with the kids—although you may be the butt of a few of the jokes.

♦ **Sloooow down.** A 2008 RAND Corporation study for the National Military Family Association reported that 57 percent of postreunion children cited difficulties in getting to know their returning parent. In my view, that's at least partly due to families trying to do too much too soon to make up for lost time, especially in the first few weeks. I know there's so much you want to do and say, but let the children set the pace. Try to make your reunion as relaxed as possible, and stay away from making any sudden changes. Keep your plans simple and flexible and your expectations low. You can always do more tomorrow, slugger.

Making Time for Friends, Other Family, and Everyone Else

Once you're finally ready to get together with people outside your immediate family, prepare yourself for a shock. As with every other part of coming home, it's unrealistic to expect that their world will look exactly the way it did before you left. There's a good chance that plenty has changed: there might have been new marriages, babies born, divorces, job transfers, deaths, new political leaders, and people who may reject you because they don't support the mission you were on. On the plus side, gas may be cheaper, laptops less expensive, and all the road construction they started years ago is now done—okay, not really. They're still working on that overpass…

"How did Operation Remember to Pick Up Milk go?"

♦ **Wait till your mother comes home.** When it comes to discipline, children are pretty picky about whom they'll listen to. And for the foreseeable future that person is Mom. If you jump in and demand obedience before the kids have a chance to get used to you being around, they'll resent you every step of the way. You and your wife will have to negotiate rules and consequences that you both can live with (and, hopefully, that will produce the desired results). In the meantime, let Mom take the lead for a few more weeks.

Children—especially young ones—often have a pretty limited understanding of themselves and how their actions affect those around them. So when your child acts out, spend a little time trying to figure out what's really going on, what the true feelings behind the bad behavior are. You

So, If Your Kids Are Having Some Trouble Adjusting, What Can You Do for Them?

♦ Remind them that you're happy to see them, that you love them, and that you're overjoyed to be able to hug them again. Do this every day—more often if necessary. Should you write notes on their hard-boiled eggs or draw a smiley on their lunch bags every day? Use your best judgment here. Probably yes in grades 1 to 3, probably no in grades 10 to 12.)

♦ Show them that you're interested in their activities and interests. Show them the pictures of them that you carried in your wallet or your helmet. Tell them how proud you are of them. Ask to see some of the pictures, art projects, and other schoolwork they completed while you were gone.

♦ Tell them how grateful you are that they were such a big help to Mom while you were away.

♦ Stick close to home for the first few days after you get back. If you arrive, then suddenly leave, even if it's just for a day, the kids may get confused or worry that you've left again—and that it must have been something they did that made you go.

♦ Encourage the kids to talk to you about their fears and anger. If they're too young to articulate their thoughts and emotions, help them draw something. Let them know that they can tell you anything they want, and that you won't punish them for it.

can fall back on the old "Drop and give me twenty," but in doing so you may be sending the message that it's not okay for children to express their emotions or that you don't care about their feelings. However, if *you* drop and do twenty, the silliness may diffuse the situation.

♦ **Smile and don't criticize.** Your kids missed you a huge amount when you were gone, and they really, really want things to be great when you come home. They're proud of their new responsibilities and how grown up they are. Mom has been praising them and telling them how proud she is for months, and they want *you* to be proud too. But if you blow into town and start complaining about the way people are loading the dishwasher and insisting that you're in charge and that from now on things are going to get done *your* way, they'll be devastated. The kids have been loading the dishwasher their own way for the better part of a year, and the dishes somehow got clean. No one likes to be told that they're doing something—or everything—wrong. And no child ever wants to disappoint Dad. So compliment your kids as much as you can, and bite your tongue before you make any disparaging remarks. There are usually lots of different ways of doing things. Is yours truly the only way? Maybe Junior will invent a new way to wash dishes, patent it, build a company, and you can retire rich in one year. Stranger things have happened. Criticizing for the sake of criticizing or simply to reassert your authority is one of the fastest ways of breeding resentment. Especially with teens, where the number-one way to create resentment is for you to breathe.

♦ **There really can be second chances.** Being gone a long time can really get you thinking about all the things you wish you would have or could have done before you'd left. Given that second and third tours are commonplace, there's a good chance you'll be deployed again, so take the time now to turn your post-deployment time into the best predeployment time ever, with game nights, family pizza nights, regular family meetings for no other purpose than to talk about the day, more family activities, watch family videos, and so on. Ask the kids more questions about themselves, their friends, the music they like—and really listen. Say "I love you" more, say "I'm proud of you" more, say "Yes" more often, and build up a reserve of love and affection for the next time you're gone. The kids might freak out that you've turned into Mr. Nice Guy, but they'll get over it.

♦ **They're observing.** As we talked about in the predeployment section, your children will model their behavior on yours. Before you shipped out, if you or your wife seemed scared or angry, the kids probably would too. Now that you're home, the kids are still paying close attention to you and Mom. The more they see you working with each other, communicating openly, negotiating respectfully, and compromising when necessary, the faster they'll adjust to your being back. And if you start doing your patented happy dance in the kitchen, well, expect quite a lot of happy dancing in their future too.

Some Specific Activities to Do with Your Children

♦ **Birth to twelve months.** No agenda here. Just hold, hug, bathe, change, feed, play, relax, play some more, and just marvel at all the cool things babies can do.

♦ **One to three years.** Hug, hold, and kiss as much as you can, but understand that your child may not know you and could cry, seem afraid, or go running off to Mom. Give your toddler plenty of space; get down on the floor and play on her level.

♦ **Three to five years.** Lots of play, lots of praise, lots of I-love-yous. Read—especially the stories you recorded before leaving—do art projects, talk, and listen.

♦ **Six to twelve years.** Same as above, plus lots of questions about the child's life while you were gone. Ask to see schoolwork, scrapbooks, trophies, and more. And tell your child, in an age-appropriate way, about what you went through.

♦ **Thirteen-plus years.** Be prepared for some long talks about politics, war, casualties, and justice. Talk about your experiences and listen to your child's, without making judgments or criticizing. Learn 2 text-message. It's gr8. 4 real.

♦ **The great outdoors.** If you like the outdoors—or even if you don't— check out the Military Family Outdoor Initiative (sierraclub.org/military), which provides outdoor camping experiences for returning servicemen and their children. Cosponsored by the Armed Services YMCA and the Sierra Club, the MFOI project offers a great way for you and your kids to reconnect, bond, and have a ton of fun hiking, camping, swimming, boating, and a lot more.

♦ **Maintain family routines as much as possible.** Besides craving routines and patterns, your kids need to keep up-to-date on homework, extracurricular activities, and social obligations. But don't go overboard—take a hint from the school and celebrate backwards day or silly hat day once in a while.

♦ **Go back to school.** Tell your children's teacher(s) that you're back. If you can, drive the kids to school, coach their sports teams, and volunteer in the classroom. The more you're involved, the more your children will know you love them and that you're glad to be back.

♦ **Make a coupon book.** Fill it with vouchers the kids can redeem for an extra chapter of reading, an evening of stargazing, five kisses on each elbow and one on the nose, baking chocolate chip cookies, and anything else you know your kids will love. This might work for your wife as well. "Good for one night of unlimited…" Well, that's between the two of you.

♦ **Pull out those old photos or videos.** Looking back at the happy times you had as a family often makes it easier for kids (and adults, for that matter) to see that life can be good again.

♦ **Grab your calendar.** Try to schedule some one-on-one time with each
child. It doesn't have to be an all-day affair. Just taking a walk around
the block, reading a story together, or going out for lunch can be great. If
you have more time, go to the zoo, a museum, a concert, or the movies, go
shopping and make dinner together, or take a weekend camping trip. The
most important thing is that you do things that your children really want
to do and that each one has your undivided attention, without annoying
brothers or sisters to distract you.

While you've got your calendar open, line up some babysitters and
schedule some date nights with your wife. (Keep contact info for good sitters on your list of important phone numbers, right underneath the pediatrician and the poison control hotline. Sitters are pretty darn important,
and they're a lot easier to get hold of.) The two of you need some quality
time to reconnect with each other. And you need to thank her for everything she did while you were away.

9.

Putting Humpty Dumpty Together Again

The Challenges of Getting Back to Your Old Life

Challenges to reintegrating

Getting back into the swing of things with your family is one thing, but there are also a number of challenges that can make reintegrating harder than it really should be.

Mental Health Issues

Coming back from a combat deployment is far more complex than just packing your bags, shaking sand out of your skivvies, and heading home. You'll likely get hit with a host of challenges, ranging from the relatively minor (such as exhaustion, getting used to a new diet after a year of eating scorpions, and

adjusting to the peace, quiet, and boredom of life at home after having lived in a high-stress, fast-paced combat zone) to the more significant (such as sleep problems, feelings of social isolation, physical injury, and guilt that you survived while some of your buddies may not have).

Many people who experience traumas—and deployment in a combat zone or rescue work after a natural disaster such as a hurricane or earthquake definitely qualifies—recover quickly and get back to their normal lives without any problems. But not everyone. Some returning service members relive the traumatic event they experienced over and over, in nightmares at night and scary thoughts during the day, and they may go to extraordinary lengths to avoid any reminder (people, places, smells, etc.) of the events. These symptoms, and others we'll talk about below, are part of what's called post-traumatic stress disorder (PTSD).

PTSD is not always the result of a single traumatic event. For some veterans, the cumulative effects of being deployed, separated from family, living in severe conditions, and constantly being afraid for your life is more than enough to leave some long-term emotional and/or psychological scars. Overall, 15 to 20 percent of service members returning from combat zones are diagnosed with PTSD.

Symptoms of PTSD usually start cropping up around three months after the traumatic event or events, although you might not see any for a year or longer. Early symptoms are typically fairly minor and can include headaches, stomach trouble (nausea, indigestion, constipation, or diarrhea), shortness of breath, and sleep issues (either too little or too much). Ignored or untreated, those symptoms could gradually get worse, and may include:

- Physical symptoms, such as chest pain, unintended weight loss or gain, loss of interest in sex, and ulcers.
- Antisocial behavior. You may feel that you can't trust other people. That could make you withdraw from friends or family, or cause relationship problems at home, school, or work.
- Maladaptive behavior, such as drinking too much, smoking, eating unhealthy food, thrill-seeking or dangerous behavior, and not getting enough exercise.
- Intrusive symptoms, such as flashbacks and nightmares. These are often so vivid that it may feel like you're going through the trauma again. You may feel as scared as you were when it actually happened. Instead of (or in addition to) flashbacks and nightmares, you may suddenly feel waves of fear, panic, anger, or crying that come completely out of the blue.
- Avoidance of activities and situations that remind you of the event, or that you worry *might* remind you or trigger a flashback. For example, if you served in combat, you would probably try to stay away from any place where there might be loud noises.
- A constant agitated state or a feeling you can never relax, which may cause elevated blood pressure, muscle tension, difficulty falling or staying asleep, irritability, outbursts of anger, sweating, and being easily startled.
- Emotional numbness. In an attempt to avoid remembering or reliving the event, people with PTSD often shut down their emotions—the good ones as well as the bad.
- Exaggerated startle responses to loud noises or to being approached or touched.

Getting the Help You Need

Although men and women both suffer from stress, we have very different ways of coping with it. Women generally do what mental health professionals call "tend and befriend," meaning that they reach out to others around them, look for friends and family to lean on, and talk about what's bothering them.

Men, on the other hand, have a tendency to cope with stress in pretty much the same way that we cope with other problems. We bottle it up and refuse to talk about it. We escape, either by trying to get away physically or by denying to ourselves and everyone else that there's a problem at all (It's nothing... I'm sure the bleeding will stop soon). We try to cover it up, often with drugs or alcohol. Or we get angry and aggressive. (Note: none of these approaches are particularly successful, yet men keep trying them over and over. I suggest you skip this step and move right on to healthier behaviors.)

The result is that far too many veterans with PTSD—and other trauma-related conditions such as traumatic brain injury (TBI)–don't get the help they need. Sometimes it's because they aren't paying attention or they're in a state of denial. Other times it's because of the idiotic view that still exists within the military that asking for physical or psychological help is a sign of weakness, or is a demonstration that you can't handle things on your own. Here are a few more reasons I've heard from service members who felt uncomfortable asking for help.

- ♦ I'm concerned that my request for help and my treatment will show up in my service record.
- ♦ I'm worried that everyone will find out and that others will judge me.
- ♦ I asked for help, but they told me I was just depressed and sent me back to work.
- ♦ The doctors all say it's confidential, but I don't trust them.
- ♦ If I ask for help, I'll be trashing my career or ruining my chance of getting a security clearance.
- ♦ My superiors will use my asking for help as an excuse to pass me over for promotions.
- ♦ I'm a very private person, and my problems are none of anyone else's business.
- ♦ It's not that big a deal. I'm only feeling stress, like 90 percent of the time. Not always.

To be fair, the military has made significant strides in removing these

The Dogs of War

You've probably seen guide dogs for the blind, and you might have heard of hearing guide dogs for the deaf. But if you're suffering from PTSD, you'll definitely want to know about psychological (or psychiatric) service dogs. These specially trained canines can do absolutely amazing things, like keeping strangers from coming too close—especially from behind— nudging you if they sense you're having a panic attack, and snuggling up with you when you're depressed or anxious. Some soldiers who have had psych service dogs have said that when they wake up in the middle of the night in a cold sweat, they find it very reassuring to see the dog sleeping calmly nearby. Also, since these dogs need regular exercise, you'll be forced to get out of the house at least a couple times a day.

Dogs are also trained to work with service members who have physical injuries. They can pick up dropped items, pull wheelchairs, steady you when you're walking, and even untie your shoelaces and pull your boots off. To find out more, check out Dogs for Deaf and Disabled Americans (neads.org), Service Dog Central (servicedogcentral.org), or the Psychiatric Service Dog Society (psychdog.org). And just so you know, these dogs come in more versions than stern-looking German shepherd—there are beagles, poodles, and plenty of mutt brands. They're also allowed anywhere other service dogs are, including restaurants, theaters, and airplanes. And dogs are great pals—they're upbeat, not too much chatter, and will watch hours of football with you without wanting to change the channel.

obstacles. They now proactively encourage every returning vet to get the help he (or she) needs. And the Department of Defense recently announced that it no longer denies security clearances based on receiving mental health services for "marital, family or grief issues and counseling for adjustments from service in a military combat environment."

"Having PTSD does not mean you are weak, or bad, or crazy," according to a wonderful resource called FamilyOfAVet.com. "You are having a natural reaction to living for so long in an unnatural environment. Having people shooting at you or trying to blow you up on a regular basis is not fun (though it may give you a super adrenaline rush)—and it's also not great for your overall mental health."

Not getting help with PTSD can undermine your relationships with family,

Field-Tested Ways of Helping Your Kids

Brannan Vines, the wife of a soldier who developed PTSD after returning from Iraq, told me about a number of things she and her husband did to try to help their young daughter:

+ We bought our daughter a portable DVD player and several of her favorite movies. When we're having a bad PTSD day and noise is particularly hard for my hubby to handle, we get the DVD player out for quiet time. It's become something she enjoys, something I feel okay about (most of the movies are educational), and it helps until my husband is able to work through things and get a handle on the day.

+ Whenever my husband reacts too harshly or abruptly to something, or scares our daughter, he picks her up, tells her he's sorry, and gives her a hug as soon as possible. This is a coping technique we learned from his counselor, and since overreacting is a common trait in PTSD and TBI (traumatic brain injury), we use this one a lot.

+ We worked to find a calm, enjoyable activity for Dad and daughter to do together. For them, it's coloring and painting with watercolors. This has been really important, not only to help them continue building a good relationship, but because it gives them something positive to do together. It makes the harder times easier for her to cope with because she knows without a doubt her dad loves and adores her.

+ We have a network of family and friends that our daughter is extremely comfortable with. Besides helping us, this support system also ensures that she always has somewhere she loves to go on those days that Dad (or Mom!) needs a break. A lot of guys who suffer from combat PTSD say that that the natural noise children make can really grate on them at times. This system gives my daughter something fun to do when my hubby needs time to de-stress.

+ We start long car trips just before our daughter's bedtime. Driving on crowded roads can be a huge source of stress for veterans with PTSD. Add in the noise of a crying toddler, and it's a real disaster. Leaving after most of the rush-hour traffic has cleared, and knowing our daughter will be asleep in a few minutes, makes for a much more calm, peaceful ride for everyone.

friends, and others. It also greatly increases your risk of developing other mental health issues (about 80 percent also suffer from depression and/or anxiety), or of committing suicide. So if you notice any of the signs we've discussed, please do yourself and your family a favor: put your worries and fears aside, and schedule an appointment with a medical professional. Now. Listen, I know us guys don't love a visit to the doc and tend to put it off until never. But, and I promise you this, you will feel better. Plus, no rectal exam required.

Coping with PTSD

For some veterans, PTSD symptoms begin to fade on their own within a few months after returning home. But that's the exception. For most, it's going to take a lot of work, a lot of time, and a lot of support.

There are a number of ways of treating PTSD, and your health-care provider should be able to recommend the one, or the combination, that's best for you. The first line of defense will probably involve some talk therapy. Individual cognitive behavior therapy can help by teaching you techniques for controlling your thoughts and feelings about the trauma. And group therapy can help by connecting you with others who know exactly what you're experiencing. Your health-care provider may also prescribe antidepressants or antianxiety medication.

At the same time, there are a number of things you can do on your own, such as practicing relaxation or meditation, getting exercise, eating a healthy diet, and learning as much as you can about your condition. But by far the most important is to get support from family and friends. Research has shown that the more social support you have, the better you'll do.

It's important to understand that there are no treatment options that will make you magically forget what you experienced, or that will make your symptoms disappear completely—that's just not going to happen. It's very possible, however, to make the symptoms less severe and more manageable. Doing *something* is a good idea here. Doing nothing is what is known in the field of psychology as *a really bad idea.*

You, Your PTSD, and Your Kids

Tens of thousands of children have seen dad or mom come back from a deployment with physical or psychological injuries. Or both. Even if they don't (or can't) understand exactly what's going on, your children have an uncanny ability to know when something's not right. And nothing will confirm their suspicions more quickly than having you dive for cover every time a car backfires

Civilian Contractors: The Hidden Victims of PTSD

Since many civilian contractors are engaged in combat support (and even outright combat) missions, it's not surprising that they experience some of the same traumas that can lead to PTSD in military personnel. And it's not surprising that many of them come home with physical or mental injuries.

Any American company that employs civilians outside the United States is required by the Defense Base Act (DBA) to provide a special insurance policy. The DBA program theoretically "provides disability, medical, and death benefits to covered employees injured or killed in the course of employment, whether or not the injury or death occurred during work hours." I say "theoretically" because I've heard from a number of civilian contractors that actually getting benefits under the act is a lot harder than it sounds. And those who are able to get coverage find that most civilian health-care providers have no experience treating PTSD and no idea what to do with people who suffer from it.

Unfortunately, returning civilians who need care are pretty much on their own. Unlike the military, which provides routine physical exams, PTSD screenings and treatment, and access to support groups, there is no formal safety net for returning civilians. There is no civilian counterpart to the Department of Veterans Affairs, whose mission it is to help vets access all the benefits they're entitled to. And civilians don't have powerful lobbying organizations like the American Legion and Veterans of Foreign Wars. If you're interested in finding out more about this, take a look at American Contractors in Iraq (americancontractorsiniraq.com).

or a door slams, wake up screaming in the middle of the night, or explode in anger if someone comes up from behind and touches you. As I'm sure you can imagine, this kind of behavior can scare the hell out of your kids and create a huge amount of stress in their young lives. This is why it's essential that you do the following as soon as you possibly can:

- Talk with your children in an age-appropriate way and tell them what's going on and why, what you're doing about it, and what it might mean to them.
- Give them lots of opportunities to ask questions. Don't assume they know it's okay to ask—come right out and say so.

If Mom Has PTSD

Women generally have an easier time asking for help than men do, but if you think your wife is suffering from severe stress or PTSD and isn't taking active steps to seek out treatment, she needs you. The most important thing you can do is to be understanding and supportive. Talk with her about what she's feeling and remind her that stress—even PTSD—is treatable and doesn't mean she's weak or flawed in any way. (Isn't it nice to know that moms can be as bullheaded as we are?) Encourage her to go out for a walk with you, or suggest low-stress, just-plain-fun activities. Helping her keep her expectations and goals reasonable can be huge.

If you feel that your wife needs more assistance than you can provide, help her get what she needs. This may mean that you'll have to take the initiative and make medical appointments for her, and take her there if she's unwilling or unable to do it herself. Most important, be patient. Recovering from stress will take some time. When it comes to PTSD, there is no cure. But the condition can be effectively managed, and symptoms greatly reduced.

Finally, be sure to take care of yourself. Your wife's stress can spill over into the lives of everyone around her. Caring for another person requires love, commitment, and patience. And you can't possibly take care of someone else if doing so is stressing you out. Consider this your official permission to spend some quality time with your Xbox.

♦ Let them know that what's going on with you is *not* their fault. Many children, regardless of their age, try to make sense of your behavior by blaming themselves.

♦ Spend some time doing fun things with each child. They may be feeling left out and could resent the amount of attention being focused on you and your problems instead of on them, which (in their mind) is where it really belongs. Of course your PTSD may make it hard for you to do activities that involve a lot of noise. Simple kid stuff like coloring, watching Barney videos, and playing with the remote are good options.

♦ Let them know that even if you say or do something that scares them, you will always love them.

♦ Forgive yourself when (not if) you slip.

♦ More hugs, more kisses, more reassurances.

♦ Pay close attention—with your wife—to their behavior. Children of parents with PSTD can develop their own stress symptoms. Individually, each of the symptoms below is a normal reaction to stress. But if your child is exhibiting more than one, or they last for more than a week or so, talk to your child's pediatrician.

◊ Fear of being with you or of being alone.

◊ A significant drop in school performance.

◊ A significant change in friendships.

◊ Behavioral regression, such as bed-wetting or daytime accidents after having been toilet trained, or a return to baby talk.

◊ Nightmares, insomnia, or excessive sleep.

◊ An increase in angry outbursts, temper tantrums, or violence toward others.

◊ Unexplained aches and pains.

◊ Trouble concentrating or focusing.

◊ Read "Field-Tested Ways of Helping Your Kids," on page 237.

◊ Send 'em to camp. Camp COPE (which stands for courage, optimism, patience, and encouragement) was created specifically to help children of injured service members deal and come to terms with a parent's problems. To see whether there's one near you, visit camphope.org.

Physical Injuries

As with psychological injuries, physical injuries can have a real impact on your relationship with everyone in your family. With your wife, frequent, open communication, of course, is key. Couples who aren't able to talk about the injury and how it affects the family may find themselves drifting apart. In addition, the stronger your relationship with your wife was before the injury, the better the two of you will cope afterward. If your relationship wasn't all that great, you've got some work to do, but there's still hope.

Helping your children cope with your injuries is a little more complicated. To start with, it really depends on their age. Because young kids have generally not experienced huge amounts of stress in their lives, they don't have the intellectual and emotional tools to deal with the upheaval your injury could cause in their life. As a result, they may not fully understand what being injured (in a way that requires more than a Band-Aid or a cast) means, or how being injured will affect you.

When Mom Is Injured

Even though women are officially banned from fighting on the front lines, more and more female service members are facing enemy fire. And people—regardless of gender—who are in combat are at risk of physical and/or psychological injury. So if your wife is the one who was deployed and injured, here's how you can help with her recovery:

- **Foster hope.** While it may sound silly, numerous studies have shown that a patient's mental and emotional attitude plays a huge role in his or her recovery process. No one's sure why that is, but does it matter? Injured or not, life is always much more enjoyable when you feel hope. Sounds flaky? Yes. True? Yes again.

- **Encourage friends and family to help.** If your wife is like many women, she may feel guilty that you've been put in a position of having to care for her and your children at the same time, or worried about how all that extra work will affect you. Obviously, these thoughts aren't completely rational (although you might have the same ones if the situation were reversed). Nevertheless, having some other folks around to lend a hand will make her feel a little better. It will also give you a welcome break—one you may not feel comfortable asking for otherwise. As you're assembling your team, try to line up support throughout the entire recovery period. Too often

Starting at about age seven or eight, children will have a firmer grasp of what injury, recovery, and even brushes with death mean, and how your physical wounds could affect the family, their daily lives, and you. (If your injuries are fairly cosmetic—*not* amputations—and are healed, they might be interested in seeing your scars.)

Understanding what your children are going through and what they need will help you give them the support they need to cope. I know that sounds weird—after all, you're the injured one, and they should be helping you, right? Ideally, yes. But the fact is that, injured or not, you're still their dad, and they'll still be looking to you for guidance and comfort. Here are some things your child may experience:

- **Stunted development**. The time your child spends caring for you comes at the expense of activities and interactions that would have encouraged his own physical and/or social development. Of course, in small doses, this isn't a big problem and won't do any long-term damage. But make friends and family will be there in droves immediately following a tragedy, but over time the level of help will tail off.

- **Learn.** Talk to her doctors and read everything you can get your hands on about her injury or illness, treatments, and recovery timelines. The more you know, the more in control you'll feel. It's also important that you help your wife follow the doctors' orders, take her medication, and do every single exercise her physical therapist prescribes.

- **Help her become more independent.** Over time, you should gently encourage your wife to start doing simple tasks on her own. Depending on the nature of her injury, the first step might be something as simple as brushing her teeth. As her recovery progresses, move on to more complex tasks. She may be afraid at first to push herself, but with every accomplishment, her sense of hope will grow.

- **Be patient.** For major injuries, the road to recovery is rarely a straight and level path. Sometimes it's two steps forward and one step back. Other times—such as if a new condition develops during recovery, or a treatment stops working—it's going to be more like one step forward and two back. If she does experience a setback of any kind, keeping her focused on the recovery instead of on the problem is critical.

sure your kids get plenty of time to just be kids. Children—especially young ones—should not be thrust into the role of caretaker. They may feel they need to take care of you, but they need to know that although you appreciate their help, adults are ultimately responsible for other adults.

- **Boys and girls may cope differently**. Studies show children are more likely to take on some of the household responsibilities of a same-sex injured parent than an opposite-sex one. That doesn't mean your daughters won't lend a hand—it's just that they may be more interested in helping you recover than in taking out the garbage or doing the other chores you aren't able to do now.

- **They might become bitter.** If your children feel that they're having to shoulder too great a burden, they may feel resentful and angry. So be sure to talk with the kids about what they think is "fair" (keeping in mind that in most kids' minds, the word *fair* is a synonym for "the same as.") If one child really is being treated unfairly, be prepared to redistribute the work load. If the unfairness is just a perception issue, you may need to convince your child that she plays an important role in the family. And you may need to stress that you are proud of how responsible and helpful he is. A little bit of appreciation goes a long way. A lot goes even further.

♦ **Kids need outside support too.** Watch your children for signs of stress (as described on pages 238–41), and make sure they get whatever support and help they need.

Returning to Military Life after Deployment

There's nothing like shared experiences—especially life-threatening ones—to create deep and powerful bonds. And that's exactly what happened between you and the guys in your unit. So now that you've had a little post-deployment leave or R&R and you're back at home station, you should still be a pretty tight group, right? Well, maybe. Being in a different environment, with different work conditions, different distractions, and different stressors, will definitely shake up the system that seemed to work so well downrange. For example:

♦ **Family commitments now mean less time with the guys.** The bonds you built with your team during deployment will most likely take a back seat to reconnecting with the wife and children—yours and theirs. Some of the single guys (who don't have the same kind of family commitments) may try to keep up frequent, intense social interactions with you during your off-duty hours, but remember: your top priority right now is your family.

♦ **Missions change.** Now that you're back at home station, your unit has a totally different mission, shifting from combat operations to recovery and peacetime ops. This usually entails some personnel reshuffling as some people get promoted and transferred to different units and others take on new roles and responsibilities. These changes can be a little uncomfortable at first, but over time, you and the newly constituted unit will find a comfortable balance.

♦ **Friendships change.** After returning from deployment, it's common for units to turn over as much as 90 percent of the personnel assigned to them. As you can imagine, that means that *everything* about the unit will change. If you're one of the remaining "old-timers" in the unit, it may be tough to welcome the new guys as friends and coworkers. They weren't around for the deployment, and they didn't experience the unit's challenges, hardships, and successes. Eventually, though, you'll find that some of the new guys have been through challenges of their own, and you'll all create a new unit together. Just remember, giving the new guy a nickname like "Stud" is much better than giving him one like "Pimple."

If you're one of those being transferred out of the unit (or you're separating from the military completely), you'll still feel the void created by the sudden absence of those close friendships. When you've been living, working, eating, working out, and goofing off with the same guys twenty-four hours a day for a year, just walking away isn't going to be emotionally easy. You may feel lonely, out of your element, bored, or just plain dissatisfied with your new situation. In short, you'll miss the guys. One solution to try is to reconnect with old friends. Perhaps start a bowling team, a book club, or a sewing circle. Just kidding about the book club.

♦ **Your job changes.** Coming back from deployment can involve some work-related letdowns as well. For example, instead of contributing to the freedom and prosperity of a Third World country or emerging democracy, you might find yourself cleaning and counting equipment, trimming hedges outside the unit headquarters, or planning a training exercise that pales in comparison to real-world missions. This is bound to have an impact on your sense of purpose and job satisfaction.

National Guard and Reservists Return to the Workplace

If you're in the Reserve or Guard and just getting back from deployment, it's tempting to think that transitioning back into your civilian job will be pretty simple. Think again.

The reality is that you'll be walking into a number of emotional and psychological challenges. You may, for example, experience some of the same issues that active duty service members do when they return home, including a kind of withdrawal as you separate from the guys you may have fought alongside for a year or two (see "Returning to Military Life after Deployment," above, for more). You may also find that reconnecting with your former civilian coworkers is almost as hard as reconnecting with your family. Think of a job as one big happy dysfunctional family. Does that help?

Given that Guardsmen and Reservists accounted for as much as 40 percent of the troop strength in Iraq throughout much of Operation Iraqi Freedom, these military-to-civilian integration issues are nothing new. Here are some of the issues you might face:

- **Your old coworkers could seem wary as they try to assess how your deployment may have changed you.** This is a completely natural reaction, so don't hold it against them. You may be able to help the situation along by spending some time reminiscing about the great times you had working together before the deployment, or simply getting them to talk about what they were up to while you were gone.

- **You'll probably want to tell your coworkers all about your deployment, and a lot of them may want to know (some may even come right out and ask).** But don't go overboard with the stories. For now, keep the focus on reestablishing the bond you shared with them before you left. You can always tell them all about your adventures later.

- **Get ready for some big changes.** It's almost certain that you're not going to be able to pick up exactly where you left off. Some of your coworkers may have divided up your duties and responsibilities, or the company may have hired a new person to do your job during your absence. Either way, don't expect your workplace to operate as it did before you left, and try to keep the "But that's not how we did it before!" comments to a minimum. Things will definitely have changed, and you may have to quickly get up to speed on all the new procedures.

  As you slowly work your way back into the swing of things, tread lightly. The guy who had been doing your job (or at least part of it) may not be in any hurry to give it up, and may resent having to do so. He's got some adjusting to do too, so try to be understanding if he behaves like a hungry shark circling his next meal, critiquing everything you do and waiting for you to make a mistake.

- **Be prepared for some retraining.** If everything in your workplace is just as you left it, consider yourself lucky. But don't count on it. Software and hardware are constantly being upgraded, and being out of loop for even a year can leave you feeling hopelessly out of touch. Besides having to get trained on the latest hardware and software innovations and features, you may find that things such as personnel policies procedures, industry best practices, and the entire organizational chart may have changed as well.

- **Know your rights.** If you came home with an injury and your disability prevents you from qualifying for your old position, your employer must move you to another job with equal status, pay, and seniority, if such a position exists. Most employers have no problem doing whatever they can to ensure that your work area or conditions meet your new demands. Just in case you meet some resistance, it's worth spending a few minutes learning about the Americans with Disabilities Act, the Uniformed Services Employment and Reemployment Rights Act (see page 39 for more on USERRA), and the Fair Employment and Housing Act (FEHA).

♦ **Don't jump back into your job too quickly.** The stresses of adjusting to life at home after deployment can negatively affect your job performance. And the stresses of being back at work can negatively affect life at home. So take a vacation day or week or—well, a year is probably a bit much.

♦ **No more saluting!** Hey, you've got to look on the bright side.

♦ **Be patient.** There's a good chance that the skills you learned or refined while you were on active duty have increased your value to your employer. You may be a stronger leader, a more committed team player, or a more creative problem-solver. And you may even have outgrown your previous position. Having confidence in yourself is always good, but although you're very aware of your new skills and talents, your employer and coworkers will probably still want to see those changes in action before they adjust their impressions of you or give you a promotion. Maintain open communication with your supervisor. Don't be afraid to discuss your concerns or your new aspirations. This will allow them to understand what you're thinking and what you're hoping for.

♦ **Understand that your perspective may have changed.** One of these days you'll be sitting with a bunch of coworkers and one of them will start complaining about how tough his job has been and how your employer really should be doing blah, blah, blah. And you're going to think to yourself, "Oh, quit your bitching and shut up. You think this job is tough? Try living in a tent and getting shot at every day like I did for the last year...." Of course you won't actually say that, but it's going to be tough to restrain yourself. Fact is, being in or near combat is really and truly a you-had-to-be-there kind of thing. No one else will fully get it.

♦ **Boredom alert.** Chances are your experiences during deployment involved more excitement, intensity, danger, and focus than you'll see back home at your old workplace. This may make you feel that it's time to find a new career, something more challenging. But before you do anything hasty, give yourself some time to get readjusted to your old job. It's going to be slower than being on the front line, but that just might be a good thing.

Conclusion

I know that this last chapter is largely a downer, but it's hard to dismiss post-traumatic stress, physical disability, and traumatic brain injury. Fortunately, though, it's not all gloom and doom. In fact, most returning service members don't have long-term psychological or physical problems. And most rejoin their families and get their lives back on track pretty quickly. No, it's not easy, and yes, it'll take plenty of patience and understanding from everyone. But it can be done.

The real key to a smooth post-deployment transition is in the preparation. And that's true whether you're active duty military, in the Reserve, a government employee, or a civilian contractor. If you know what to expect from yourself and your family before you leave, the run up to the deployment and the actual tour itself will be a lot easier to cope with. You'll understand their odd behavior (okay, and yours as well), you'll be confident that your family will be all right, and you'll be better able to focus on your mission.

If you manage to remain a part of your family's life—and keep them a part of yours—while you're gone, you'll be able to support your wife and be an active, involved father to your children. And when you come home, you'll know how to deal with the "new normal," and your family ties will be as strong or stronger than ever.

My foremost goal in writing *The Military Father* was to provide you with clear insights and appreciation for the many ways your deployment affects everyone in your entire world, and to equip you with a whole arsenal of field-tested strategies for staying connected to your family. I'm confident that the time you've invested in reading this book was well spent—especially if you were lucky enough to start before you actually shipped out. But even if you tuned in while you were already gone or even after you came home, remember: it's never too early to start preparing for the next deployment.

From the bottom of my heart, I thank you for your service and for the sacrifices you and your family have made for our country.

Appendices

Predeployment Checklists

Before you leave, you and your spouse should go through the following check-lists carefully. Collect all the required information, put all the necessary documents into one easy-to-find file, go through them slowly and thoroughly with your spouse, and make sure everything is ready to go. It'll take a couple of hours to put all this together, but it'll be time very well spent. Once you're wheels-up, it's too late to get your signature on an important piece of paper or to show your spouse the way you have to kick the dishwasher to get it to stop clanking.

After you've collected all of the following, consider making a copy of the whole file and put it in a safety deposit box. Better yet, scan everything and either burn it to a CD or DVD (which you'll store someplace else than your home), or upload it all to an online data storage service such as GoogleDocs (docs.google.com). That way you'll be able to access your information from any computer, anywhere in the world.

Basic Stuff about the Deploying Spouse

	Got It	Need It	N/A
Spouse's unit			
Home base location	☐	☐	☐
Commander, first sergeant, administrator	☐	☐	☐
Contact information	☐	☐	☐
Emergency contact number	☐	☐	☐
Rear detachment commander	☐	☐	☐
Rear detachment contact info	☐	☐	☐
Deployment location (if available)	☐	☐	☐

Mailing address _____

_____

Phone_____

Other emergency contact info

Red Cross: (703) 206-6000, redcross.org

	Got It	Need It	N/A
Chaplain _____	☐	☐	☐
Family assistance center _____	☐	☐	☐
Legal assistance office _____	☐	☐	☐
Family Readiness Group, support group _____	☐	☐	☐
Contact person_____	☐	☐	☐
Contact number _____	☐	☐	☐

Spouse's

	Got It	Need It	N/A
Social Security number _____	☐	☐	☐
ID card number _____	☐	☐	☐
Rank _____	☐	☐	☐
Date and place of birth_____	☐	☐	☐
Blood type _____	☐	☐	☐

Medical

	Got It	Need It	N/A
Immunizations for the whole family (including pets) are up-to-date.	☐	☐	☐
I know where the immunization records are.	☐	☐	☐
I know where medical, dental, vision, and other records are:			
For children	☐	☐	☐
For adults	☐	☐	☐
Babysitter for emergencies Contact info	☐	☐	☐

_____

Providers

Location of hospital	☐	☐	☐

_____

Doctor's name and number	☐	☐	☐

_____

Pediatrician's name and number	☐	☐	☐

_____

Dentist's name and number	☐	☐	☐

_____

Location of dentist	☐	☐	☐

_____

Others (orthodontist, eye care specialist, etc.)	☐	☐	☐

_____

_____

Location and phone number for 24-hour pharmacy	☐	☐	☐

_____

Auto and Home

	Got It	Need It	N/A
I know the year, make, and model of all vehicles.	☐	☐	☐
I know the schedule for routine maintenance, oil changes, tire rotation or replacement, tune-up, and other major and minor service.	☐	☐	☐
I know any quirks about the vehicles.	☐	☐	☐
I know the kind of gas all vehicles use.	☐	☐	☐
I know where we usually take the car for service and repairs.	☐	☐	☐
I have a spare set of keys someplace safe.	☐	☐	☐
I know where all title, registration, loan, insurance, and inspection documents are.	☐	☐	☐
I know when to renew policies and registrations.	☐	☐	☐
I have a valid license to drive all vehicles.	☐	☐	☐
All vehicles have stickers that will allow them to be driven on base. (Make sure these are valid through the end of the deployment.)	☐	☐	☐
I know how to handle basic emergency repairs, such as replacing a tire and charging a battery.	☐	☐	☐
I have a valid AAA, auto club, or other roadside service plan.	☐	☐	☐
I've done a complete home walk-through with my spouse.	☐	☐	☐
I know where the emergency shutoffs are for water, gas, electricity.	☐	☐	☐
I know where the breaker panels and/or fuse boxes are.	☐	☐	☐
I know how to contact the home warranty company.	☐	☐	☐
I have contact info for an emergency plumber, electrician, handyman.	☐	☐	☐
I know where the fire extinguishers are in the house and how to use them.	☐	☐	☐

Auto and Home *continued*

	Got It	Need It	N/A
We have an up-to-date earthquake or natural disaster survival kit. This should include a week's worth of nonperishable food for each member of the family, self-powered flashlight and radio, spare batteries if necessary.	☐	☐	☐
I know where extra lightbulbs are and how to replace them.	☐	☐	☐
I know where all the smoke and CO detectors are, when to change the batteries, and how.	☐	☐	☐
I have a spare key hidden someplace safe and/or with trusted neighbors.	☐	☐	☐
If we live on base, I know the emergency repair numbers of the on-base housing office.	☐	☐	☐
I know when and how to change furnace filters.	☐	☐	☐
We have a family fire escape plan (including emergency ladders), and everyone in the family knows the procedures.	☐	☐	☐
Everyone in the family knows how to dial 9-1-1.	☐	☐	☐
Every phone in the house has a sticker with the number for emergency poison control or, if 9-1-1 isn't available, contact info for police and fire departments.	☐	☐	☐
I know how to set and operate our home security system.	☐	☐	☐
I have log-ins, passwords, and any other security information I need to use all the computers and other technology devices in our home.	☐	☐	☐
I've put together a basic tool kit, including hammer, screwdrivers (Phillips and flat), wrenches, pliers, extra batteries, tape measure, and a variety of nails and screws.	☐	☐	☐

Money, Finances, and Banking

	Got It	Need It	N/A
I have names, account numbers, balances, statements, bankbooks, checkbooks, Web sites, log-in info, passwords, and PINs for all joint and individual accounts at:			
Banks	☐	☐	☐
Credit union	☐	☐	☐
Money market	☐	☐	☐
Brokerage accounts	☐	☐	☐
Other	☐	☐	☐
I know where our safety deposit boxes are located, and I have the keys.	☐	☐	☐
I have names, account numbers, statements, Web sites, log-in info, passwords, and PINs for all joint and individual:			
Credit cards	☐	☐	☐
Debit cards	☐	☐	☐
ATM cards	☐	☐	☐
I have emergency contact phone numbers in case any cards are lost or stolen.	☐	☐	☐
My spouse has set up allotments and/or direct deposits to ensure that we have money coming in on a continuing basis during deployment.	☐	☐	☐
The money that's coming in is enough to take care of all regular household expenses.	☐	☐	☐
I have copies of my spouse's leave and earnings statement (LES).	☐	☐	☐

Money, Finances, and Banking *continued*

	Got It	Need It	N/A
I have a power of attorney that allows me to make any and all necessary financial decisions for our family during the deployment.	☐	☐	☐
I know how to change the address to which allotments are sent.	☐	☐	☐
I know whom to contact and how in case an allotment check doesn't arrive, a direct deposit doesn't happen, or there is some other financial emergency.	☐	☐	☐
I have payment information (account numbers, statements, contact information) for all of our regular bills, including:			
House payment or rent	☐	☐	☐
Utilities (gas, water, trash collection, electricity)	☐	☐	☐
Phone (including Internet, cable, cell phone)	☐	☐	☐
Car payment	☐	☐	☐
Insurance (auto, fire, home, property, life)	☐	☐	☐
Security system	☐	☐	☐
Home warranty	☐	☐	☐
Taxes (property, auto, federal and state income)	☐	☐	☐
Any other credit card or revolving credit accounts	☐	☐	☐
We have set up automatic bill pay for as many regular bills as possible.	☐	☐	☐

Important Documents

	Got It	Need It	N/A
Military orders	☐	☐	☐
Leave and earnings statements	☐	☐	☐
Birth certificates for everyone in the family	☐	☐	☐
Social Security cards for everyone	☐	☐	☐
Marriage certificates	☐	☐	☐
Divorce decrees, including child custody orders or agreements, alimony, child support	☐	☐	☐
Citizenship papers	☐	☐	☐
Adoption papers	☐	☐	☐
Medical records, including shot/immunization records for family and pets	☐	☐	☐
Passports and any required visas (in case you have to make an emergency trip to visit a wounded spouse)	☐	☐	☐
Insurance policies (life, home, fire, property, auto, etc.)	☐	☐	☐
Real estate deeds, leases, loan documentation	☐	☐	☐
Auto deed, title, registration	☐	☐	☐
Home rental leases or rental agreements	☐	☐	☐
Giving nondeployed spouse authorization to get medical treatment, take care of school and extracurricular program registration, and anything else for stepchildren	☐	☐	☐

Important Documents *continued*

	Got It	Need It	N/A
Powers of attorney:			
General—for everything	☐	☐	☐
Special (limited)—just for specific transactions or situations	☐	☐	☐
Medical—for medical decisions	☐	☐	☐
Current wills and trusts for both spouses	☐	☐	☐
Contact info for:			
Immediate family on both sides	☐	☐	☐
Next of kin	☐	☐	☐
Attorney	☐	☐	☐
Friends to contact in case of emergency	☐	☐	☐
Federal, state, and business tax returns (at least the past three years—five is better)	☐	☐	☐
Armed forces ID cards for everyone in the family. Make sure they are valid at least through the expected end of the deployment.	☐	☐	☐
DEERS enrollment forms	☐	☐	☐
Copies of all banking/finance/credit card documents	☐	☐	☐
School registration information and all required paperwork	☐	☐	☐
Copies of all medical, dental, and vision records, including prescriptions for medication and glasses	☐	☐	☐

A Brief Overview of Your Child's Development

What's Going on with Your Unborn Baby

Going from *man* to *father* is one of the most dramatic changes you'll ever experience. It'll force you to rethink who you are, what you do, and what it means to be a man. Your relationships—with your partner, your parents, your friends, your coworkers—will change forever as you begin to reevaluate what's important to you and reorder your priorities. Meanwhile, as you and your wife are making your transitions to parenthood, your future child is on an even more amazing journey—from sperm and egg to living, breathing infant. Here's how it happens.

Month 1

Just because you can't feel anything doesn't mean that things aren't action-packed. Only about two hours after you and your partner had sex, the egg is fertilized, and a day or so later you've got a tiny bundle of quickly dividing cells. By the end of the month the embryo will be about a quarter of an inch long and will sport a heart (but no brain), and stumpy little arm and leg buds.

Month 2

This month your baby changes from an embryo to a fetus. By month's end, his or her (it's way too early to tell which) stubby little arms develop wrists (but no fingers yet), sealed-shut eyelids appear on the side of the face, along with ears, and a tiny, beating heart (albeit on the outside of the body). Not exactly the bouncing baby one normally envisions. If you bumped into a six-foot-tall version of your baby in a dark alley, you'd run the other way.

Month 3

By now, your little fetus looks pretty much like a tiny person—except that he or she (a really sharp ultrasound technician might be able to tell you which, but don't count on it) is only about two or three inches long, weighs less than an ounce, and has transparent skin. Teeth, fingernails, toenails, and hair are developing quite nicely, and the brain is not far behind. By the end of this month, the baby will be able to curl its toes, turn its head, and even frown.

Month 4

By the end of month four, your baby will grow to about four or five inches long. The heart is now fully developed and will start pounding away at

120–160 beats per minute—about twice as fast as yours. In addition, the whole body is covered with smooth hair called *lanugo*. The fetus can swallow, suck his thumb, and kick like nobody's business. Your baby also knows when your partner is eating sweet things or sour things and may have a lot to say about it. He also reacts to light and dark at this stage. Shine a strong light on your partner's abdomen, and the baby will turn away.

Month 5

Your baby's eyelids are still sealed, but her eyebrows and lashes are fully grown in, and you might be able to see the beginnings of a head of hair. By the end of this month your future darling is about nine inches long and weighs in at close to a pound. She kicks, punches, grabs at the umbilical cord, and has developed something of a regular sleep pattern—waking and dozing at regular intervals. In between, she'll spend her time doing somersaults and eavesdropping on what's going-on outside the womb. No kidding—she can hear at this point.

Month 6

Your baby's lean and mean and covered with *vernix*, a thick, waxy, protective coating. His eyes are starting to open; he coughs and hiccups and already has unique footprints and fingerprints. The movements of your now foot-long two-pounder are getting more controlled and stronger—especially when he starts responding to sounds from the outside world. He may even jump at the sound of a door slamming or a car backfiring.

Month 7

Your baby has bulked up to three pounds or so—she's about fifteen inches long, and sports red, wrinkly skin and two functional lungs. If she were born right now, she'd have a pretty good chance of survival. In fact, being born right now might sound good to her, since it's getting a little cramped inside—especially if she's bunking with a womb-mate. Her eyes are fully open and her irises react to light and dark. She can even dance, moving in time to music played outside the womb. Her brain is developing incredibly quickly, but the surface of it is still fairly smooth, and she's not really capable of much rational thought. Given her living situation, that's probably a good thing.

Month 8

At this point, your baby's about eighteen inches long and weighs five pounds or so (a little less if he's got a sibling or two), and his body now looks more like it belongs with that huge head. He's probably assumed a head-down, duck-and-cover position, and will stay that way for the rest of the pregnancy. With practically no room to maneuver, movements become less and less frequent but are often so powerful that you can tell which part of his body is doing the poking. His hearing is getting so good that he now responds differently to your and your partner's voices. Chances of survival outside the womb are excellent.

Month 9

During this final month, your baby grows like a maniac, putting on about half a pound a week. By the time she finally decides to leave the nice, warm uterus, she'll weigh six to nine pounds (less if she's a twin or triplet) and be about twenty inches long—so big that there will be hardly any room to kick or prod your partner anymore. Her fingernails and toenails are frequently so long they have to be trimmed right after birth, and the lanugo and vernix that have been covering and protecting her little body are starting to slough off. And despite the widespread myth that babies are born blind, her sight is just fine. If you shine a bright light (which you *really* shouldn't do) at her mother's abdomen, she'll blink.

Birth

Squiiiiiish, plop, cooo, coooo.

What's Going on with Your Infant (Birth to Twelve Months)

The first year of your child's life may be the most important one in your development as a father. It's the time when the initial parent-child bond and the foundation of your lifelong relationship with each other are formed. But just because you're going to miss some of that first year *does not* mean that you'll never be a good father or that you and your child will ever have a strong relationship. Not at all. As with so much of life, the more you know, the better off you are. If you understand how your child is developing physically, intellectually, emotionally, and socially while you're gone, you'll know what to expect—and what not to expect—when you get home. Doesn't sound like much, but having realistic expectations—especially at this stage—can make a huge difference in how quickly you're able to start building that bond with your baby.

1–3 months

PHYSICAL

In your baby's first week, she's pretty much a bundle of reflexes. She wants seven or eight feedings a day and takes the same number of naps, spending 80 percent of her time asleep. She can, however, focus her eyes for a few moments on an object eight to ten inches from her head.

By the end of the first month she'll accidentally discover her hand and realize that sucking, even if it doesn't result in any milk, is just plain fun.

During her second month she starts grasping for objects voluntarily (as opposed to reflexively) and will even hold on to some for a few minutes at a time. She can't hold her head up for more than a second or two. Her vision gets better, and she'll track you with her eyes everywhere you go.

By the end of the third month she'll have learned how to keep her hands open (before she used to keep them clenched), her head is a lot steadier on her neck, and she'll use those new grasping skills to bring objects in for a closer look.

INTELLECTUAL

Crying is her favorite means of communication, but she's very interested in exploring her new world and will stare at new objects for longer than ones she's seen before.

In her first few weeks of life she prefers simple patterns to complex ones, and the borders of objects (such as your jaw or hairline) to the inner details (mouth and nose). She can't differentiate herself from the other objects in her world. When she's grasping your hand, for example, her little brain doesn't know whether it's yours or her own.

In her second month she'll take to more complex patterns. Just a few weeks ago she'd try to suck on anything that touched her cheek. This month she's learned to tell the difference between nipples and other things (like your fingers). She has no sense of "object permanence," meaning that once something is out of sight, it doesn't exist for her anymore.

At three months your baby can now make associations between certain things and the qualities associated with them; he may associate your partner with food and you with play and reacts differently to each of you. He now uses his voice to communicate—you should be able to tell the difference between the "I'm hungry," "I'm tired," and "Change my diaper right this minute" cries.

EMOTIONAL/SOCIAL

Even in her first month, your baby has a lot to say and is trying to say it. If she hears a noise she'll often quiet down and focus, and she'll usually calm down if you pick her up. Her expression is fairly blank, so it won't always be entirely clear to you what she's thinking.

She sleeps sixteen to twenty hours a day and sometimes uses sleep as a defense mechanism, short-circuiting when she gets overstimulated.

At two months she can smile for real (until now what you thought were smiles were probably just gas). She expresses excitement and distress, is stimulated more by touch than by social interaction, and will stay awake longer if there are people around to amuse her.

At three months she already has strong likes and dislikes, crying or calming down depending on who holds her. She'll also smile at familiar people and gawk at strangers.

4–6 months

PHYSICAL

He can now coordinate the movement of his head and eyes to track moving objects just like you do. He still grasps at everything he can and tries to shove it into his mouth for further analysis. He's figured out that the two sides of his body are separate, and to prove it to you will pass objects back and forth between his hands. While on his tummy he can raise his head and prop himself up on his forearms.

In his fifth month, the big discovery is toes—every bit as exciting as the finger discovery of a few months ago. He may be able to roll from tummy to back and might occasionally lift himself up on hands and knees. He now manipulates objects in his hands to study them from all sides.

By the end of the sixth month he probably sits by himself and might even right himself if he tips over. He can clap his hands and bang two objects together. Whatever's not being banged goes straight into his mouth. He moves to his hands and knees with ease and gets tremendous enjoyment from rocking back and forth.

INTELLECTUAL

At the grand old age of four months, he's learning about cause and effect. If he kicks a toy and it squeaks, he may just try to kick it again, hoping to get the same reaction.

He's trying to communicate. He may respond to your speech, and may even initiate a "conversation" of his own. He also recognizes the difference between speech and other sounds.

At five months, he does a lot of reaching, which reinforces his knowledge that he's separate from other objects.

Handling and turning objects teaches him that even though things look different from different angles, their shape remains the same. As a result, he may get excited at seeing a corner of a familiar object. He knows about gravity, and if he drops something he may look down for it. But if he can't find it in a few seconds, it ceases to exist for him.

At six months, he still thinks he has absolute control over all he sees or touches. He'll endlessly drop toys, dishes, and food from his high chair, and revels in the way he can make you pick them up.

He kinda sorta understands and responds to his name, and he'll spend fifteen or twenty minutes at a time testing out his newfound ability to make vowel sounds.

He also cries for attention—whether he needs it or not—just to prove that he can get you to come. This all shows that he can formulate plans and anticipate consequences of his actions. Verbally, he's added consonants and makes single-syllable "words" like *ka, ma, la, pa, ba.*

EMOTIONAL/SOCIAL

At four months your baby is a pretty happy kid, smiling regularly and spontaneously and anticipating pleasurable encounters by vigorously kicking his arms and legs. He's such a social animal at this point that he'll suppress other interests in order to play. Talk to him while he's eating, and he's glad to stop and chat for a half hour or so. He'll even try to extend playtime by laughing or staring at a desired object, and may protest loudly if you stop doing what he wants you to.

At five months he's expressing a broad spectrum of emotions: fear, anger, disgust, and satisfaction. He'll cry if you put him down and become calm if you pick him up. He has—and expresses—strong preferences for toys and people.

If he feels you're not paying enough attention to him, he'll try to interrupt whatever you're doing with a yelp or a cry. If he does start crying, you can usually stop the tears just by talking to him.

Before now your baby didn't really care who fed him, changed him, played with him, or hugged him—just so long as it got done. But at six months, 50–80 percent of babies start caring about *who's* doing the satisfying and have a definite A and B list of people who can go through the velvet ropes and get near them. Welcome to stranger anxiety.

7–9 months

PHYSICAL

A true expert at getting from tummy to sitting position, she now can sit on her own without support. And (sometimes unfortunately) she's figured out how to use her opposable thumb, which means she'll be yanking up even more stuff than before.

In her eighth month she's a master of crawling and will follow you everywhere. She might even start trying to pull herself upright. But to get down she'll have to fall. Manual dexterity is excellent now, and she'll use her brand-spanking-new pincer grip to pick up ever-tinier things. She's not too bad at feeding herself with her hands and may even be able to hold a bottle or cup.

In her ninth month she won't learn many new tricks, preferring to spend her time perfecting what she knows. By the end of this month she crawls forwards and backwards and maybe up a flight of stairs (childproofing is essential now, if you haven't done it already). She can even crawl and hold on to something at the same time. After pulling herself upright, she can now unlock her knees and sit down—sort of.

INTELLECTUAL

At seven months her ability to make associations is getting better. She recognizes the sounds of your footsteps and gets excited before you even come into her room. "Object permanence" (understanding that things exist even when they can't be seen) is slowly dawning on her. If an object falls, she'll spend as much as 15–20 seconds looking for it. Helium balloons are endlessly amusing—and confusing.

She's now making multisyllable words (*babababababababa*) and understands her name and a few other words.

At eight months, her newfound mobility gives her a chance to explore objects she's seen only from afar. Crawling around the floor, she'll stop and examine (including taking bites to test texture) things from every possible angle. She now babbles using adult intonation and rhythm, and responds to familiar sounds like a car approaching, a refrigerator opening, or a telephone ringing.

By nine months she's starting to get that she's not all-powerful and may bring you a wind-up toy to wind. She's also beginning to shake her "if I can't see it, it doesn't exist" attitude. If she watches you hide a toy, she'll look for it. But if you hide the same toy somewhere else, she'll keep looking in the first place. In her mind, something out of sight may be able to exist, but only in one specific place. She's also learning more about actions and consequences. If she sees you put on a coat, she knows you're going out and may start howling.

EMOTIONAL/SOCIAL

At seven months the fascination with objects continues, but she much prefers the same one-on-one social activities that your dog does: namely chasing and fetching.

She knows the difference between adults and members of her own species (other babies her age) and may be interested in playing with (actually, alongside) them. She recognizes, and reacts differently to, positive and negative tones of voice and your happy or sad facial expressions.

At eight months she's so busy with her physical development that she doesn't nap much during the day, leaving her cranky. But when she's in a good mood, she really wants to be included in everything; she may crawl into the middle of a conversation, sit up, and chatter.

At nine months, she may be able to get you to understand—by pointing, grunting, squealing, or bouncing up and down—that there's something specific on her mind. Preferences are more distinct, and she pushes away things (and people) she doesn't want.

Frightened of the new world she's discovering, she clings to you more than ever, and cries if you leave her alone; it's the beginning of separation anxiety, which is different from the stranger anxiety of the past few months.

10–12 months

PHYSICAL

There are few major physical advances in the tenth month. Most important, he gets to a standing position easily, and cruises sideways while holding on to something for support. He also shows a preference for one hand over the other, using one to manipulate things, the other to hold them.

By the end of the eleventh month he gets himself upright from a squat, and may stand unsupported for a few seconds before crashing down. He gets up and down from chairs and couches with ease and loves wrestling and being held upside down.

By his first birthday he may take a tentative step or two (although many babies won't for a few more months). Hand preference is more obvious.

If you put an object into his "weak" hand he'll transfer it to the "strong" one.

INTELLECTUAL

At ten months his world is categorized into "things I can chew on" and "things that are too big to get into my mouth." This adds some predictability and control to his life. He thinks symbolically (associating things he can see with things he can't). A few months ago he cried when seeing a nurse at his doctor's office because he associated the nurse with shots. Now he recognizes the doctor's office from the street and will start crying as soon as you pull into the lot.

In his eleventh month, he recognizes the symbolic use of words—he'll say "yum" if you're talking about ice cream, or "meow" if you point to a cat. He babbles in long paragraphs, tossing in a recognizable word once in a while.

By his first birthday he knows for sure that objects exist even though he can't see them. He'll search—in more than one place if necessary—for objects he's seen but didn't see you hide. He uses trial and error to solve problems and overcome obstacles. He has a vocabulary of six to eight words, as well as a few other sounds like "moo," "woof," or "boom."

EMOTIONAL/SOCIAL

At ten months he's a real mimic, saying "brr" after getting out of the bath and taking power calls on the phone just like you. He's sensitive to your emotions and expresses plenty of his own. If you're happy, he is too; if you scold him, he'll pout; if you do something he doesn't like, he shows real anger; and if you leave him alone for too long (only he knows how long that is), he might just "punish" you.

At eleven months he shows genuine tenderness and affection for you— and his stuffed animals.

He understands approval and disapproval, looking for your praise when he does something good, hanging his head sheepishly when he's misbehaved.

Around his first birthday he gets less cooperative, regularly testing your limits and your patience.

He's developing a sense of humor, especially for incongruities. Pretend to cry, tell him a dog says "moo," or crawl like a baby, and he'll laugh hysterically. He plays nicely around other kids at home, where he feels safest. But in less secure environments he's less sociable and may not leave your side.

What's Going On with Your Toddler (One and Two Years)

What image comes to mind when you hear the word *toddler*? Probably that of a small child, not nearly as helpless as an infant, walking, falling, walking again. A child brimming with confidence and eager to learn. Well, that's exactly right. And much the same could be said about you, too. You've learned a huge amount in the year since your child was born, and you're getting a pretty good grip on this parenting thing. But as confident as you are, something still happens every day to remind you that there's still plenty more to learn.

1 year

PHYSICAL

Your bouncing baby is still expanding, but not nearly as fast as in her first year. Less growing means less eating.

At the start of the first half of the year she can walk by herself—hands out and teetering—and she'll insist on doing so. She can run by eighteen months, but mostly stops by falling down.

She can hold two objects in her hands at the same time, and if you draw her a straight line, she can copy it.

She uses legs all the time, running and jumping and kicking. By her second birthday she may even be able to pedal a small tricycle.

Favorite activities include emptying and filling (emphasis on the emptying)—especially things you don't want emptied, such as your refrigerator and sock drawer.

She's fascinated by action-reaction and adores turning the lights on and off, opening doors and slamming them, and flushing the toilet repeatedly.

She loves all sorts of physical games: chase me/catch me, rolling balls back and forth, and wrestling are big favorites.

After eighteen months or so she starts and stops running without a problem, but corners present some difficulty.

She stoops to pick things up and most of the time doesn't fall. She can go up stairs by herself, holding on to the railing, but usually comes down backward.

Fine motor coordination is improving. By now she can sort shapes with a shape sorter and build a fine tower as much as six blocks tall, and is really good at undressing. Dressing is an entirely different story.

She makes a formidable mud pie, spends hours opening and closing screw-top containers, and stacks, piles, tears, and pours anything that isn't tethered down.

She is better at handling silverware, but she's no Emily Post. She holds her fork in one hand, picks up a piece of food, and pushes it onto the tines with the other.

INTELLECTUAL

At the beginning of her second year your baby has an active vocabulary of six to ten words—mostly body parts, a few animals, a few familiar people, and show-stoppers like *yes* and *no*.

Her passive vocabulary (what she understands) is much bigger, though. When asked, she can point to her eyes, nose, and other body parts, and may even respond to simple directions, such as "Bring me my pipe and slippers."

She will try to repeat everything you say, using a kind of shorthand. For example, if you say, "No, you can't pour your milk on the floor," she'll probably reply, "Pour milk floor."

She's starting to grasp the symbolic use of words: if she knows the word *pool*, she may use it when she sees a duck pond, a puddle on the street, or even the ocean. She also might refer to every cat, horse, goat, pig, llama, or other hairy, four-legged animal as a "dog."

By eighteen months she'll be trying to put phrases together ("Gimme book" or "Up me"). Near her second birthday she'll begin using language where she once used emotions: this is nice, especially when she says "Change my diaper" instead of just shrieking.

Nursery rhymes are very well received, and if you pause for a few seconds, she'll fill in the last word of a couplet ("Hickory, dickory, dock / The mouse ran up the ___"). Unfortunately, this also means that if you're reading a familiar book and make a mistake, she won't let you get away with it.

As her imagination develops, so will her capacity for pretending. She may crawl around the house pretending to be a dog, or may "eat" the drawings of food in your cookbooks.

She'll start trashing your home by picking up, rotating, dropping, tasting, stacking (and knocking over), and throwing. Be patient—by touching everything she can get her hands on, she's giving herself a crash course in shape, texture, taste, density, balance, and aerodynamics.

It finally dawns on her that things exist even if she can't see them, and she'll search for objects she thinks might be hidden.

A word of advice: toddlers love routines. Establishing rituals now, such as bath-story-bedtime and park-lunch-nap, will help you minimize some of the problems you're likely to encounter later on.

EMOTIONAL/SOCIAL

Her never-ending search for independence starts—tentatively—now. She'll stroll a few yards away, casually looking back over her shoulder to make sure you aren't going anywhere. But independence is scary, so every few seconds she'll scamper back and cling to you for all she's worth. She'll repeat the process of going away and coming back at least through college.

As she gets more secure with the idea that you'll always be there for her, fear of separation and shyness around strangers should decrease.

Establishing independence involves a lot of limit-testing, such as refusing to do just about anything you want her to—including eating and napping.

She still plays alongside, rather than *with*, other toddlers. In fact, the only people she really wants to socialize with are you and your wife. She watches kids a lot and tries to imitate them.

She may show her interest in other kids by physically exploring them, sometimes hitting, pushing, shoving, and hair-pulling. But she's not really being mean: she's still learning about the difference between animate and inanimate objects and is fascinated by cause and effect.

She doesn't know how to share, so don't spend a lot of time trying to force her. She just hasn't yet picked up the ability to think about others' feelings or wants.

She understands verbal humor now, particularly when it deals with incongruities. After refusing your lunchtime offer of a banana, a bowl of cereal, and a cheese sandwich, she may laugh hysterically if you suggest a spoonful of dirt. (After all, *even babies* know that people don't eat dirt....)

She's developing a wider range of emotions: she's now quite affectionate with friends, family, stuffed animals, and pictures in books—she loves to "baby" dolls (and even parents), covering them with blankets and putting them to "bed." Her whole body lights up when she's praised, and her feelings are genuinely hurt when she's criticized.

2 years

PHYSICAL

Your toddler's appetite tapers off and he starts getting picky, preferring the "white food group"—like rice and plain pasta.

Enjoy his baby fat while you can, because it's melting fast. His little pot-belly is mostly gone, and so are those wonderful little fat cushions on the bottoms of his feet.

Gone too is his disproportionately giant head, as his body lengthens. And suddenly, there are all these teeth in his mouth.

He doesn't need his hands for balance anymore, and he's losing that endearing Frankensteinian lumber. He runs without falling down, walks up and down stairs by himself, jumps off a low step, and rocks or marches in time to music.

He's also adept at squatting and stooping and can even bend over to pick something up without crashing down.

His attention span is still a bit iffy, so he seems to think with his feet—wandering aimlessly, stopping to engage in some activity or other, then moving on to something else. He can kick a ball, and sometimes even control where it goes.

Now that his hand-eye coordination is improving, his fork-handling abilities are much better, and so are his construction skills. He moves from simple block towers to long walls, houses, forts, and horse corrals.

Pushing is nice. So is pulling, filling, and dumping everything he can get his hands on. He can turn the pages of a book, but almost never only one at a time. Give him a crayon and he'll scribble emphatically, but without an agenda. By his third birthday, though, he'll try to imitate your writing and will be able to draw a fabulous X.

Early this year he still won't be able to differentiate between one side of his body and the other—when he points to something he sticks out the fingers of both hands. But about six months from now he'll be able to control each side independently.

Think your house is childproofed? You might want to revisit some of those door knobs, cabinets, and window locks. You can bet that he has.

INTELLECTUAL

Your child talks, and talks, and talks. Until now, he learned about his world *physically*: he had to touch, feel, or taste things before he could truly understand them. But now, *language*—questions, answers, explanations—begins to take over as the primary means of acquiring information.

He uses twenty to a hundred words and is learning two or three new ones every day. *Why* and *no* are his hands-down favorites. He can also do some pretty good animal imitations.

Listening is another story. Most of his words announce things that he's doing or seeing, and he doesn't respond much when you talk to him.

He'll start this year with a passive vocabulary of 200–500 words, but by his third birthday he'll be able to understand the majority of the conversational language he'll use for the rest of his life, which means you'd better start spelling things out if you want to keep secrets from him.

One of the more interesting steps in language-related development, according to child psychologist Selma Freiberg, is that "language makes it possible for a child to incorporate his parents' verbal prohibitions, to make them part of himself." This isn't always 100 percent successful, though. You may find him sitting on the floor, eating sugar out of the box, and saying "No, baby not eat sugar" between mouthfuls.

He wants it and he wants it now and he wants to do everything himself, which means he gets insanely frustrated every time his desires outstrip his physical capabilities, which is most of the time. If you offer to help, you'll make him mad. If you don't offer to help, you'll make him mad too. Good luck.

Expect some spectacular tantrums as the "terrible twos" kick in. Most arise out of the frustration of having too few words to express what he wants.

Routines, patterns, and symmetry are a must for the latter half of this year. Half an apple (or a cookie with a bite out of it) is completely unacceptable. And if you forget to fasten your seat belt before starting the car, you're likely to get a stern talking-to.

He learns the vocabulary of time between age two and a half and three. At this point he regularly uses "soon," "in a minute," and the always-endearing "this day" (instead of "today").

He can now count to three and may even be able to recite numbers up to ten, but he has no idea what they mean.

EMOTIONAL/SOCIAL

The first few months of this year are happy and delightful. But starting at about two and a half, your child becomes rebellious, defiant, negative, and exasperating. He doesn't know what he wants, but knows that he *doesn't* want to do whatever it is that you want him to. Get used to this now, because you'll be seeing it again when he's thirteen.

He expresses his emotions physically more than verbally. If happy, he may jump up and down with glee; if angry, he may hit someone or throw something. Tantrums and mood swings happen daily as he struggles to gain some kind of control over his thoughts and actions. Offering a limited number of choices (red sweater or blue one?) can help reduce tantrums by giving him more control over his world.

Being contrary and ornery is a tough job for a kid, and he's likely to be tired a lot. Unfortunately, tiredness makes tantrums worse....

He still plays alongside rather than with other kids. But, hard as it is to tell, he's slowly becoming more interested in them. You'll see this for yourself when he starts making a strange noise or using a word he never did before—the same noise or word used a few days before by the two-year-old at the park your child seemed to be ignoring completely.

He'll start off the year very possessive of his toys—offering them to others and then snatching them back. But by the end of this year, he'll show the first signs of cooperation—helping a playmate build or dig something instead of just trashing it.

He's incredibly proud of the things he can do, and constantly seeks your approval. He'll beg you a hundred times a day, "Look at me!!!" as he climbs up stairs, fills a bucket with sand, draws a straight line, or rides his trike.

His imagination is wild, and he can pretend to do anything with any kind of prop. Boys may turn dining room chairs into racing cars and chew toast into the shape a gun. Girls may wrap a toy truck in a blanket and pretend it's a baby.

He still finds the incongruous incredibly funny: try to put your foot into his shoes or wear his pants on your head, and you're likely to reduce your toddler to hysterical laughter.

What's Going On with Your Preschool and Early School-Age Child (Three to Seven Years)

The primary focus of your child's preschool years is going to be on growing and perfecting skills—physical as well as linguistic. You're changing too, of course, in ways you never would have if you hadn't become a father. During your child's preschool years the most significant interactions you'll have with him are going to be physical, through play. Yes, you'll miss some of that time while you're deployed, but fortunately, this stage of your child's life lasts a few years, so there'll be lots of fun to be had before you leave and after you get back. This is also a time when you'll be figuring out exactly what your priorities are, what kind of dad you want to be, and how on earth you're going to accomplish what you want to in life.

3 years

PHYSICAL

He's taller and thinner and has a full set of baby teeth.

He spends most of his waking hours exploring the world and honing his motor skills. This means spending half the morning going up and down the same flight of stairs and the other half screwing the lid on and off his favorite jar.

His average night's sleep is ten to twelve hours. He usually wakes up dry, but accidents are still de rigueur. A few girls may show some interests in potty training, but most boys won't.

His dressing skills are improving. The shoes, he can put on himself. Snaps and zippers still frustrate him. And buttoning? Forget it!

He can catch a large ball if it happens to land on his outstretched arms.

He walks and runs like a champ—usually without having to hold his arms out for balance. In fact, he's so good that he can even take corners at full speed. Once he does slow down, you might catch him practicing walking on tiptoe.

And how 'bout those fine motor skills. Somebody's feeding himself with a spoon, and most of the food is getting inside him. He holds a crayon sort of like we do, and traces some (very basic) shapes, most of which bear an uncanny resemblance to Mr. Potato Head.

INTELLECTUAL

Your child will not stop talking. By now he has an active vocabulary of over 600 words and likes to arrange them in three-to-five-word sentences.

He's still not much of a conversationalist and prefers announcements and demands to give and take.

He loves stories and rhymes, over and over and over and over. Not to worry: if you need a break, he's perfectly able to "read" you the book in his own words, using the pictures as a guide.

He understands sequences much better than before: We went to the park, then we came home, then we watched a video.

He's becoming aware of gender differences and stereotypes and understands that certain activities are "boy" things and others are "girl" things.

He associates people with places, which means he may not recognize his favorite pediatrician if you bump into him in line at grocery store.

He's got "now," "soon," and "in a minute" down pretty well, but he's a little fuzzy on more abstract time words such as "tomorrow" and "today."

He counts "One, two, a lot."

Buy puzzles. He loves the relationship between whole objects and the parts that make them up.

His imagination is soaring, and he loves dressing up. Cross-dressing is still common at this age.

EMOTIONAL/SOCIAL

Whew, the "terrible twos" are pretty much over. Your toddler now says yes more than no. His improved coordination and his growing control over his own actions mean he's less frustrated and a lot nicer to be with.

Sometimes timid, sometimes adventurous, he may still have some trouble making up his mind—demanding to be taken to the car and then refusing to get in.

He may also spend some time testing your limits, pushing you just to see what kind of reaction he can produce. Luckily, he's got a fairly short attention span, and you can easily distract him, which makes it easier to avert a crisis. This is also a good time to remember the very important advice: Choose your battles. Before reacting, take a second to figure out whether it's really worthwhile to stand your ground on some little thing like whether he's wearing matching socks or not.

He's becoming a little less self-centered, changing from "I want..." demands to "Let's do..." requests.

He craves your approval and often does what you ask him to the first or second time instead of the seventeenth or twenty-fifth. When he does ignore you or misbehave, he may express some guilt or embarrassment later.

Interestingly, your toddler may express a preference for the opposite-sex parent. This stage usually doesn't last very long.

He still plays nearby rather than with other kids and isn't great at sharing. But by his fourth birthday he may actually do it without being prompted.

He's becoming very aware of differences in race and gender, and the kids he does play with are more likely than not to be same-sex.

His active fantasy life still includes dress-up and role playing. It may also include some imaginary friends. These characters serve a very important purpose, helping him try out different behaviors and emotions and giving him someone to blame if things don't go right.

4 years

PHYSICAL

No, you aren't imagining it: your four-year-old is even more active than she was at three. She will run and jump and hop on one foot and crawl and climb and skip and balance and do somersaults, and she will want you to do this with her.

Roller skating is a distinct possibility, as is pedaling and steering her tricycle (or even a two-wheeler with training wheels) at breakneck speed. Thankfully she's a little more cautious on the stairs, putting both feet on each step.

Using the abovementioned activities, she'll begin navigating impromptu obstacle courses. Make sure she has plenty of time and space to blow off steam.

Meanwhile, on the small motor front, she loves painting with big, broad strokes and is getting pretty handy with spoons, forks, and knives.

She can get herself dressed and tie her shoes (if not in bows, then in knots) without much help, but she may not want to do either.

INTELLECTUAL

She's up to about 1,500 words now and will boost that to 2,500 by the end of this year. She still uses most of those words to tell you what's going on, but she begins to participate in—and even initiate—small conversations with other kids. If you ask her about her day, she may tell you, but chances are she'll make it up and exaggerate all sorts of details.

She tailors her speech to her audience. She'll tell *you*, "I fell down outside and cut my toe." But she'll tell the baby, "Me hurt foot."

She's so proud of her language abilities that she starts playing language games, making up silly names for objects she doesn't know. She'll be driven to hysterical laughter by the name-game song (Bill Bill bo bill, banana-fana-fo-fil, mee my mo mill, Bill).

She identifies a few numbers and most letters—especially the ones that make up her name, which she may even be able to print. She also recognizes a few simple words that she sees regularly, such as STOP.

Her grammar improves. She picks up some irregular plurals (one mouse, two mice, not mouses). But she still has trouble with some irregular past tenses, saying things like "I goed to the zoo and seed a rhino," instead of "I went" and "I saw." When she makes this kind of mistake, don't correct her; simply repeat the sentence correctly.

She's very curious and asks lots of questions, particularly about birth and death.

She loves making big things out of little ones and is especially fond of connect-the-dots games.

She still loves dressing up, but cross-dressing decreases as boys and girls tend to prefer "gender-appropriate" clothes.

EMOTIONAL/SOCIAL

Her ability to feel and express emotions is increasing faster than her ability to manage them. She's often oversensitive, breaking into tears or becoming enraged at something insignificant or laughing for twenty minutes about something that wasn't that funny.

She now plays *with* other kids. Actual friendships are developing, almost all of which are with same-sex kids. She has a new best friend every day.

Along with friends comes peer pressure. Your child absolutely *must* have all those cool things her playmates have, and they can't live without what she's got.

She's still not great at sharing, partly because she doesn't really get that other people have feelings that may be as important as hers. Locking a friend up in a closet so she won't be able to leave is a pretty typical four-year-old way of keeping a play date going.

She understands simple rules for games and usually follows them. But she'll often change the rules to suit herself.

Until now, most imaginative play had to do with house and pretending to be mommy or daddy. Now, your child will more likely pretend to be an astronaut or a doctor or a police officer or butcher.

She's still pretty self-centered, bragging about her accomplishments and getting jealous if you pay attention to anyone else.

In an attempt to remain the center of attention, she tries to shock people by swearing, using her own made-up profanity, such as "doo-doo head."

Your preschooler now prefers the same-sex parent and tries to be like him or her in every way. But no matter what gender you are, she loves to hear stories about your childhood—especially the times when you got into big trouble.

She's more interested in sex now and may ask you about the mechanics. Long explanations are *not* necessary at this stage. Boys and girls both may extend their curiosity about sex into the pants of their friends. That's normal. Still, it may be time for a talk on privacy.

5 years

PHYSICAL

He's down to ten or eleven hours of sleep a night, but not because he's any less active than before. In addition to everything he was doing last year, he can catch balls on a bounce, throw overhand, jump rope, and stand on his head. He can even come down a flight of stairs alternating his feet (as opposed to last season's two-feet-per-step approach).

He's now able to take on more complex physical activities such as swimming or skiing.

He may still like riding his trike, but if he hasn't already ridden a two-wheeler with training wheels, he's going to want to soon. But that phase will be short—by the end of the year he'll be ready to get rid of the training wheels.

As his baby teeth fall out, you'll find yourself paying good money in the name of someone called the Tooth Fairy. And since the permanent teeth won't be along for a bit, you'll have plenty of time to enjoy the gaping holes in his smile.

New, improved fine motor skills include zipping, buttoning, and shoe tying.

Everything is easier than last year. He can cut a pattern with scissors and even draw fairly intricate pictures. So what if his people have eyes on the tops of their heads? At least they have necks....

INTELLECTUAL

Your five-year-old is a real thinker. He loves to argue, reason, and prove his points. *Because* is the big word now.

He still loves to be read to, but he's a lot more interested in trying to read for himself. He understands that books go from left to right and top to bottom. He especially likes jokes, nonsense rhymes, and silly stories.

He draws letters and shapes and loves to write, especially his own name and short sentences like "I (heart) Daddy."

He begins to understand that actions have consequences. This won't keep him from misbehaving, of course, but at least it's on some back burner for later.

He can memorize his address and phone number—and should, for safety reasons.

He can count up to ten and may even have memorized a few more numbers past that. He loves to count and sort and organize everything he can—the number of squares on the sidewalk between your house and the park, the number of dogs you pass on the way there, how many green cars you drove by, how many kids have long hair in his preschool class, how many days till his birthday, and on and on.

EMOTIONAL/SOCIAL

Friends are getting to be very important. They continue to be almost exclusively same-sex. Preschoolers love to get together and construct elaborate fantasy games. But they spend more time talking about the rules and who's going to be whom than actually doing anything.

He's pretty good at sharing and taking turns but may occasionally exclude some kids from the play group.

He's much more interested in others in general. He now has conversations with people and may even ask a question now and then.

His sense of empathy is growing. He notices when others are upset and may try to soothe them.

Your preschooler has developed a fondness for rules—they offer some security in a world that he seems to have less and less control over. He likes to invent games and the rules that go with them, and has no problem changing the rules if things aren't going his way. He can't always remember the rules he's supposed to follow, though: Wash your hands after going to the bathroom, use a fork instead of your hands...

He still has some trouble telling fantasy from reality and may be developing a fear of the unknown, which could include loud noises, the dark, strangers, and even some things he didn't use to be afraid of, like the mailman or the neighbor's dog.

He likes to test his strength and show off how strong and capable he is. But he's not ready for competition, even with other kids—his ego is still pretty fragile, and he can't stand not to win.

He's becoming more aware of the world around him and will notice differences between his family and other families—this one has two daddies, that one doesn't have any...

He's also becoming more self-aware. He instinctively knows that he needs a little down time every once in a while, and he will go to his room or another quiet place where he can be alone.

6–7 years

PHYSICAL

Your six-year-old is still very much a child, and her mouth is filled mostly with baby teeth.

Her right- or left-handedness is pretty well established, and her hand-eye coordination and dexterity are getting better all the time.

She can tie her shoelaces by herself, print her name and a lot of other words, handle a pair of scissors without drawing blood, and most of her art actually looks like what it's supposed to be. Control over small muscles (fingers, for example) is lagging, and she prefers doing things that work out the more developed large muscles (legs and arms).

She's not gaining weight as fast as before (probably three to six pounds per year). That, combined with lots of physical activity, has eliminated most of her baby fat and makes her look gangly.

Her balance is excellent now, and she's ready to learn to ride a bicycle. She can catch small balls and connect fairly regularly with a baseball bat.

INTELLECTUAL

There are pouts galore as your six-to-seven-year-old becomes increasingly taken with the notion that people are unfair and favor everyone else—especially younger siblings.

Taking responsibility isn't her strong point, and she's quick with excuses. Still, she's starting to show some guilt about misbehaving. It's hard for her to make up her mind, but she's stubborn once a decision has been made.

She lives in a black-and-white world with very little gray. She finds security in rules and makes up complicated games with extensive, ever-changing regulations.

The notion of "men's work" and "women's work" is beginning to dawn on her, and she may have some trouble dealing with the idea of a male nurse or female firefighter.

She's getting mighty curious about reproduction and birth, but (thankfully) that's about as far as her interest in sex goes.

She can tell time on an analog clock, yet persists in asking time-related questions (How long till we get home?).

She can separate fantasy and reality, but may not want to—especially when fantasy yields money, as in the case of tooth fairies or Santa Claus.

She craves knowledge and loves learning, adventure, and new ideas. Her vocabulary is over 2,000 words, which means she's got plenty of words to use when talking back to you. Questions are constant. With her increased attention span, she spends a lot of time reading and writing, though she may still reverse *b* and *d*.

She loves magic, card tricks, and competitive games but can't stand losing.

EMOTIONAL/SOCIAL

Your six-to-seven-year-old is a highly emotional creature, given to angry outbursts, mood swings, and difficult behavior.

She wants to be the biggest, strongest, and have the most. She adores being flattered and becomes infuriated if you don't notice—and praise— her often. She's discovered that tattling is a great way to attract your attention.

Her emotional range is fairly limited, and she tends to express herself physically more than verbally (hitting and pushing rather than discussing problems).

She constantly starts more projects than she finishes, but by her eighth birthday will be much better.

Though still fairly self-centered, she can now (sometimes) see things from others' point of view and has a greater (but not too great) respect for their needs.

"Real" fears, such as not having friends, or that something horrible that happened somewhere else will happen to her, begin replacing garden-variety childhood fears of witches and goblins and being flushed down the toilet.

Her first steps away from her insulated little world and into the big world of school and peers scares her and even undermines her confidence. Her fragile ego doesn't deal very well with failure or criticism from others.

Her playmates are generally of the same sex. She plays better with one friend at a time and demands loyalty (If you play with her, you can't be friends with me).

She wants to tell you all about her day and everything that happened to her. And she does.

What's Going On with Your School-Age Child (Eight to Twelve Years)

Even though your child has been trying to establish her independence since she was born, she's still spent most of her time at home, with you and your partner. And you still had a lot of control over her life—where she went, who her friends were, what she learned. But now that she's in school, that will be the focus of her life. And over the next few years she'll go from barely being able to read her name to plowing through two-hundred-page novels. The ongoing process of separating from you and joining the outside world is getting more obvious by the day. Your school-age child has her own social life—one that often doesn't include you—and she's perfectly capable (or at least she thinks she is) of scheduling her own engagements and other activities.

8–10 years

PHYSICAL

Your baby's looking like an adult! By ten, girls are getting softer around the edges while boys are getting firmer.

But she still acts like a child, with energy to burn, fidgeting, and in constant movement. She does everything fast, shifting quickly between activities. Endless projects are started, few get finished.

All this activity takes its toll on both of you. She'll crash hard at the end of the day and may still be tired in the morning. So are you.

She's between growth spurts, and the slower growth makes it easier for her to control her body. Coordination and small muscle control are excellent. She can use both hands at the same time, which should help her make great advances in playing musical instruments.

She's proud of her physical strength, agility, and stamina and loves to show them off.

She's getting a little more adventurous when it comes to eating, and she may occasionally try something that isn't white (rice, noodles).

Most of her baby teeth have been replaced by permanent ones. So a quick trip to the orthodontist and some squirreling away of money for braces may be in order.

Now that she's using the computer and doing a lot more reading for school, watch out for eyestrain.

INTELLECTUAL

She still loves praise but is starting to grasp the painful notion that the entire world doesn't revolve around her. She still loves competitive games, but can now tolerate losing once in a while.

Her awareness of time is growing. She knows her bed- and wake-up times and may write out detailed hour-by-hour schedules of her day. Sequence and order make sense to her now, which enables her to concoct very elaborate stories about why she was late for school. It also enables her to comprehend death.

Money intrigues her, and the more she understands what it does, the more interested she becomes in getting some of her own.

Girls are more sex-aware than boys. Boys love to tell dirty jokes. Both genders are a little shy when it comes to sexual themes.

Her mind is growing, and she loves to use it. She loves memorizing and now reads to acquire information as opposed to entertainment. She prefers active learning (going to see the lions at the zoo) to listening to an adult drone on and on. Beware of the know-it-all attitude this new facility gives her.

Mathematical concepts are making more sense. She now understands about odd and even, larger and smaller, and groups (Ford, Chevy, and Lexus are all cars). She'll make endless lists of everyone she knows, organized by hair color or height.

She defines herself in terms of what she can do (I can tap-dance, I can torture my brother, I can lift my daddy off the floor).

Her stubbornness blossoms into perseverance, and she begins working on skills repeatedly until she masters them.

Occasionally she thinks of the future, though mostly in terms of doing the same things that Dad or Mom have done in their lives.

She's developing a sense of right and wrong! She tells the truth more often, exaggerates less, and has a pretty good understanding of actions and consequences.

She may show couch potato tendencies, enjoying TV, videos, and video games so much that she'll often pass up a chance to play outside in favor of sitting passively in front of a screen.

EMOTIONAL/SOCIAL

She's outgoing and cheerful most of the time but seesaws back and forth between emotional highs and lows. Pouting is replacing violence as a way of expressing anger.

She can be impatient too. She often has some trouble delaying her own gratification and is jealous of the time her younger siblings spend with you.

Her confidence is growing, particularly about what she's learning at school. Her teacher can do no wrong, which means that should you ever disagree with either of them, you'll suffer her wrath.

As her desire to fit in to the group increases, her confidence in herself decreases. She wants to control younger kids, but she's usually worshipful to the older kids. She still tattles and often exaggerates the wrongs people are doing to her.

She's more empathetic of others, but more critical of herself at the same time.

She still enjoys spending time with her family but as friends take on a more central role in her life, she'll spend less and less time with you.

Guess what? She craves recognition from her peers more than from you, and they frequently resolve their problems by judging each other.

There's little if any play with kids of the opposite sex. Boys' friendships are fairly smooth. Girls have endless spats, breakups, and makeups. She has a handful of friends and a worst enemy. The lineup changes daily.

She craves heroes—usually a teacher, coach, one of the adults who drives the carpool, or even a really cool teenager from the neighborhood—whom she'll try to please all the time.

She's self-conscious, worried that everyone is looking at her all the time. Perfectly ordinary things become embarrassing. You, for example.

She worries about the unknown—death, divorce, abandonment, high school, not being popular, growing up.

11–12 years

PHYSICAL

Girls are slouching toward maturity and are two years ahead of boys in maturity. Most girls have started puberty; most boys have not.

Fidgeting tapers off as he approaches his thirteenth birthday—a cause for celebration all around.

He's still very active, though, is often ravenous, and needs a lot of sleep (ten or eleven hours a night). Watch out for unnecessary dieting or skipping meals, which may indicate a predisposition toward bulimia or anorexia.

Reaction time improves, and he gets stronger. He loves to learn complex physical tasks.

He understands why exercise is good for him and may even see the value in warming up.

Beware of his bite! He has most or all of his permanent teeth (twenty-eight), unless his orthodontist has pulled some. Regular dental checkups are important.

Enter pimples. And now that his sweat glands are fully operational, you may want to invest in some deodorant.

INTELLECTUAL

As he careens into teenhood, he becomes less cooperative, often doesn't respond when asked to help out, and is quick to criticize anything less than perfection in anyone else (especially you). Get used to the phrase "Why should I?"—you'll be hearing it a lot.

His behavior may remind you of the terrible twos: he does the opposite of whatever he's asked, cries hysterically for no apparent reason, has tantrums, uses the word *no* more than any other in his rather large vocabulary, and slams doors a lot. Thankfully, he may also want to cuddle up on your lap and have you read him a bedtime story.

He's ever more curious about sex but wants to get the skinny from all the wrong places: friends, magazines, television.

His mathematical skills have taken him beyond fractions and decimals to algebra, geometry, statistics, and probability. Hopefully he's learning the basic computer, library, and research skills he'll use in high school.

He actively participates in adult conversation when he wants to, listening to what people say, asking questions, and making well-thought-out arguments. He also thinks critically and uses reason and logic, and he'll jump all over any mistake you make.

His sense of right and wrong is pretty solid, but he still adores getting away with whatever he can.

He compares your family to his friends' ("But Jimmy's father lets him…"), and you'll almost always come up short.

He makes plans, sometimes weeks in advance, now that his abstract thinking skills are developing.

EMOTIONAL/SOCIAL

He's an emotional chameleon on two legs, ranging from murky frustration to burning passion to blinding fury (generally reserved for younger sibs, whom he sees as worthless creeps).

He becomes less embarrassed by your mere existence as he gains confidence with his friends. He still likes to spend time with his family, but complains that you don't ever have time for him.

He knows he's changing, and peer pressure will affect both you and him. "Fitting in" is a big deal, and requires keeping up with the latest fashions, movies, music, and trends. Aimless hanging out increases, and individualized activities decrease.

Friends are getting more important, which makes sense because it's about the only area of your child's life that he has complete control over. Both genders usually have only a few close friendships, though. Secret clubs and passwords are used to deepen friendships by keeping others out. Boys and girls live in very different social worlds. Boys go to parties to eat and hang out, girls go secretly hoping something will happen.

Girls' friendships are intense and marked by spats and fights and tearful reunions. Boys quarrel with each other a little more than they did before, but still less than girls.

He's codifying his world, and the rules (for you, anyway) just got more stringent. He may swear like a sailor, but parents should never swear in front of kids.

Your eleven-to-twelve-year-old actually wants to grow up! In fact, she may even hate being seen as a child. So what if her hygiene slips a little or if she skips an occasional bath or shower?

What's Going On with Your Teenager (Thirteen to Eighteen Years)

One of the horrid little secrets about fatherhood is that sometimes it's...not fun. I know, I know, I shouldn't say things like that, but it's true. Throughout our children's lives, all parents have the occasional why-did-I-ever-have-kids? day. But during the teen years it's not uncommon for dads to watch helplessly as those days sometimes blimp into weeks and then months. Bottom line: the teen years will likely be the least satisfying time of your life as a father. They're not going to be that much fun for your teen either.

Of course there's all the head-butting that dads and teens do. But at the same time, your child's teen years are a time of real growth and self-examination for *you*. It's during this stage that the aging process will really sink in. Before now you knew you were getting older because you kept having birthdays and you stopped getting carded at grocery stores and bars, but you probably didn't feel much different than when you were twenty. But get ready, because this is gradually starting to change—you'll have a few more aches and pains than you did before, and it might take a little longer to recover from your weekend basketball game with your buddies. At the same time, you'll watch with envy as your teen steps into a world of unlimited possibilities and choices, and you'll become aware that your options are far more limited. Your teen's largely responsibility-free life is a sharp contrast to your life, which is filled with work, mortgage payments, carpools, and other obligations. He's entering his physical and sexual prime, and you're leaving yours. And as he looks toward the future, you can't help but reevaluate the past.

13–14 years

PHYSICAL

As far as sexual development goes, girls continue screeching ahead of boys. Most girls are starting to look (or have been for some time looking) "womanly," but most boys this age still look, like, well, boys, especially when placed next to high-schoolers. No matter what they look like, though, both genders are starting to have sexual feelings, which they and you may find disconcerting.

In the beginning, these feelings tend to be directed at themselves, rather than others, which means that they'll "stumble" onto masturbation soon, if they haven't already.

As peer pressure increases, along with the belief that everyone else is doing it ten times a day, the likelihood of your teen having sex increases stratospherically.

Your teen's still getting taller and heavier, but thankfully, that whole four-inches-per-year thing is over. Noses, however, have their own growth spurt about now, which can be cause for great alarm. Ditto for acne.

Overall health and hygiene may start to slip a little.

INTELLECTUAL

Your teen is starting to think more about the larger world and how he fits in to it.

Teens just entering high school will have to deal with the shock of going from the top of the middle school heap to the bottom of the high school one. There are unfamiliar settings, new people, new rules, and new expectations. Those with fashion-conscious teens could find this development costly.

Overall, your teen may not seem to know whether he wants to grow up or not. He knows he's outgrowing kid stuff but may still like reading picture books or playing with younger kids (except for younger siblings, who are the perennial cause of misery).

He craves independence but isn't yet able to accept the responsibility that goes with it. As a result, bouts of poor judgment and impulsiveness are still quite common. He might suddenly announce a passion for a brand-new sport or music or art or even science.

Likewise new religious and moral beliefs. Experimentation is common at this stage, so don't panic if you hear some talk of a God you've never heard of.

The "Get away from me" versus "I need you" syndrome begins as your teen vacillates between the belief that he knows everything and can do anything, and his fears of inadequacy, helplessness, and failure.

As he tries to separate himself from you, he may temporarily veer into a path of rudeness, arguments, and defiance—stopping along the way to break as many rules as possible.

With the above syndromes in place, privacy will become the catchword of the day. And he needs it. Private time allows him to exert some modicum of control over his thoughts and environment without having to suffer through all those lectures on what you did when you were his age.

And who knows, a day—or an hour—later, your teen may be respectful, cooperative, and responsible, and will come looking for your advice, guidance, or even just a hug.

As worries about the world beyond high school begin to take hold, your teen will take a greater interest in career and in education.

EMOTIONAL/SOCIAL

The flip side of your teen's need to separate from you is his need to be accepted by his peers. As he begins to rely on them for emotional support, they will have a great influence on his choice of clothing, hair color, music, activities, and on whether or not he starts smoking, drinking, or experimenting with drugs. (This threatens to bankrupt you too.)

This struggle to find his moorings in the social scene and fit in with the "in" crowd is accompanied by much blushing and multiple bouts of crushing loneliness.

At this state, the dating thing is still a little unclear. Friendships and group activities tend to be with members of the same sex and are usually driven by common interests such as sports.

Still, kids have opposite-sex friends, and making out at parties is always a crowd pleaser. Most attempts to go further are usually pretty clumsy.

On the emotional front, your teen is a lot better able to manage his emotions than he did only a year ago, and he's now quite adept at articulating his emotions verbally—especially when expressing his judgments of you.

None of this prevents him from acting like a much younger child once in a while, probably in an attempt to get more attention from you as the occasional terror of growing up sets in.

15–16 years

PHYSICAL

Girls are still more physically mature than boys. And by now most teens have had sex, or at least gotten to third base (which today means oral sex, not heavy petting as it used to when we were all chaste teens). Info on STDs, condoms, AIDS, and so on is essential.

Raging hormones may have your teen flip-flopping between hysterical laughter, tears, oversensitivity, and complete insensitivity.

The only constant is her self- consciousness about her body, whether what's going on is normal, and whether she's attractive enough. Even more time will be spent in front of mirrors than before. Girls may start dieting (which can lead to eating disorders), and boys start bulking up (which can lead to steroid abuse).

Hygiene may improve along with the desire to impress new love interests.

Teens need more sleep now than at any other time since they were infants, so oversleeping is common.

INTELLECTUAL

All those moral and religious beliefs are firming up. Many teens get very involved in social causes, serving meals in soup kitchens, organizing AIDS walks, volunteering, and so on. Many teens get rigid and judgmental, lecturing you on the lousy religious and moral choices you've made at this point. Others continue to dabble.

Thankfully, your teen will start taking more responsibility for her actions and may look for role models (sorry, not you). Rebelling against you and everything you stand for is a crucial pastime.

Even though deep down inside she knows she needs structure, she'll complain that your stupid rules are limiting her freedom. True independence—at least in her mind—can only be won through being "different" from the rest of the family. If that doesn't work, conflict will have to do.

She wants a relationship with you on her own terms. That means that you are demoted from actually controlling her life to the menial position of on-call consultant, available to answer questions, but only when asked for.

Struggling with the "Who am I?" question, she may spend countless hours staring off into space, thinking about herself, her hopes, and her dreams. She'll start projects and drop them halfway through. She'll also "try on" different identities: changing the spelling of her name or asking to be called something else altogether; adopting phony mannerisms, handwriting, or a bizarre accent; sporting clothes or a new hairstyle just for the shock value; and wanting (or even getting) a tattoo or body piercing. Some sexual experimentation is common at this stage.

A lot of teens will take a particular class because they heard it was easy or because someone they have a crush on is taking it or the teacher is supposed to be cool. Since school guidance counselors are working triple time, it's your responsibility to make sure your child is taking the classes it'll take to get her where she wants to go in life.

EMOTIONAL/SOCIAL

The peer group becomes even more important than before. She'll confide in them more and more as her opinion of you and your credibility slips. At the same time, she starts breaking away from her peers, or at least trying to carve out her own identity.

Social circles broaden one day, then shrink the next, as your teen's focus shifts from simply being popular to creating and maintaining closer, lasting friendships.

Friendships deepen in the middle teen years as kids develop more emotional depth. Your teen will have her first experiences with powerful positive and negative emotions (compassion, love, hate) directed at nonfamily members.

Pairing off with members of the opposite sex now goes into high gear.

She'll seek out more role models and mentors. Even though she's rejecting you, she knows that she still needs to have an adult around to give her some guidance.

Your teen isn't good at taking criticism from anyone. But because of your privileged status, just about everything you say will be "stupid" or "annoying." She'll also interrupt you a lot, claiming she knows everything you say before you even finish the thought.

17–18 years

PHYSICAL

Boys have finally caught up to girls physically, and sexual energy is rampant.

Physically, most teens are fairly comfortable with their body.

Although they feel and look like fully developed adults, teens' brains are still growing. The frontal lobes, which regulate little things like self-control, emotional maturity, and emotion, are in a period of rapid expansion.

Most teens have experimented with drugs and/or alcohol, and they're in real need of support and honest information—especially about the dangers of driving under the influence of drugs or alcohol.

Overall health and hygiene become downright adult as teens prepare themselves to leave home and enter college or the work world.

INTELLECTUAL

Congratulations, the high-conflict days of your relationship with your teen are almost water under the bridge.

Amazingly enough, he's beginning to see you as a real, live person, and— even though he'd never admit it in public—he values your opinion.

This does not mean he will listen to you, however. It is still imperative that he reject your world, if only to show you how responsible he is (especially if he needs the car keys).

Be wary of an overt display of self-confidence—it may just be an act. Believe me, he's questioning the important choices he's made, like where to go to college. He's excited but scared about leaving home and worried whether he'll be able to make it without the safety net you've been providing for so long.

The search for identity narrows from "Who am I?" to "Which is the real me—the way I am with my friends, the way I am with my family, or the way I feel inside?"

He also has a much clearer picture of his assets and inadequacies and is beginning to feel bad if he hasn't lived up to his own or others' expectations.

Moral views are pretty solid now, as are empathy for others, and an ability to compromise and to work with others toward a common goal. He still may suffer from a wide-eyed idealism and announce plans to rid the world of racism, poverty, and other societal ills.

Interests are more stable, and he'll now finish most projects that he starts.

EMOTIONAL/SOCIAL

By now your teen has had at least one significant romantic relationship, and at least one significant breakup.

Your teen increasingly relies on role models and mentors—usually teachers, coaches, or other adults. The fact that you may have given the same advice weeks ago means nothing.

His friends still play a major role in giving him the courage to stand up to you. The theory being that if things don't work out at home, the supporting friends will always be there to provide the emotional support he needs during tough times but can't ask you for.

As a graduating senior, he's finally made it to the top of the social ladder. But dread ensues at the prospect of leaving good friends behind, and the fear that new ones will be hard to make, and there's trepidation about having to start over again at the bottom of a new social ladder in college.

Driving becomes a big issue here. Not letting him drive is pretty much your only remaining method of wielding control.

Slowing hormones mean more emotional stability—just in case you do take away the car keys.

Resources

This section contains the most helpful, informative resources we could find for deployed service members, veterans, civilian contractors, and their families. However, it's only a snapshot, capturing what was available as we went to press. Things change all the time, so in order to keep these resources as current and relevant as possible, we're posting frequent updates on our website, at www.mrdad.com/miltary. Do you know of any resources that really should be here but aren't (or that are but shouldn't be)? Please send an email to resources@militarydad.com

Benefits

Department of Veterans Affairs
oefoif.va.gov

For returning vets of Operation Enduring Freedom and Operation Iraqi Freedom, and others. For survivor benefits, visit vba.va.gov/survivors.

GovBenefits.gov
govbenefits.gov/

The official benefits Web site of the U.S. government, with information on over 1,000 benefit and assistance programs.

Guard and reserve benefits
nga.org/Files/pdf/07GUARDSURVEY.PDF

An excellent resource provided by the National Governors Association listing everything a reservist or National Guardsman needs to know on state-by-state programs and benefits.

Tricare
tricare.mil

Information on the military's health-care benefits, including eligibility and enrollment.

Blogging

Blogger
blogger.com

MilBlogging.com
milblogging.com

A searchable collection of hundreds of military-themed blogs.

WordPress
wordpress.com

Civilian Contractors

Civilians in Iraq Yahoo! group
groups.yahoo.com/group/civiliansinraq (yes, there's a letter missing in Iraq)

American Contractors in Iraq
americancontractorsiniraq.com

Communication and Keeping in Touch

BabbleSoft
Babblesoft.com

Web/mobile applications that help new parents communicate about child care, baby photos, milestones, etc.

Blankets for Deployed Daddies
blanketsfordeployeddaddies.com

Sends blankets to deployed dads who have newborns or very young children at home. Dad sleeps with the blanket, then sends it to his baby, who gets a chance to bond with him through scent.

Freedom Calls
freedomcalls.org

Free video conference calls between service members stationed in Iraq and friends and family.

Google Calendar
calendar.google.com

Oovoo
oovoo.com

Skype
skype.com

Tatango and eMail Our Military
Tatango.com and emailourmilitary.com

> A partnership that gives U.S. troops overseas the ability to communicate with their friends, family, and loved ones back in the States using text-messaging.

United through Reading
unitedthroughreading.org/military

> Helps ease the stress of separation for military families by having deployed parents read children's books aloud via DVD for their child to watch at home.

Education

Military Child Education Coalition
www.militarychild.org

> Its work is focused on ensuring quality educational opportunities for all military children affected by mobility, family separation, and transition.

Military K-12 Partners
militaryk12partners.dodea.edu

> Projects to enhance student learning opportunities and achievement. Also lots of education-related links and tools for families.

Operation Military Kids
operationmilitarykids.org

> A bit more for parents than kids themselves, Operation Military Kids is the U.S. Army's collaborative effort with America's communities to support the children and youth impacted by deployment.

Our Military Kids
ourmilitarykids.org

> Provides tangible support to the children of deployed and severely injured National Guard and Military Reserve personnel through grants for enrichment activities and tutoring that nurture and sustain the children during the time a parent is away in service to our country.

Parents as Teachers
ParentsAsTeachers.org

> A parent education and family support program serving families throughout pregnancy until their child enters kindergarten, usually age five.

Emergency Aid and Support

Good sources for help with low-interest loans, transportation, food, rent, and any other unforeseen emergencies.

Air Force Aid Society
afas.org

American Red Cross
redcross.org

Army Emergency Relief
aerhq.org

Coast Guard Mutual Assistance
cgmahq.org

Navy-Marine Corps Relief Society
nmcrs.org

Family Connections, Support, and Activities

Air Force Crossroads
afcrossroads.com

"The official community website of the United States Air Force." Provides information on deployment, parenting, and more.

Army Families Online
armyfamiliesonline.org

Army One Source
myarmylifetoo.com

The Integrated Army Family Support Network. Everything—tons of info for families and kids.

Army Reserve Family Programs
arfp.org

Soldier readiness + family readiness = mission readiness.

Kids Across Parents Down
kapd.com

Great crossword puzzles that dad and kid can do together.

LifeLines Services Network
lifelines.navy.mil

Answers for sailors, Marines, and their families, complete with links to support and services outside the military as well.

Marine Corps Community Services
usmc-mccs.org

Serves Marines and their families around the world. Offers a variety of programs to build strong families.

The Military Family Network

emilitary.org.

Works with community organizations, local governments, and businesses to support the families of our armed services.

The Military Family Outdoor Initiative Project

sierraclub.org/military

Cosponsored by the Armed Services YMCA and the Sierra Club. Offers a great way for you and your kids to reconnect, bond, and have a ton of fun hiking, camping, swimming, boating, and more.

Operation Homefront

operationhomefront.net

Supporting our troops and helping the families they leave behind.

General Information

Military Family Resource Institute at Purdue University

mfri.purdue.edu

A fantastic source of information. The Institute conducts studies that provide insight into the experiences of military members and their families. It also designs and implements outreach activities that assist military families in Indiana and beyond.

Military Home Front

militaryhomefront.dod.mil

The official Department of Defense Web site for reliable quality of life information designed to assist troops and their families.

Military One Source

militaryonesource.com

This site is designed to help military families deal with life's issues. Consultants are available twenty-four hours a day, seven days a week, 365 days a year, and can be reached by phone or e-mail.

National Military Family Association

Nmfa.org

NMFA's goal is to educate military families concerning the rights, benefits, and services available to them and to inform them regarding the issues that affect their lives. They also seek to promote and protect the interests of military families by influencing the development and implementation of legislation and policies affecting them.

Surviving Deployment

survivingdeployment.com

> Tons of information and resources for military families.

The Navy Fleet and Family Support Center

nffsp.org

> Provides services to strengthen personal and family competencies to meet the unique challenges of the military lifestyle.

Navy and Marine Welfare and Recreation

mwr.navy.mil

Administers a varied program of recreation, social, and community support activities on U.S. Navy facilities worldwide.

Legal Issues

U.S. Armed Forces Legal Assistance

legalassistance.law.af.mil

> Provides general legal information to the military community.

Official Military Web Sites

Air Force

af.mil

Air Force Reserves

airforcereserve.com

Army

army.mil

Coast Guard

uscg.mil

Coast Guard Reserves

uscg.mil/reserve

Marines

marines.com

Marine Reserves

mfr.usmc.mil

National Guard Association of the United States

ngaus.org

Navy
navy.mil

Navy Reserves
navyreserve.navy.mil

Health (Mental and Physical)

Deployment Health and Family Readiness Library
deploymenthealthlibrary.fhp.osd.mil/home.jsp

This library offers service members, families, leaders, health-care providers, and veterans an easy way to find deployment health and family readiness information.

Family of a Vet
FamilyOfAVet.com

Dedicated to helping vets and their loved ones survive and thrive after combat.

Hooah 4 Health
hooah4health.com

Run by the Army and targeted toward reservists—but there's plenty of great info for everyone. This site promotes health and wellness in four areas: body, mind, spirit, and environment.

Military Mental Health Screening Tool
militarymentalhealth.org

Online screening tools for anonymous inquiry into possible needs for counseling.

National Center for Posttraumatic Stress Disorder
ncptsd.va.gov

Aims to advance the clinical care and social welfare of U.S. veterans through research, education, and training on PTSD and stress-related disorders.

Reserve and Guard

Employer Support of the Guard and Reserve (ESGR)
esgr.org

Resources and advice for citizen soldiers on avoiding job conflicts.

National Guard Association of the United States
ngaus.org

National Guard Family Program
guardfamily.org

Geared to National Guard and families, yet pertinent to all deploying soldiers. Helps military personnel and their families prepare for deployment.

National Guard and Reserve Health Care Site
tricare.mil/reserve

Office of the Assistant Secretary of Defense
defenselink.mil/ra

Loads of info for reservists.

Strategic outreach to families of all reservists
www.sofarusa.org

A unique and innovative program to aid the families and loved ones of army reservists and National Guard deployed in Afghanistan, Iraq, and Kuwait.

Spouses

Deployment Lessons
deploymentlessons.org

Support and information for wives of deployed military.

MilSpouse.org
milspouse.org

A huge collection of resources on spouse employment, education, and relocation.

Homefront Online
homefrontonline.com

Operation Homefront's community of military wives and women in uniform.

Resources for Children

BOOKS
An Army ABC Book, by Kristen T. Pirog

Daddy Is a Soldier, by Kirsten Hallowell

Daddy's in Iraq, But I Want Him Back, by Carmen R. Hoyt

Daddy, Will You Miss Me? by Wendy McCormick

Daddy You're My Hero, by Michelle Ferguson-Cohen

Deployment Journal for Kids, by Rachel Robertson (ages 5–adult)

H Is for Honor: A Military Family Alphabet, by Devin Scillian

Hurry Home, by Leah McDermott

I Miss You! A Military Kid's Book about Deployment, by Beth Andrews

The Impossible Patriotism Project, by Linda Skeers

Love, Lizzie: Letters to a Military Mom, by Lisa Tucker McElroy (ages 4–12)

The Magic Box: When Parents Can't Be There to Tuck You In, by Marty Sederman and Seymour Epstein

A Marine ABC Book, by Kristen T. Pirog

Mommy You're My Hero, by Michelle Ferguson-Cohen (ages 4–8)

My Hero: Military Kids Write about Their Moms and Dads, by Allen Appel and Mike Rothmiller

My Red Balloon, by Eve Bunting (ages 3–12)

Night Catch, by Brenda Ehrmantraut (ages 3–8)

A Paper Hug, by Stephanie Skolmoski

Red, White and Blue, Good-bye, by Sarah Wones Tomp (ages 3–8)

The Soldier's Tree, by Stephanie L. Pickup

Uncle Sam's Kids: When Duty Calls, by Angela Sportelli Rehak

We Serve Too! A Child's Deployment Book, by Kathleen Edlick (ages 3–8)

When Dad's at Sea, by Mindy Pelton (ages 4–8)

While You Are Away, by Eileen Spinelli

The Wishing Tree, by Mary Redman

A Year without Dad, by Jodi Brunson

A Yellow Ribbon for Daddy, by Anissa Mersiowsky

WEB SITES

Deploymentkids.com

deploymentkids.com

> Offers free downloadable activities, including a time-zone chart, distance calculator, and spotlights on different areas of the world where a parent might be deployed.

Hooah4Kids

hooah4health.com/4life/hooah4kids

> Games, resources, and info for military kids.

Hooah4Teens

hooah4health.com/4life/hooah4teens

> Games, resources, and info for military teens.

National Guard Child and Youth Program

guardfamilyyouth.org

> Supports the social, emotional, and academic needs of National Guard children and youth.

Sesame Workshop

sesameworkshop.org/tlc/index.php

> A partnership between Sesame Workshop and Wal-Mart, this is an excellent resource designed to help military families and their young children with the concerns they experience before, during, and after deployment.

Military Teens on the Move

defenselink.mil/mtom

> This site features a chat room, bulletin board, and other resources and information for military teens around the world to assist them with relocating and other teen issues.

Selected Bibliography
and References

Books

Adler-Baeder, F., L. Taylor, and K. Pasley. *Marital Transitions in Military Families: Their Prevalence and Their Relevance for Adaptation to the Military.* West Lafayette, Ind.: Military Family Research Institute, Purdue University, 2005.

Anthony, E. James, and Therese Benedek. *Parenthood: Its Psychology and Psychopathology.* Amsterdam: Jason Aronson, 1990.

Ashley, Steven. *The Long-Distance Dad: How You Can Be There for Your Child—Whether Divorced, Deployed, or on the Road.* Avon, Mass.: Adams Media, 2008.

Benedek, Therese. *Insight and Personality Adjustment: A Study of the Psychological Effects of War.* New York: Ronald Press, 1946.

Booth, Bradford, Mady Wechsler Segal, and D. Bruce Bell. *What We Know About Army Families: 2007 Update.* Alexandria, Va.: Family and Morale, Welfare and Recreation Command, 2007. http://www.army.mil/fmwrc/documents/research/whatweknow2007.pdf.

Dandeker, C., C. French, C. Birtles, and S. Wessely. "Deployment Experiences of British Army Wives Before, During and After Deployment: Satisfaction with Military Life and Use of Support Networks." In *Human Dimensions in Military Operations: Military Leaders' Strategies for Addressing Stress and Psychological Support*, 38-1–38-20. Papers prepared for the RTO Human Factors and Medicine Panel (HFM) Symposium, Brussels, Belgium, April 24–26, 2006. http://www.rto.nato.int/abstracts.asp.

Dawalt, Sara. *365 Deployment Days: A Wife's Survival Story.* Austin, Texas: Bridgeway Books, 2007.

de Haan, M., and C. A. Nelson. "Discrimination and Categorization of Facial Expressions of Emotion during Infancy." In *Perceptual Development: Visual, Auditory, and Language Perception in Infancy*, edited by A. M. Slater, pp. 287–309. London: University College London Press, 1998.

Dumler, Elaine Gray. *I'm Already Home: Keeping Your Family Close When You're on TDY.* Westminster, Colo.: Frankly Speaking, 2003.

———. *I'm Already Home, Again: Keeping Your Family Close While on Assignment or Deployment.* Westminster, Colo.: Frankly Speaking, 2006.

Etheridge, R. M. *Family Factors Affecting Retention: A Review of the Literature.* Research Triangle Park, N.C.: Research Triangle Institute, 1989.

Hammer, L. B., J. C. Cullen, G. C. Marchand, and J. A. Dezsofi. "Reducing the Negative Impact of Work-Family Conflict on Military Personnel: Individual Coping Strategies and Multilevel Interventions." In *Military Life: The Psychology of Serving in Peace and Combat*, edited by C. A. Castro, A. B. Adler, and C. Britt. Vol 3, *The Military Family*, (220–42) Bridgeport, Conn: Praeger Security International, 2006.

Harrell, Margaret C., Nelson Lim, Laura Werber Castaneda, and Daniela Golinelli. *Working around the Military*. Santa Monica, Calif.: RAND Corporation, 2004.

Hosek, James R., Jennifer Kavanagh, and Laura Miller. *How Deployments Affect Service Members*. Santa Monica, Calif.: RAND Corporation, 2006.

Huebner, A. J., and J. A. Mancini. *Adjustments among Adolescents in Military Families When a Parent Is Deployed*. West Lafayette, Ind.: Military Family Research Institute, Purdue University, 2005.

Huffman, A. H., and S. C. Payne. "The Challenges and Benefits of Dual-Military Marriages." In Castro, Adler, and Britt, *Military Life*. Vol 3. (115–37).

Jensen, P., and J. Shaw. *The Effects of War and Parental Deployment upon Children and Adolescents*. In *Emotional Aftermath of the Persian Gulf War: Veterans, Families, Communities, and Nations*, edited by R. Ursano and A. Norwood, pp. 83–109. Washington, D.C.: American Psychiatric Press, 1996.

Karney, B. R., and Crown, J. S. *Families under Stress: An Assessment of Data, Theory, and Research on Marriage and Divorce in the Military*. Santa Monica, Calif.: RAND Corporation, 2007.

Kelley, M. L. "Single Military Parents in the New Millennium." In Castro, Adler, and Britt, *Military Life*. Vol 3. (93–114).

Leyva, Meredith. *Married to the Military: A Survival Guide for Military Wives, Girlfriends, and Women in Uniform*. New York: Fireside, 2003.

Musheno, Michael, and Susan M. Ross. *Deployed: How Reservists Bear the Burden of Iraq*. Ann Arbor: University of Michigan Press, 2008.

National Institute for Building Long-Distance Relationships. *Helping Your Kids Connect: 250 Activities to Help Your Children Stay Connected to Their Long-Distance Mom or Dad*. Provo, Utah: A&E Family Publishers, 2002.

Norwood, A. E., C. S. Fullerton, and K. P. Hagen. "Those Left Behind: Military Families." In Ursano and Norwood, *Emotional Aftermath*, pp. 283–315.

Pavlicin, Karen M. *Life after Deployment: Military Families Share Reunion Stories and Advice*. Saint Paul, Minn.: Elva Resa, 2007.

———. *Surviving Deployment: A Guide for Military Families*. Saint Paul, Minn.: Elva Resa, 2003.

Pennebaker, J. W. *Opening Up: The Healing Power of Confiding in Others*. New York: William Morrow, 1990.

Pryce, J. G., D. Ogilvy-Lee, and D. H. Pryce. "The Citizen-Soldier and Reserve Component Families." In *The Military Family: A Practice Guide for Service Providers*, edited by J. A. Martin, L. N. Rosen, and L. R. Sparacino. Westport, Conn.: Praeger, 2000.

Resick, P. A., and K. S. Calhoun. "Posttraumatic stress disorder." In *Clinical Handbook of Psychological Disorders: A Step-by-Step Treatment Manual*, edited by D. H. Barlow, pp. 60–113. 3rd ed. New York: Guilford Press, 2001.

Schindler, Michael. *Operation Military Family: How to Strengthen Your Military Marriage and Save Your Family.* New York: Aviva, 2007.

Sherman, M. D., and D. M. Sherman. *Finding My Way: A Teen's Guide to Living with a Parent Who Has Experienced Trauma.* Edina, Minn.: Beavers Pond Press, 2006.

Stolz, Lois. *Father Relations of War-Born Children: The Effect of Postwar Adjustment of Fathers on the Behavior and Personality of First Children Born While the Fathers Were at War.* Stanford, Calif.: Stanford University Press, 1954.

Tuttle, William M. *Daddy's Gone to War: The Second World War in the Lives of America's Children.* New York: Oxford University Press, 1993.

Vandevoorde, Shellie. *Separated by Duty, United in Love.* New York: Citadel, 2006.

Watanabe, H. K., and P. S. Jensen. "Young Children's Adaptation to a Military Lifestyle." In Martin, Rosen, and Sparacino, *Military Family.*

Weins, T. W., and P. Boss. "Maintaining Family Resiliency Before, During and After Military Separation." In Castro, Adler, and Britt, *Military Life. Vol. 3 The military family* (pp. 13–38).

Wright, K. M., L. M. Burrell, E. D. Schroeder, and J. L. Thomas. "Military Spouses: Coping with the Fear and Reality of Service Member Injury and Death." In Castro, Adler, and Britt, *Military Life, Vol. 3. The military family* (pp. 64–90). Praeger Security International: Westport, Connecticut.

Articles

Agaibi, C. E., and J. P. Wilson. "Trauma, PTSD, and Resilience: A Review of the Literature." *Trauma, Violence, and Abuse* 6 (2005): 195–216.

Albano, Sondra. "What Society Can Learn from the U.S. Military's System of Family Support." *National Council on Family Relations Report* 47, no. 1 (2002): F6–F8.

Amen, D. J., L. Jellen, E. Merves, and R. E. Lee. (1988). "Minimizing the Impact of Deployment on Military Children: Stages, Current Preventive Efforts, and System Recommendations." *Military Medicine* 153 (1988): 441–46.

Applewhite, L. W., and R. A. Mays. (1996). "Parent-Child Separation: A Comparison of Maternally and Paternally Separated Children in Military Families." *Child and Adolescent Social Work Journal* 13 (1996): 23–39.

Behnke, A. O., S. M. MacDermid, J. C. Anderson, and H. M. Weiss. "Ethnic Variations in the Connection between Work-Induced Family Separation and Turnover Intent." Military Family Research Institute, Purdue University, West Lafayette, Ind. http://www.cfs.purdue.edu/mfri/pages/research/ethnicity_and_turnover.pdf.

Blaisure, K. R., and J. Arnold-Mann. "Return and Reunion: A Psychoeducational Program aboard U.S. Navy Ships." *Family Relations* 41, no. 2 (1992): 178–85.

Blount, B. W., A. Curry, and G. Lubin. "Family Separations in the Military." *Military Medicine* 157, no. 2 (1992): 76–80.

Bowen, G. L., J. A. Mancini, J. A. Martin, W. B. Ware, and J. P. Nelson. "Promoting the Adaptation of Military Families: An Empirical Test of a Community Practice Model." *Family Relations: Interdisciplinary Journal of Applied Family Studies* 52 (2003): 33–44.

Bowen, G. L., and D. K. Orthner. "Single Parents in the U.S. Air Force." *Family Relations* 35, no. 1 (1986): 45–52.

Bowen, G. L., D. K. Orthner, and L. I. Zimmerman. "Family Adaptation of Single Parents in the United States Army: An Empirical Analysis of Work Stressors and Adaptive Resources." *Family Relations* 42, no. 3 (1993): 293–304.

Carver, Leslie, and Brenda Vaccaro. "12-Month-Old Infants Allocate Increased Neural Resources to Stimuli Associated with Negative Adult Emotion." *Developmental Psychology* 43 (2007): 54–69.

Chandra, Anita, Rachel Burns, Terri Tanielian, et al. "Understanding the Impact of Deployment on Children and Families: Findings from a Pilot Study of Operation Purple Camp Participants." Working paper, RAND Health series, prepared for the National Military Family Association, 2008. http://rand.org/pubs/working_papers/2008/RAND_WR566.pdf.

Chartrand, Molinda M., Deborah A. Frank, et al. "Effect of Parents' Wartime Deployment on the Behavior of Young Children in Military Families." *Archives of Pediatric and Adolescent Medicine* 162, no. 11 (2008): 1009–14.

Cohn, J. F., and E. Z. Tronick. "Three-Month-Old Infants' Reaction to Simulated Maternal Depression." *Child Development* 54 (1983): 185–93.

Cozza, S. J., R. S. Chun, and J. A. Polo. "Military Families and Children During Operation Iraqi Freedom." *Psychiatric Quarterly* 76, no. 4 (2005): 371–78.

Defense Department Advisory Committee on Women in the Services (DACOWITS). Washington, D.C.: DACOWITS, 2005.

Defense Manpower Data Center (DMDC). "Overview of the 1999 Survey of Spouses of Active-Duty Personnel." DMDC Report No. 2000-014, DMDC Survey and Program Evaluation Division, Arlington, Va., 2002.

Department of Defense. "Report on Military Spouse Education and Employment." Office of the Deputy Under Secretary of Defense, Military Community & Family Policy, Washington, D.C., January 2008.

Drummet, A. R., M. Coleman, and S. Cable. "Military Families under Stress: Implications for Family Life Education." *Family Relations* 52, no. 3 (2003): 279–87.

Fallon, T. J., and M. A. Russo. "Adaptation to Stress: An Investigation into the Lives of United States Military Families with a Child Who Is Disabled." *Early Childhood Education Journal* 30, no. 3 (2003): 193–98.

Fiore, Faye. "Troops' Struggles in Iraq Include Failing Marriages." *Seattle Times*, July 17, 2005.

Frankel, H., L. R. Snowden, and L. S. Nelson. "Wives Adjustment to Military Deployment: An Empirical Evaluation of a Family Stress Model." *International Journal of Sociology of the Family* 22 (1992): 93–117.

Fricker, Ronald D., James Hosek, and Mark E. Totten. "How Does Deployment Affect Retention of Military Personnel?" Rand Research Brief, 2003. http://www.rand.org/pubs/research_briefs/RB7557/RB7557.pdf.

Greenhaus, J. H., and N. J. Beutell. "Sources of Conflict between Work and Family Roles." *Academy of Management Review* 10, no. 1 (1995): 76–88.

Hillenbrand, E. D. "Father Absence in Military Families." *Family Coordinator* 25, no. 4 (1976): 451–58.

Hoehl, Stephanie, L. Wiese, and T. Striano. "Young Infants' Neural Processing of Objects Is Affected by Eye Gaze Direction and Emotional Expression." *PLoS ONE* 3, no. 6 (2008): e2389. http://www.plosone.org/article/info:doi/10.1371/journal.pone.0002389.

Hoge, C. W., C. A. Castro, S. C. Messer, D. McGurk, D. I. Cotting, D. I., and R. L. Koffman, R. L. (2004). "Combat Duty in Iraq and Afghanistan, mental health problems, and barriers to care." *New England Journal of Medicine* 351 (2004): 13-22.

Hood, Bruce M., J. Douglas Willen, and Jon Driver. (1998) "Adults Eyes Trigger Shifts of Visual Attention in Human Infants." *Psychological Science* 9 (1998): 131–34.

Jakupcak, M., L. J. Roberts, C. Martell, P. Mulick, S. Michael, R. Reed, et al. "A Pilot Study of Behavioral Activation for Veterans with Posttraumatic Stress Disorder." *Journal of Traumatic Stress* 19 (2006): 387–91.

Jensen, P. S., D. Grogan, S. N. Xenakis, and M. W. Bain. "Father Absence: Effects on Child and Maternal Psychopathology." *Journal of the American Academy of Child and Adolescent Psychiatry* 28 (1989): 171–75.

Jensen, P. S., D. Martin, and H. Watanabe. "Children's Response to Separation during Operation Desert Storm." *Journal of the American Academy of Child and Adolescent Psychiatry* 35 (1996): 433–41.

Jensen, P. S., H. K. Watanabe, J. E. Richters, R. Cortes, M. Roper, and S. Liu. "Prevalence of Mental Disorder in Military Children and Adolescents: Findings from a Two-Stage Community Survey." *Journal of the American Academy of Child and Adolescent Psychiatry* 34, no. 11 (1995): 1514–24.

Johnson, S., M. Sherman, J. Hoffman, L. James, P. Johnson, J. Lochman, T. Magee, and D. and Riggs. "The Psychological Needs of U.S. Military Service Members and Their Families: A Preliminary Report." APA Presidential Task Force on Military Deployment Services for Youth, Families and Service Members, February 2007. http://www.apa.org/releases/MilitaryDeploySvcsTFReport-ExecutiveSummary02-2007.pdf.

Kelley, M. L. "Military-Induced Separation in Relation to Maternal Adjustment and Children's Behaviors." *Military Psychology* 6, no. 3 (1994): 163–76.

Kelley, M. L., P. A. Herzog-Simmer, and M. A. Harris. "Effects of Military-Induced. Separation on the Parenting Stress and Family Functioning of Deploying Mothers." *Military Psychology* 6, no. 2 (1994): 125–38.

Kelley, M. L., E. Hock, K. M. Smith, J. F. Bonney, and M. A. Gaffney. "Internalizing and Externalizing Behavior of Children with Enlisted Navy Mothers Experiencing Military Induced Separation." *Journal of the American Academy of Child and Adolescent Psychiatry* 40 (2001): 464–71.

Kerner, Timothy. "Mail Call: A Look at Communication for the Deployed U.S. Soldier." *MAIL: The Journal of Communication Distribution*, May/June 2003.

Leppänen, J. M., and C. A. Nelson. "The Development and Neural Bases of Recognizing of Facial Emotion." In *Advances in Child Development and Behavior*, edited by R. Kail, pp. 207–46. Amsterdam: Elsevier Press, 2006.

Levai, M., S. Kaplan, R. Ackerman, and M. Hammock. "The Effect of Father Absence on the Psychiatric Hospitalization of Navy Children." *Military Medicine* 160 (1995): 103–6.

Levin, Diane E., Carol Iskols Daynard, and Beverly Ann Dexter. "The 'SOFAR' Guide for Helping Children and Youth Cope with the Deployment and Return of a Parent in the National Guard and Other Reserve Components." Strategic Outreach to Families of All Reservists, 2008. http://www.sofarusa.org/downloads/SOFAR_2008_Final.pdf.

Lincoln, Alan, Erika Swift, and Mia Shorteno-Faser. "Psychological Adjustment and Treatment of Children and Families with Parents Deployed in Military Combat." *Journal of Clinical Psychology* 64, no. 8 (2008): pp. 984–92.

Loughran, David, Jacob Klerman, and Craig Martin. "Activation and the Earnings of Reservists." RAND Research Brief, 2006. http://www.rand.org/pubs/research_briefs/2006/RAND_RB9183.pdf.

Lyle, D. S. "Using Military Deployments and Job Assignments to Estimate the Effect of Parental Absences and Household Relocations on Children's Academic Achievement." *Journal of Labor Economics* 24, no. 2 (2006): 319–50.

MacDermid, Shelly. "Multiple Transitions of Deployment and Reunion for Military Families." Military Family Research Institute, Purdue University, West Lafayette, Ind., 2006. http://www.cfs.purdue.edu/mfri/pages/research/DeployReunion.pdf.

MacDermid, S. M., T. M. Olson, and H. Weiss. "Supporting Military Families throughout Deployment." Military Family Research Institute, Purdue University, West Lafayette, Ind., 2002. http://www.cfs.purdue.edu/mfri/pages/research/MFRI_Brief_Deployment_Support.pdf.

Maguire, Katheryn. "Bridging the Great Divide: An Examination of the Relationship Maintenance of Couples Separated during War." *Ohio Communication Journal* 45 (2007): 131–57.

Manguno-Mire, Gina, Frederic Sautter, J. Lyons, L. Myers, D. Perry, M. Sherman, et al. (in press). (2007) "Psychological Distress and Caregiver Burden in Partners of Veterans with Combat-Related PTSD." *Journal of Nervous and Mental Disease.* 195(2):144-151.

Medway, F. J., K. E. Davis, T. P. Cafferty, K. D. Chappell, and R. E. O'Hearn. "Family Disruption and Adult Attachment Correlates of Spouse and Child Reactions to Separation and Reunion Due to Operation Desert Storm." *Journal of Social and Clinical Psychology* 14 (1995): 97–118.

Merolla, Andy, and Dan Steinberg. "Relational Maintenance during Military Deployment: A Qualitative Analysis of U.S. Military-Affiliated Romantic Relationships." Paper presented at the annual meeting of the International Communication Association, San Francisco, Calif., 2007.

Mumme, Donna, and Anne Fernald. "The Infant as Onlooker: Learning from Emotional Reactions Observed in a Television Scenario." *Child Development* 75 (2003): 221–37.

Murray, J. S. "Helping Children Cope with Separation during War." *Journal for Specialists in Pediatric Nursing* 7, no. 3 (2002): 127–30.

Myers-Walls, J. A., K. S. Myers-Bowman, and A. E. Pelo. "Parents as Educators about War and Peace." *Family Relations* 42, no. 1 (1993): 66–73.

National Military Family Association. "Serving the Home Front: An Analysis of Military Family Support from September 11, 2001, through March 31, 2004." http://www.nmfa.org/site/DocServer?docID=362.

Orthner, D., and Bowen, G. "Attitudes toward Family Enrichment and Support Programs among Air Force Families." *Family Relations* 31, no. 3 (1982): 415–24.

Orthner, D. K., and R. Rose. "SAF V Survey Report: Reunion Adjustment among Army Civilian Spouses with Returned Soldiers." University of North Carolina, Chapel Hill, 2005.

Patterson, J. M. "Integrating Family Resilience and Family Stress Theory." *Journal of Marriage and the Family* 64, no. 2 (2002): 349–60.

Paulovich, Janet M. "Managing Sudden Deployment." Original presentation at 2003 Commander's Conference, NAS Fallon, updated October 8, 2007.

Peebles-Kleiger, M. J., and J. H. Kleiger. "Reintegration Stress for Desert Storm Families: Wartime Deployments and Family Trauma." *Journal of Traumatic Stress* 7, no. 2 (1994): 173–94.

Pflanz, Steven. "Military Deployments Are HARD: The Four P's of Helping Patients Cope with Deployment Stress." *Academy of Organizational and Occupational Psychiatry Bulletin* 11, no. 1 (2003). http://www.aoop.org/archive-bulletin/2003spring01.shtml.

Pierce, P. F., A. D. Vinokur, and C. L. Buck. "Effects of War-Induced Maternal Separation on Children's Adjustment during the Gulf War and Two Years Later." *Journal of Applied Social Psychology* 8 (1998): 1286–1311.

Pincus, S. H., R. House, J. Christensen, and L. E. Adler. "The Emotional Cycle of Deployment: A Military Family Perspective." *Journal of the Army Medical Department*, April–June 2001, pp. 615–23.

Pincus, S. H., and T. S. Nam. "The Emotional Cycle of Deployment: The Bosnian experience." *Journal of the Army Medical Department*, January–March 1999, pp. 38–44.

Reid V. M., and T. Striano. "Adult Gaze Influences Infant Attention and Object Processing Implications for Cognitive Neuroscience." *European Journal of Neuroscience* 21 (2005): 1763–66.

Reid, V. M., T. Striano, J. Kaufman, and M. H. Johnson. "Eye Gaze Cuing Facilitates Neural Processing of Objects in 4-Month-Old Infants." *Neuroreport* 15 (2004): 2553–56.

Renn, Paul. "Attachment Theory, the Transmission of Affect and the Therapeutic Process." *Counselling Directory*, March 30, 2007, http://www.counselling-directory.org.uk/counselloradvice3.html.

Schnurr, P. P., and B. L. Green. "Understanding Relationships among Trauma, Post-Traumatic Stress Disorder, And Health Outcomes." *Advances in Mind-Body Medicine* 20 (2004): 18–29.

Schumm, Walter R., D. Bruce Bell, and Benjamin Knott. "Predicting the Extent and Stressfulness of Problem Rumors at Home among Army Wives of Soldiers Deployed Overseas on a Humanitarian Mission." *Psychological Reports* 89 (2001): 123–34.

Spera, Christopher. "Spouses' Ability to Cope with Deployment and Adjust to Air Force Family Demands." *Armed Forces and Society* 35, no. 2 (2009): 286–306.

Stafford, E. M. "Supporting Families in the Face of Trauma: War and Deployment." PowerPoint presentation, Tripler Army Medical Center, 2006.

Stafford, E. M., and B. A. Grady. "Military Family Support." *Pediatric Annals* 32, no. 2 (2003): 110–15.

U.S. Army Community and Family Support Center. "2004/2005 Survey of Army Families V." http://www.army.mil/cfsc/documents/research/safv/intro.ppt.

U.S. Army Medical Research Unit-Europe. "Soldier Attitudes: Military Deployments." In *USAREUR Soldier Study*, May 10, 1999. Walter Reed Army Institute of Research, U.S. Army Medical Research and Materiel Command. http://www.per.hqusareur.army.mil/services/MPPD/Soldier%20Study%20I%20-%20%20Kosovo%20Predeployment.pdf.

Vinokur, A. D., P. F. Pierce, and C. L. Buck. "Work-Family Conflicts of Women in the Air Force: Their Influence on Mental Health and Functioning." *Journal of Organizational Behavior* 20, no. 6 (1999): 865–78.

Vormbeck, J. K. "Attachment Theory as Applied to Wartime and Job-Related Marital Separation." *Psychological Bulletin* 114, no. 1 (1993): 122–44.

Walker-Andrews, A. S. "Infants' Perception of Expressive Behaviors: Differentiation of Multimodal Information." *Psychological Bulletin* 121, no. 3 (1997): 437–56.

Wheeler, E. "Self-Reported Mental Health Status and Needs of Iraq Veterans in the Marine National Guard." Ms., 2007.

Wood, S., J. Scarville, and K. Gravino. "Waiting Wives: Separation and Reunion among Army Wives." *Armed Forces and Society* 21 (1995): 217–36.

Yeatman, G. W. "Parental Separation and the Military Child." *Military Medicine* 146 (1981): 320–22.

Index

Illustration Credits

About the Author

A nationally recognized parenting expert and former Marine, **ARMIN BROTT** has devoted the last 15 years to providing men with the tools, support, and knowledge to help them become the fathers they want to be—and their families need them to be. His seven critically acclaimed books for fathers have sold well over a million copies. Titles include *The Expectant Father: Facts, Tips, and Advice for Dads-to-Be* and *The New Father: A Dad's Guide to the First Year* (also available as audiobooks). He has written on fatherhood for hundreds of newspapers and magazines and is a frequent guest on such television programs as the Today Show. He also writes a nationally syndicated newspaper column, "Ask Mr. Dad," and hosts a syndicated radio show, "Positive Parenting." He lives with his family in Oakland, California. To learn more, please visit his Web site, www.mrdad.com.

About the Cartoonists

MARK BAKER
Mark Baker is a retired U.S. Army Master Sergeant. He initially signed up as a 19D Cavalry Scout, but changed his job to Signals Intelligence Analyst after the first Gulf War. In the early '90s he started drawing a series of cartoons based on a character he named Pvt. Murphy. The first Pvt. Murphy cartoon was published in 1993, and in November 2000 the series began running on a regular basis in *Army Times*, where it is read by a quarter of a million people each week. His cartoons are also posted online at his Web site: www.pvtmurphy.com.

VICTOR L. CASTRO
Veteran of the Afghanistan and Iraq campaigns, Victor now lives in Orange County, NY, with his wife Heather and son Nicolas. He is the illustrator of the graphic novel *Scionic* and the creator of *The Warrior Chronicles*, a compilation of soldiers' real world stories transformed into graphic art. His work has been published in the Comic Geek Speak anthology *"U" is for United*.

STEVE DICKENSON

Steve Dickenson grew up a military brat, moving from base to base, and having to face the mean kids at each new school. He managed to cash in on all that stored up angst by becoming a professional cartoonist, with seven comic strips syndicated nationally to date. He also writes for a number of established cartoon strips ("Dennis the Menace," "Wizard of Id," "Beetle Bailey," just to name a few). He currently resides in Tennessee with his five cats, who gleefully provide the background noise. Visit his Web site at www.stevedickenson.com.

JULIE NEGRON

Julie Negron is the creator of "Jenny," the only comic strip about life as a military spouse, which is published worldwide weekly by *Stars & Stripes* and by approximately fifty other military publications. A lifelong Air Force brat who has lived all over the world, from the Philippines and Taiwan to Germany and Alaska, Julie based the strip on her experiences abroad with her active-duty Air Force husband. The Negrons recently relocated back to the U.S., where Julie continues to create "Jenny." Visit her Web site at www.jennyspouse.com.

CHARLES WOLF

GySgt Charles Wolf served in the Marine Corps from 1987 to 2007. "Semper-Toons" are read worldwide and are dedicated to those that serve, have served, their families and their morale since 1994. Charles lives with his wife Amelia and son Joshua. For your daily morale, please visit www.sempertoons.com.

BASIL ZAVISKI

After many years in the Co. F 425 Airborne Infantry Unit, Basil Zaviski was deployed to Iraq, where he served as an Airborne Infantry Long Range Surveillance Soldier. He has been drawing comics for more than twenty years and hopes that service members enjoy his comics, particularly the comic strip "Gunston Street"—made for soldiers by a soldier. Visit his Web site at www.GunstonStreet.com.